THE MEANING OF SALVATION

THE EERDMANS Michael Green COLLECTION

Adventure of Faith:
Reflections on Fifty Years of Christian Service

Baptism:
Its Purpose, Practice, and Power

The Empty Cross of Jesus:
Seeing the Cross in the Light of the Resurrection

Evangelism:
Learning from the Past

Evangelism in the Early Church:
Lessons from the First Christians for the Church Today

Evangelism through the Local Church:
A Comprehensive Guide to All Aspects of Evangelism

I Believe in Satan's Downfall:
The Reality of Evil and the Victory of Christ

I Believe in the Holy Spirit:
Biblical Teaching for the Church Today

The Meaning of Salvation:
Redemption and Hope for Today

Thirty Years That Changed the World:
The Book of Acts for Today

THE MEANING OF SALVATION

Redemption and Hope for Today

Michael Green

William B. Eerdmans Publishing Company
Grand Rapids, Michigan

Wm. B. Eerdmans Publishing Co.
4035 Park East Court SE, Grand Rapids, Michigan 49546
www.eerdmans.com

First published 1965 by Hodder and Stoughton, London
This Eerdmans Michael Green Collection edition published 2023

Printed in the United States of America

29 28 27 26 25 24 23   1 2 3 4 5 6 7

ISBN 978-0-8028-8258-5

Library of Congress Cataloging-in-Publication Data

A catalog record for this book is available from the Library of
Congress.

Biblical quotations are taken from the Revised Standard Version
(1952) unless otherwise stated.

Foreword

I have read Mr. Green's study of *The Meaning of Salvation* with very great pleasure, and it is with equal pleasure that I commend it to other readers. Theological students in particular will find it a most helpful handbook, but other readers, who have no examination in History of Doctrine to prepare for, will discover much that is interesting and informative in Mr. Green's treatment of an important area of biblical theology.

What I like especially about this book is the historical handling of the biblical material. The successive phases of the biblical concept are presented in their contemporary context, and can thus be much more readily understood. Of particular importance in this regard are the chapters which deal with the Jewish and Gentile backgrounds of the New Testament doctrine of salvation.

Yet Mr. Green's interest is not exclusively historical. Salvation – or whatever alternative term may be used in its place – is something of urgent relevance to the predicament of our own generation, and in the last few pages of the book some timely things are said on this score. I should like to underline the last sentence of Chapter 11, with double underlining beneath the words "a translation into modern idiom"!

F. F. BRUCE,
*Rylands Professor of Biblical
Criticism and Exegesis,
University of Manchester*

Author's Preface

This book is intended to fill a gap. The concept of salvation is clearly central to Christianity, although it is often either neglected or misunderstood. The term "salvation", moreover, is often used to cover a wide area of related subjects. Most of the books on salvation embrace the covenant, the sacraments, the doctrine of the atonement, eschatology and much else. My aim is much more modest.

I have sought primarily to examine what the biblical writers understood by the *yesha'-sōtēria* roots and their cognates, and how they used them. If, therefore, it be objected that I have paid insufficient attention to the fall, the sacrificial system or the eucharist, this will be found to be because the biblical words for "salvation" are not closely connected to these subjects. There seemed to be no book on what the Bible teaches about "salvation" in this restricted sense. Even the standard work on the subject, the late Professor C. Ryder Smith's *The Bible Doctrine of Salvation*, first published in 1941, ranges much farther afield than the strict concept of salvation. It is, moreover, avowedly written to sustain certain psychological presuppositions. There seemed to me, therefore, to be room for a book of this sort.

The subject is one which is both important for Christian doctrine and relevant to Christian evangelism. I have tried to bear these two factors in mind while writing the book, and I hope that it may be of some use both to the student who is concerned to understand and to the minister who is concerned to interpret the gospel of salvation. With the general Christian public in mind I have tried to avoid excessive heaviness of style and undue technicality of content – but I know I have not completely succeeded. Some of the major issues raised by so important a subject are touched upon in the last chapter of the book, but for the most part I have been concerned less with hermeneutics than the exegesis and arrangement of the biblical material.

I want to thank many kind friends for their help, and particularly three former teachers: J. P. V. D. Balsdon, Fellow and until recently Senior Tutor of Exeter College, Oxford, who taught me Classics and made helpful suggestions on chapter 4; Professor H. Chadwick, of Oxford, and Professor C. F. D. Moule, of Cambridge, who taught me Theology, and gave me advice and encouragement for this project.

Indeed, the latter made time to read part of the book in MS. I am very grateful to Professor W. Foerster of Münster for the gift of his articles on the subject of salvation in the *Theologisches Wörterbuch zum N.T.*, Professor A. S. Herbert of Birmingham, and my colleagues, Prebendary Hugh Jordan and the Rev. P. H. Buss, have given me kind assistance with the Old Testament teaching on salvation, while Professor F. F. Bruce of Manchester not only made available to me his essay, *Our God and Saviour—a recurring biblical pattern* before its publication, but has also most generously contributed a Foreword.

I am more than grateful, too, to my friend, the Rev. R. C. Lucas, for first suggesting to me the theme of this book, and to the Rev. E. J. H. Nash both for teaching me many years ago that salvation had a present and a future as well as a past tense, and also for showing me that it could be preached with power and effectiveness in this twentieth century. I am deeply indebted to my father and four of my students, the Rev. W. O. Steele, the Rev. C. H. B. Byworth, Mr. T. Thake and Mr. J. Simons for their willing help in proof-reading, compiling Indices and checking biblical references—no easy task! Last, but by no means least, I want to thank my wife for reading through the whole book as it emerged, and removing some of the more glaring pedantries and obscurities. For those that remain, I must, of course, take full responsibility.

E. M. B. GREEN

Christmas, 1964

Contents

CHAPTER 1

The Language of Salvation in the
Old Testament

"The creed of Israel is, in brief, 'Yahweh saves'."[1] So wrote T. B. Kilpatrick half a century ago, and he was not far wrong. Salvation is the great central theme not only of the Old Testament but of the whole Bible. From the story of God's rescue of Noah and his family from the flood (Gen. 6-9) to that graphic picture of the final destiny of God's saved people as the Bride of Christ in the heavenly Jerusalem (Rev. 21), God is seen to be at work in the rescue of men.[2]

For the greater part of the Christian era, scholars have tended to follow the Alexandrian exegetes in regarding the events of the Old Testament as prefiguring the salvation which Christ came to bring. Thus Isaac bearing the wood for sacrifice up Mount Moriah was thought of as a shadowy foreboding of Jesus, carrying his cross up Golgotha. As a matter of fact this is a somewhat restrained example of the typology employed. It was not beyond the skill of a second-century Christian[3] to make the 318 members of Abraham's household (Gen. 14.14) a numerical cipher denoting Jesus and his cross! In this way much of the Old Testament could be seen as a veiled prediction of the salvation later achieved through the life, death and resurrection of Jesus. This method of interpretation had a value; it emphasized the continuity between the Old and New Testaments. But it had two great weaknesses. It enabled the commentator to read what he liked into the Old Testament text; and it hardly allowed the Old Testament message to mean anything to its original hearers.

With the rise of modern critical scholarship has come a strong reaction against this sort of approach, and a refreshing recognition that the makers of the Old Testament were *men* speaking from God to the

[1] *Encyclopaedia of Religion and Ethics* (1920), article "Salvation".
[2] "Salvation is the central theme of the whole Bible, and as such is related to every other biblical theme," A. Richardson, *Interpreter's Dictionary of the Bible* (1962), *s.v.* "Salvation".
[3] *Ep. Barn.* 9.8.

situation of their own day – and not mere machines recording a time-less echo of his voice. Much greater attention is paid today to the writer himself, the political and historical situation to which he addressed his message and the philosophical and cultural heritage in which he was nourished. The Old Testament is seen nowadays less as the *Book of the Oracles of God* than the *Book of the Acts of God*;[1] God's self-disclosure is seen less in biblical statement than in biblical history. While there is a danger of overemphasis in this direction, it cannot be denied that God's acts in rescuing his people are even more important than the inter-pretation given to those acts in the pages of the Bible. This theme of *Heilsgeschichte*, "salvation history", is what the Bible is all about.

However, so far as the study of salvation is concerned, it makes very little difference whether one adopts the old static conception of the Old Testament as first and foremost a *praeparatio evangelica*, or the newer, more dynamic approach,[2] which sees it as the record of God visiting and redeeming his people. On any showing, salvation is basic.

On this the theologians are agreed; not so the man in the pew. To him, "salvation" carries one of two connotations. It may conjure up in his mind the open-air preacher, the high-pressure evangelist, or that earnest but rather daunting acquaintance who is always enquiring whether he is yet saved. His immediate reaction is to resent this un-warrantable intrusion into his private life, and indeed to defer all such ungentlemanly considerations of ultimate issues.

On the other hand, mention of salvation may induce in the modern churchgoer a soporific, numinous feeling of well-being; it is a word which he associates with church and clergy, with archaic prayer-books and black-bound Bibles. It belongs, in short, to the world of religion, not of life.

This is of course a caricature of the ordinary Christian's attitude to salvation, but it is not a misleading distortion. It serves to emphasize how far we have strayed in our religious thinking from the teaching of the Bible. The Hebrew would not understand the distinction we so often make (at all events by implication) between religion and life.

[1] See G. E. Wright, *God Who Acts* (1952), and Wright and Fuller, *The Book of the Acts of God* (1960).
[2] It is illuminating to compare this modern emphasis on salvation, such as one finds in scholars like R. Davidson (*The Old Testament*, 1964), W. Eichrodt (*The Theology of the Old Testament*, E.T. 1961), A. R. Johnson (*Sacral Kingship in Ancient Israel*, 1955), S. Mowinckel (*He That Cometh*, E.T. 1960 and *The Psalms in Israel's Worship*, E.T. 1962), with the theologians of a generation ago, who rarely mentioned it. Thus one can study the index in vain for any mention of salvation in, e.g. Buchanan Gray's *Sacrifice in the Old Testament* (1925), or Max Loehr's *History of Religion in the Old Testament* (1936). It was, apparently, thought irrelevant to a study of the religion of the Old Testament!

What would be the good of a religion that made no difference to life? The Hebrew would find it hard to understand our familiar distinction between the sacred and the secular. To him, the worship of Yahweh was not something confined to the great annual festivals, and, later on, to worship at the synagogue or prayers in the home. It embraced the whole of life. He saw God in his battles with the enemy, God as the ultimate source of his daily bread, God everywhere. The sacred and the secular were inextricably intertwined. And nowhere is this insight more clearly demonstrated than in the way the Hebrew understood and spoke of salvation.

A number of words are used in the Old Testament to express salvation, and it will be necessary to examine them with some care if we are to discover what this important subject meant to Hebrew man. In so doing, it will be important to bear in mind Professor James Barr's strictures on the merely lexical approach to biblical study. It is not enough, as he points out, to get to work with a concordance, and then suppose that one has elicited a biblical theology.[1] Attention must be paid to the context as well as the word itself, to the usage as well as the semantics.

A. ḤAYAH

There is, first of all, *ḥayah*, a word which used statively (*qal*) means "to be alive", but in the causative sense (*pi 'el* and *hiph 'il*) means "to preserve", "to keep alive" or "to give full and prosperous life" to someone. Seven times it is used in the formula "God save the king" (e.g. 1 Sam. 10.24). Here at once we meet an emphasis which is constant throughout Scripture. It is *God* who saves. Whatever salvation may mean, and it comprises various shades of meaning, it is basically seen as the proper function of God himself.

Of course, the word *ḥayah* is also used in a non-religious sense, "to spare the life of", "to give new life to". Indeed this meaning predominates in the historical writings of the Old Testament. Thus "Joshua saved Rahab the harlot alive" (Josh. 6.25).

But the refusal of the Hebrew to divorce physical from spiritual life is illustrated in the way Ezekiel uses the word. He can use it for ordinary physical life (13.18, 19); he can also give it strong spiritual overtones, for if the wicked man turns away from his wickedness, he will save his soul alive (3.18 and 18.27). It may readily be granted that Ezekiel had little idea of a future life, and was thinking primarily in terms of this life when he spoke of the sinner responding to the call of the watchman in repentance, and so saving his life. But it certainly means far more than the purely physical usage above in 13.18, 19. And

[1] James Barr, *Biblical Words for Time* (1962), especially pp. 161ff.

13

this talk of a saved life in contrast to death, in a context of righteousness and iniquity, of warning and response, had far-reaching effects in the development of the New Testament doctrine of salvation (cf. Acts 20.24-27). The use of this word in Genesis, where it appears frequently, is also significant in view of later usage. Basically, as we have seen, it means "to preserve alive", or, intransitively, "to live". It is used in this perfectly natural sense in 5.3, "Adam lived an hundred and thirty years." But in 19.19 Lot's prayer for rescue is prefaced by this statement, "Behold now, thy servant hath found grace in thy sight, and thou hast magnified thy mercy, which thou hast shewed unto me in saving my life." The reference is to Lot's supernatural deliverance from the wicked city of Sodom, and comprises two elements in particular which reappear throughout later salvation history – judgement and mercy.

In the first place, salvation is seen against the backcloth of divine judgement which is justly meted out upon persistent and flagrant wickedness. It is God who judges; it is God who saves, exactly as in Rom. 1.17, 18.

Secondly, the safety which Lot found depended entirely on God's mercy, and not at all on his own merits. The Genesis account does not even claim with 2 Pet. 2.7 that Lot was a just man vexed with the filthy conversation of the wicked. He appears simply as a man of the world (13.10-14, 19.16) who had strayed a long way from the God of his fathers. Though hospitable (19.1f.), he was weak (19.6, 7), morally depraved (19.8) and drunk (19.33, 35); indeed, his heart was so deep in the world that he had to be positively dragged out of Sodom by the heavenly messengers (19.16). Time and again (e.g. 19.16, "the Lord being merciful unto him", and 19.19, "thou hast magnified thy mercy") it is emphasized that his salvation rested entirely upon the unmerited goodness of God, his ḥesed, his "faithful love", which he shows to men because of what he is, not because of what they are.

We see a final aspect of this word in Gen. 45.7, 47.25, 50.20. Once again, at first sight, it appears to refer to a purely natural phenomenon. The lives of Jacob and his tribe are saved from death by famine through the providential position which Joseph occupies as controller of the granaries of Egypt. But the writer is at pains to point out that there is more at stake here than the preservation from premature death of a few Semitic nomads. "God sent me before you to preserve you a posterity in the earth, and to save your lives by a great deliverance," said Joseph (45.7). God acts as the saviour of his people, through the hand of his chosen delegate. It is God who is in control of the whole chain of events which culminates in Joseph's elevation to this position of influence. It is God, and not Joseph's scheming brothers, who holds the initiative, and is the real actor in the drama. "Ye thought evil against me," says Joseph to his brothers, "but God meant it unto good, to bring to pass as it is this day, to save much people alive" (50.20). It is God who contrives salvation.

B. YASHA', YESHU'A, YESHA'

The sovereign rescue of men and nations by God is the main burden of the most common and important Old Testament root concerning salvation. The word *yasha'* and its cognates has the basic meaning of "bringing into a spacious environment", "being at one's ease, free to develop without hindrance." It is the opposite of the verb *tsarar*, "to be in discomfort, in cramped or distressing circumstances." It deserves close attention, not only because it is normative for the whole concept of salvation in the Old Testament, but because it forms part of several of the best-known names in the Bible, such as Isaiah, Hosea, Joshua, and supremely Jesus. If we are to understand what is implied by Matt. 1.21, "Thou shalt call his name Jesus, for he shall save his people from their sins", it will be imperative to grasp something of what this word *yasha'* had come to mean to the Hebrews.

(i) Salvation is the work of God

One cannot help being struck from the very outset of any study of this word by the remarkable fact that in the vast majority of references to salvation, however it was conceived, God was seen as its author. It is God who saves his flock (Ezek. 34.22), who rescues his people (Hos. 1.7). He alone can do it (Hos. 13.10-14), for, in the last analysis, there is none else (Isa. 43.11).[1] Wherever we look in the books of the Old Testament this fact stares us in the face. It is the Lord who hears from heaven and saves his anointed with the saving strength of his right hand (Ps. 20.6). It is the Lord who saved his people from Egypt (Ps. 106.7-10). He it is who saves them from Babylon (Jer. 30.10). He will always be true to his saving character (Deut. 20.4). For he is the high tower, the refuge, the Saviour of his people (2 Sam. 22.3). He is their God and their Saviour (Isa. 43.3), the Hope of Israel and his

---

[1] Whereas in the Ugaritic pantheon different elements in salvation are shared out among many deities, in Judaism they are all taken over by Yahweh. It is Yahweh, not Asherah, who divides the sea and "works salvation" by slaying the dragon (Ps. 74.12-14). It is Yahweh, not Baal, who controls the storm clouds (Ps. 29 – see H. L. Ginsberg in *The Biblical Archaeologist* (1945), no. 2, p. 53, Isa. 19.1, Deut. 33.26) and is the source of fertility (Hab. 3.8-15. See W. F. Albright 'The Psalm of Habakkuk' in *Studies in Old Testament Prophecy* (1950) pp. 1-18). On the whole subject of this virtual monotheism whereby Yahweh replaces and takes over the functions associated by the heathen with other gods, see G. E. Wright, *God Who Acts* (1952).

Saviour in time of trouble (Jer. 14.8). In short, the whole Old Testament revelation portrays a God who intervenes in the field of history on behalf of his people. To know God at all is to know him as Saviour. "I am the Lord thy God from the land of Egypt, and thou shalt know no god but me; for there is no saviour beside me" (Hos. 13.4). "God" and "Saviour" are synonymous throughout the whole of the Old Testament, not just in Deutero-Isaiah.

But in what sense did the Israelites think of God as Saviour?

(ii) *Salvation is historic*

In framing a preliminary answer to this question, it is significant to notice that the first reference to this word *yasha'* comes in Ex. 14.30, in the story of the deliverance of Israel from Egypt. "Thus the Lord saved Israel that day out of the hand of the Egyptians." It is no exaggeration to say that this rescue from Egypt, the land of bitter bondage under the threat of imminent death at the hand of harsh taskmasters, determined the whole future understanding of salvation by the people of Israel. The Exodus was a great drama in which God was the central actor. It was played out against a backcloth of divine judgement on Egypt, carried out in the plagues. Its plot was God's faithful mercy and love to Israel displayed in their rescue from judgement through the death of a lamb, sealed in the great deliverance of the Red Sea, and issuing in the covenant of Sinai in which God undertook to be their God, and they undertook to be his people (Ex. 19.1-6). As in the case of Lot, so here God comes to the rescue of his people who cannot help themselves. Once again his salvation is accompanied by judgement on the impenitent and unbelieving. Once more, throughout the long story of the wilderness wanderings, marred as it was by rebellion and even apostasy on the part of the Israelites, we see the *hesed* of God lavished upon a people who both forgot him and disobeyed him. Through this deliverance at God's hand, marked by the death of a lamb and the application to each household of its blood, they were rescued from the land of Egypt, and set apart as a people of God's own possession, a kingdom of priests, a holy nation (Ex. 19.6). This theme is taken up and developed in more than one place in the New Testament, as we shall see. It made the deepest impression on the Hebrew mind, and every loyal Jew was careful to keep that impression fresh by the annual Passover feast. "Thou shalt remember that thou wast a bondman in the land of Egypt, and the Lord thy God redeemed thee" is the repeated theme not only of Deuteronomy but of the Passover *haggadah*. The whole essence of Israel's uniqueness was her relationship with a God who saves, and this relationship was rooted and grounded in the historic event of the Exodus, where God stepped in on their behalf to save them *from* Egypt *unto* himself – two more elements in salvation which remain constant throughout the Bible. The centrality of this Exodus experience in the religion of Israel must be seen against the background of the dragon-mythology of the Near East. In the Babylonian creation myth Tiamat, the chaos monster, is destroyed by Marduk. In the Canaanite legend, Lotan or Leviathan, the dragon of chaos, is slain by Baal. The Old Testament writers had no objection to taking over this mythology, and seeing Yahweh as the victor over all the forces of chaos represented by the dragon (Isa. 27.1, Job 41, etc.). But the really remarkable transformation which they give to the myth is this: they historicize it, and see in the deliverance of the Exodus an outworking of the divine victory over the forces of chaos. Thus in Ps. 74.12-14 the "salvation" of the Exodus is seen as the breaking of the heads of Leviathan. The same motif reappears in Ps 89.8-10. Moreover, this deliverance of the Exodus was seen as the pattern for all God's future acts of salvation. When Deutero-Isaiah looks for a way of describing the new act of deliverance from bondage which God was going to effect for the captives, he can do no better than refer to the defeat of the monster of chaos in God's historic intervention at the Exodus (51.9-11). As F. F. Bruce succinctly puts it, "If at the Exodus Yahweh saved his people by making 'a way in the sea, a path in the mighty waters', now he is to save them by making 'a way in the wilderness, and rivers in the desert' (Isa. 43.16, 19)."[1]

Even when the individual worshipper is recording God's deliverance and giving him thanks (e.g. Ps. 66.13-20), he cannot refrain from beginning with a recital of God's salvation of his people in the Exodus (66.5-7); he sees the national rescue and his own as belonging together. When Habakkuk is speaking of God's deliverance from foreign enemies and from drought and pestilence, he still cannot escape from the normative influence of the Exodus (Hab. 3.8ff.). Because of the salvation of God experienced then, he has confidence in continuing preservation by the God of his salvation (3.18).

It is just the same when the king celebrates the deliverance which God has wrought for him and his people (e.g. Ps. 18). He describes the victory (or salvation) in terms coloured both by the ancient conflict-myth and by the historic Exodus. His God is the God who saves. When the prophet looks forward to the ultimate deliverance, the final salvation in the new age, he returns to the symbol of the destruction of Leviathan by Yahweh which had found historical

---

[1] " 'Our God and Saviour': a recurring biblical pattern," in *The Saviour God*, ed. S. G. F. Brandon (1963), p. 62.

expression in the Exodus (Isa. 27.1). So does the psalmist, in a song which may perhaps have been part of an enthronement ceremony of Yahweh at the New Year festival.[1] In Ps. 68, we are told how the Lord "went forth" (*yatsa*) to lead his people out of Egypt (68.7); the experience of salvation is recalled and made contemporary in the liturgy, where it is applied to the discomfiture of enemies in battle (68.12-24), and is given as the ground for the hope of future deliverance from death (68.20, 21). Past, present and future are comprised in the intervention of the Saviour God – "the eternal Now."[2]

Not only did the Exodus profoundly influence the conception of salvation to be found in prophecy and liturgy; it made an equally great impression on the creeds and the religious festivals of Israel. Wright, following von Rad,[3] has shewn how the earliest confessions of faith in the Old Testament are recitals of the saving acts of God (he draws an interesting parallel with Paul's speech in Acts 13.17-23 where this same basic Jewish creed is reproduced – and might have added Acts 7 as well). Thus in Deut. 26.5-9 we read, "A Syrian ready to perish (*or* a wandering Aramaean) was my father, and he went down into Egypt . . . and the Egyptians evil entreated us and afflicted us and laid upon us hard bondage, and when we cried unto the Lord . . . the Lord heard . . . and the Lord brought us forth out of Egypt . . . and he hath brought us into this place." Much the same pattern of belief and confession can be seen in Deut. 6.20-24, Josh. 24.2-13. The deliverance from Egypt is put in the context both of the *shema'* (Deut. 6.4, 5, 12) and of the Decalogue (Deut. 5.6ff.) as the ground on which an ethical God demands an ethical response from the objects of his saving power. As Rowley puts it, "Many peoples have believed their gods took part in the affairs of men . . . What is distinctive of Israel's faith is the belief that God revealed his *character* in his *activity*"[4] (my italics). What God is, his people must reflect.

The influence of the Exodus on the religious festivals is even more astonishing. Each year there were three occasions when all adult male Hebrews were expected to "appear before the Lord", at some local shrine. These festivals may have been adapted from Canaanite use, or may perhaps have come from before the Exodus. The first was the Feast of Unleavened Bread to mark the beginning of the barley harvest (Ex. 23.15, Lev. 23.9ff.). Originally it was nothing to do with

[1] So S. Mowinckel, *The Psalms in Israel's Worship*, i, pp. 173f.
[2] *Ibid.*, p. 187.
[3] Wright, *op. cit.*, ch. 3, and von Rad, *Das formegeschichtliche Problem des Hexateuchs* (1938), which sees this creedal formula as the principle of coherence in the Hexateuch.
[4] *The Faith of Israel* (1956), p. 59.

the Passover, but such was the impact of the Exodus that it subsequently became identified with it, apparently because unleavened bread was used at both, and both took place at much the same time of the year. Even when the old name, *Mazzoth* or Feast of Unleavened Bread is mentioned (as opposed to the *Pesaḥ* or Passover) it still is stamped with the indelible print of the Exodus upon it (Ex. 34.18, 23.15).

The second great feast was the Feast of Weeks, later known as Pentecost, because it took place "seven weeks from such time as thou beginnest to put the sickle to the corn" (Deut. 16.9). It was a harvest festival, and two loaves baked from the new corn were offered to the Lord (Lev. 23.17). Yet even this simple harvest thanksgiving was shot through with the memory of the Exodus. "Thou shalt rejoice before the Lord thy God" as is natural at harvest; but equally, "Thou shalt remember that thou wast a bondman in Egypt; and thou shalt observe and do these statutes" (Deut. 16.12).

The third great feast was Tabernacles or the Feast of Ingathering, which from the time of David onwards became the Enthronement Festival of the king[1] (2 Sam. 6, in connection with 1 Kings 8 and Ps. 132), and was thus doubly linked with salvation through the motif of victory prominent in the enthronement liturgy.[2] But the Exodus had already marked this happy vintage festival with the imprint of salvation. "Ye shall dwell in booths seven days . . . that your generations may know that I made the children of Israel to dwell in booths when I brought them out of the land of Egypt. I am the Lord your God" (Lev. 23.43).

Thus at each of the great festivals the Israelites would be reminded of the saving events which brought them into being as a nation. They would acknowledge that their God was not merely the provider of food for his people (Ps. 145.15) but he was the Saviour God who had rescued them out of the land of Egypt. It is impossible to overestimate the influence of the Exodus as the historical emblem of salvation. It pointed beyond itself to the continued saving activity of God in history for his people, and was the promise and the warrant of the great salvation of the end time. It is not without significance that when John is musing over the final defeat of evil he should see it as the destruction of the great dragon, and hear the cry raised in heaven, "Now is come salvation" (Rev. 12.9-11). Nor is it unimportant that, when Jesus makes his final assault and achieves his final victory over satanic forces in his Passion, Luke should describe it in terms of a new Exodus (Lk. 9.31, Greek). The deliverance of the Exodus both historicizes the age-old myth of the defeat of the dragon, and becomes the paradigm

[1] See Eichrodt, *op. cit.*, p. 124.   [2] See A. R. Johnson, *op. cit.*, pp. 17ff.

for all other acts of divine deliverance until the final banishment of evil from God's world.

Let us now see how the two aspects of salvation, so prominent in the Exodus, work themselves out in the rest of the Old Testament; namely deliverance from foes and consecration as a people for Yahweh.

(iii) *Salvation from enemies*

After the Exodus, God does not abandon his saving activity exercised on behalf of his people. Rather the reverse. He is represented as delivering his people from a variety of ills, particularly, though not exclusively, in the psalms. It is God who saves a man from death (Ps. 6.4, 5) and the fear of it (Ps. 107.13, 14). He saves men from the lion's mouth and from the battlefield alike (Ps. 22.21, Deut. 20.4). Sometimes it is the wicked from whom the man of God asks to be saved (Ps. 59.2), sometimes it is some terrible but unspecified anguish (Ps. 69.1, 2). Sometimes it is from sickness (Isa. 38.20), sometimes from trouble (Jer. 30.7), occasionally in the prophets and rarely in the psalms, salvation is linked with sins (e.g. Ps. 51.14, 130.8 – though in both cases a different verb, *padah*, is used – Ezek. 36.29). The most common usage, perhaps, is in the sense of salvation from enemies; so 1 Sam. 14.23, 2 Sam. 3.18, Ps. 3.7, 7.1, 44.7, 59.2, etc. Usually God effects this through raising up some human agent as saviour, such as Gideon (Judg. 6.14), or Saul (1 Sam. 9.16) or Jonathan (1 Sam. 14.45). But it is always made perfectly plain that God is the real Saviour of his people, though he normally chooses men to cooperate with him in this work. This is expressly stated in the case of Jonathan mentioned above ("Jonathan hath wrought this great salvation in Israel . . . for he hath wrought with God this day"), and it is strongly implied in the cases of Gideon and Saul. To Gideon God says, "Go in this thy might, and *thou* shalt save Israel . . . have not *I* sent thee?" "Surely I will be with thee, and thou shalt smite the Midianites" (Judg. 6.14, 16). And to Samuel God says, with reference to Saul, "*I* will send thee a man . . . and thou shalt anoint him to be captain over my people Israel, that he may save my people out of the hand of the Philistines" (1 Sam. 9.16).

Nevertheless, although God often uses human deliverers, he is not bound to them, and in this very matter of Saul, Israel is rebuked for hankering after a king, a visible saviour, rather than relying on the Lord God of Israel who brought them up out of Egypt, and delivered them from the hand of the Egyptians. They have rejected their God who himself saved them out of all their adversities and tribulations, by saying unto him, "Nay, but set a king over us" (1 Sam. 10.18, 19).

No, God is not dependent on the human agents that he chooses to employ. That is why he is so often called "the Lord God of our salvation" (Ps. 68.19, 88.1 etc., cf. 118.14). Sometimes God has to stress his sovereignty in salvation by ceasing to use some "saviour" who had become proud or disobedient. That, of course, is why Saul had to be set aside. He had deliberately disobeyed God, rebelled against him, and rejected his word; for that reason God rejected him from being king (1 Sam. 15.23).

Sometimes God makes plain that salvation is his sovereign work by dispensing altogether with human intermediaries. It was thus that he saved Jerusalem from the besieging forces of Sennacherib (2 Kings 19.34, 35 and Isa. 37.14-38). In answer to the desperate prayer for help uttered by King Hezekiah, he promised, "I will defend this city, to save it, for mine own sake, and for my servant David's sake." And save them he did, by the plague that ravaged the Assyrian camp to such an extent that when the astonished Israelites "arose early in the morning, behold, they were all dead corpses". It was the same story in God's classic deliverance of his people from Egypt. "He saved them for his name's sake, that he might make his mighty power to be known . . . He saved them from the hand of him that hated them and redeemed them from the hand of the enemy. And the waters covered their enemies; there was not one of them left" (Ps. 106.8, 10, 11). Thus the wondering psalmist delighted to tell the story of God's power, which redounded to God's glory alone. It was thus, too, that God saved his people from Moab in the days of Jehoshaphat (2 Chron. 20.17). The king sought the help of the Lord in prayer (20.6), and God's reply, through the prophet Jahaziel, was clear and prompt: "Ye shall not need to fight in this battle; set yourselves, stand ye still, and see the salvation of the Lord with you, O Judah and Jerusalem."

A good deal of attention has been focused in recent years on the royal psalms (Ps. 2, 21, 45, 72, 110) where the king is greeted in terms of highest adulation. He is the son of Yahweh, holy, victorious, like an angel of God, exercising dominion over the nations, the saviour of his people. This is not merely the courtly language of the Near East; it represents the Jewish faith in God's historical involvement with his people, the Saviour God working through his anointed representative. This is how "the right to universal dominion could therefore be ascribed to the Israelite king as the 'son' of the covenant God without risk of megalomania . . . The royal psalms proclaim the salvation which Yahweh is going to send through his chosen king".[1] And this is how the hope of salvation continued to be applied to successive kings despite frequent disappointment in their predecessors; this is how it was able to survive the destruction of the monarchy altogether. For it was God's salvation for which men looked, until he should bring in the goal of

[1] Eichrodt, op. cit., p. 478.

21

history. This is clear from Amos 5.18. People were looking (albeit in hedonistic terms; hence Amos' denunciation) for the "day of the Lord", the eschatological intervention of God into history, even during the prosperous days of Jeroboam the Second. Although men had rarely "had it so good", they were not satisfied, but looked for God's salvation which even the king was unable to bring about. This is a graphic illustration of the truth that God was conceived of as the Saviour from all foes, spiritual as well as physical.

(iv) Salvation "unto the Lord"

But this saving work which God effects from a variety of evils and through a multiplicity of agencies, is far from being a bare deliverance.[1] It is not merely rescue from a dangerous situation, but rescue for a special purpose. This is made clear in 1 Chron. 16.35. Here God is addressed as "the God of our salvation" by the people. That is to say, their experience of his rescue in the past (16.7-27) leads them confidently to trust that he will be the same in the future (16.35f.). And the salvation for which David prays ("gather us together and deliver us from the heathen") is seen to have a definite purpose – that they may, as a people, worship and praise their Saviour God. "Save us . . . that we may give thanks to thy holy name, and glory in thy praise. Blessed be the Lord God of Israel for ever and ever. And all the people said Amen, and praised the Lord." Indeed, the universal scope of the salvation envisaged is noteworthy throughout the psalm of thanksgiving attributed to this occasion when David has brought the ark of the covenant to Jerusalem.

A similar emphasis on the purpose of salvation is expressed with some frequency in the prophets. Isa. 43.11, 12: "I, even I am the Lord; and beside me there is no saviour. I have declared, and have saved . . . therefore ye are my witnesses, saith the Lord, that I am God." Curiously enough, this passage has affinities with David's psalm in 1 Chron. 16 mentioned above. "Sing unto the Lord, all the earth; shew forth from day to day his salvation" (1 Chron. 16.23) comes there immediately after an account of the mighty deliverances God has achieved on behalf of his people. It is interesting that in two such different strands of the Old Testament as Deutero-Isaiah and the Chronicler, exactly the same purpose should be attributed to the saving work of God. Men and nations are saved by him, not in order that they may sit back and be

[1] G. A. F. Knight, in *A Christian Theology of the Old Testament* (1959), pp. 248ff emphasizes this; he points out how on six successive occasions in Judges the "saviours" whom God raised up "did more than just save their people, or a section of their people, *from* trouble; they 'saved' them into 'rest', a rest which lasted in each case for forty years, that is to say, for a whole generation in the life of man".

comfortable, but that they may bring glory to God by their worship and praise, by the witness they bear to him, and by the lives of dedication in which they show their allegiance.

The voice of Zechariah after the Exile brings the same message from the Lord, "As ye were a curse among the heathen, O house of Judah and house of Israel, so will I save you, and ye shall be a blessing" (Zech. 8.13). Saved, to be a blessing. And the way in which they are to be a blessing is emphasized. "These are the things that ye shall do; Speak ye every man truth to his neighbour; execute the judgement of truth and peace in your gates" (8.16). Perhaps the most famous expression of the purpose of salvation in the whole of the Old Testament is in Isa. 49.6, 7. The obedient Remnant of Israel will fulfil the function that properly belonged to the whole nation (49.3) and so be the Servant of the Lord their Redeemer that they can actually be called his "salvation"; a people so dedicated to God that he can use them not only to summon the exiles of Israel from all the places into which they had been dispersed, but in some sense to be a light to lighten the Gentiles, and bring even kings to worship the Lord. Whatever the detailed explanation of this much-canvassed passage, it is a plain expression of the fact that salvation has a purpose. God who gives the saving power to men expects them to use it to his glory.

In other words, before the end of the Old Testament period, salvation was coming to be seen as the prerequisite rather than merely the goal of obedience. It was a case of "Save me, and I shall keep thy testimonies" (Ps. 119.146), and in that order. Salvation increasingly came to take on an ethical content. God will not save a man or a nation, and simply allow them to remain as they were. The very grace of salvation demands the response of dedication in the rescued. Why, the Decalogue itself is framed on precisely this basis.[1] It is because of what God has done, in being their God and delivering them from the land of Egypt, from the house of bondage, that he calls on them to obey his law (Ex. 20.2). Both Testaments are at pains to emphasize that divine imperative, what man must do, is grounded in the divine indicative, what God has done.

(v) Conditions of Salvation

It is time to consider the conditions of receiving God's salvation which emerge in the pages of the Old Testament. The prime condition

---

[1] "Fulfilling the commandments is thus in no wise the presupposition of salvation. Indeed, the proclamation of the commandments takes place contemporaneously with the election, and therefore obedience can in any case only follow upon the divine saving activity," G. von Rad, *Studies in Deuteronomy* (E.T. 1953), p. 72.

is a simple trusting reliance on God alone, not in any fancied goodness or strength of one's own. This applies both in the national and in the personal sphere. Israel is not to look for alliances with Assyria or Egypt as a solution to their military problems, but to God alone (Hos. 5.13-6.3, Isa. 31.1, Ps. 33.16-20). This is the way they have always received God's salvation, and this is the way they will continue to experience it. "They got not the land in possession by their own sword, neither did their own arm save them, but thy right hand and thine arm, and the light of thy countenance, because thou hadst a favour unto them" (Ps. 44.3).

In the same way, the individual, too, is to rely exclusively on God for his salvation (Ps. 55.16, 86.2, 138.7, etc.). God will not share the glory of his salvation with another, and certainly not with man, who is so quick to forget what God has done for him, and to boast of his own puny abilities and strength (cf. Ps. 106.21). Consequently, it is when men are at the end of their tether, cast solely upon the mercy of God, that he can risk saving them without the danger of their becoming proud. Thus it is the poor, the humble, the weak that God saves (Job 5.15, 22.29, 26.2). It is, the psalms assure us, those who trust in God (Ps. 17.7, 37.40, 86.2), those whose hearts are right before him (Ps. 7.10), the heartbroken and contrite (Ps. 34.6),[1] the afflicted (Ps. 18.27), those who call upon him (Ps. 107.13) and fear him (Ps. 85.9), those who know themselves to be but poor men in need of his succour (Ps. 34.6 – and this includes the king, Ps. 20.6). These are his people (Ps. 119.94). These are the men who are not too full of themselves to receive the salvation he proffers them. Nothing could make more plain than Ex. 14.13 the truth that man's place in salvation is one of trusting response to the loving initiative and intervention of God. "Fear ye not," says Moses in God's name to the people of Israel, when God is about to seal the deliverance from Egypt with the crossing of the Red Sea, "Fear ye not, stand still, and see the salvation of the Lord which he will show to you today." Such faith is the proper attitude in man towards a God who saves; and so it is represented from one end of the Bible to the other. Salvation is not something to be gained or enjoyed independently of God. It depends on a living, trusting obedience to God, and it can be forfeited by apostasy from him (Ps. 78.21ff., cf. 1 Cor. 9.27, 10.1-12).

The Old Testament does not conceal the fact that such faith can easily degenerate into superstition, just as prayer can degenerate into the attempt to force God's hand. In 1 Sam. 4 the Israelites realize that their defeat by the Philistines is to be seen as a chastening from the

[1] Persistence in sin separates a man or nation from God's saving activity (Isa. 59.1, 2).

Lord, and so they send for the ark of the covenant (4.3), the visible pledge, the sacramental symbol of God's presence in their midst. They are sure that, provided they are armed with this talisman, the victory will be theirs. Instead, they suffer a signal defeat and the ark is captured (4.11). They have to learn that God cannot be manipulated, nor will he tolerate trust in any other than he, be it never so sacred a symbol.

In contrast, as this same first book of Samuel makes plain, once men come in sincere penitence to God and are willing to obey him rather than attempt to use him for their convenience, then he does save. The following sequence of events is illuminating. "Samuel spake unto all the house of Israel, saying, If ye do return unto the Lord with all your hearts, then put away the strange gods and Ashtaroth from among you, and prepare your hearts unto the Lord, and serve him only; and he will deliver you out of the hand of the Philistines . . . Then the children of Israel did put away the Baalim and Ashtaroth and served the Lord only. . . . And the children of Israel said unto Samuel, Cease not to cry unto the Lord our God for us, that he will save us . . . And Samuel cried unto the Lord for Israel, and the Lord heard him . . . And the Philistines drew near against *Israel*; but the *Lord* thundered with a great thunder that day upon the Philistines and discomfited them, and they were smitten before Israel . . . Then Samuel took a stone. . . . and called the name of it Ebenezer, saying, Hitherto hath the Lord helped us. So the Philistines were subdued, and they came no more into the coast of Israel" (1 Sam. 7.3-13). Israel repent, trust God and are willing to obey him. Prayer is made to the Lord in the confidence that he will save. These actions bespeak an attitude which God can bless, and so God discomfits the opposition before Israel, who are not slow to follow up the advantage and do not forget to give glory to God for the victory which is rightly his. This, surely, is no inadequate insight into what salvation means in either Testament.

We have seen that salvation involves deliverance from a variety of evil situations and commitment to the God who has saved. We have seen that the basic human prerequisites are a humble recognition of our total inadequacy to save ourselves, a firm trust in God and prayer to him in an attitude of willingness to obey his will. It is now time to enquire more particularly into the content of salvation.

(vi) The Content of Salvation
Victory

One of the important èlements in the deliverance God affords to men is victory (e.g. 1 Sam. 14.45). As F. J. Taylor puts it, "To save meant to be possessed of the necessary strength, and to act on it so that it became manifest. David gained salvation when he reduced the surrounding peoples to obedience (2 Sam 8.14). Any chieftain who had sufficient strength to gain victory over the foes of the people could be described as a saviour (Judg. 2.18, 6.14), but as it was God who had raised up the saviour (Ex. 14.30, 1 Sam. 10.19), he was preeminently their Saviour ... To save another is to communicate to him one's own prevailing strength (Job 26.2), to give him and to maintain the necessary strength. Only God is so strong that his own arm obtains salvation (victory, security, freedom) for himself (Ps. 98.1, Job 40.14), and everybody else must rely on a stronger than himself (i.e. God) for salvation."[1]

Not only does the same Hebrew term (yesha' or yeshu'a) do duty both for "salvation" and for "victory", but, as we saw above, throughout the Bible the salvation wrought by God is dramatized as victory over the dragon, deliverance from the forces of chaos and evil. Salvation as victory in this sense is found in Ps. 65.5-9, and F. F. Bruce has demonstrated very clearly its persistence throughout Scripture.[2]

So crucial is the link between victory and salvation that it figures prominently in the enthronement psalms. The enthronement of the king is the emblem of the sovereignty of God. Thus Mowinckel can claim "Yahweh's universal dominion nowhere stands out so clearly as in the enthronement psalms".[3] The identification of victory with salvation in an enthronement psalm like 98.1, 2 is as clear as could be. "O sing unto the Lord a new song, for he hath done marvellous things; his right hand and his holy arm hath gotten him the victory. The Lord hath made known his salvation."

This theme, of course, is not confined to a small group of psalms of this character. It is to be found throughout the Old Testament. "Give thy strength unto thy servant, and save the son of thine handmaid," cries an unknown individual whose prayer became used in public (Ps. 86.16). Again, Ps. 44.7, which may have been composed in the Maccabaean wars, stresses the element of victory in salvation: "Thou hast saved us from our enemies, and hast put them to shame that hate us." Or take the chronicler: "They slew the Philistines, and the Lord saved them by a great deliverance" (1 Chron. 11.14). Indeed, it is no exaggeration to say that almost every reference to salvation in the Old Testament has this note of victory about it.

Vindication

Secondly, there is an element of vindication in the Old Testament

[1] *Theological Word Book of the Bible*, ed. A. Richardson (1950), s.v. 'Save, Salvation'.
[2] " 'Our God and Saviour': a recurring biblical pattern," in *The Saviour God*, a Festschrift for E. O. James (1963).
[3] *Op. cit.*, i, p. 161.

teaching on salvation. When God steps in to save a man or a people, let nobody else speak against him. When God makes a man's cause his own, he vindicates that man, he gives judgement for him. This emerges most clearly in the psalms. "God arose to judgement, to save all the meek upon earth" (Ps. 76.9); "Save me, O God, by thy name, and judge me by thy strength" (Ps. 54.1); "He shall judge the poor of the people, he shall save the children of the needy, and shall break in pieces the oppressor" (Ps. 72.4); "He shall stand at the right hand of the poor, to save him from those that condemn his soul" (Ps. 109.31). The imagery is plainly derived from the administration of justice among the Hebrews.[1] The elders would meet in the gate of the town, and decide the cases that were brought before them. Often, no doubt, they would give sentence for some poor, oppressed person (the "fatherless and widow" are the classic examples) who was being exploited by an unscrupulous but powerful neighbour. In so doing they would save that man, vindicate him, make his cause their own. And after their verdict, the rich oppressor would be very foolhardy indeed if he ventured further to oppress or disparage his erstwhile victim. Now that is what God does with his people who know their poverty and need, and seek redress and help from him. He intervenes to give judgement on their behalf, to save them. God is righteous in remembering his covenant with his people; he will make their cause his own.

The importance of the covenant idea in the religion of Israel has been well brought out in W. Eichrodt's *Theology of the Old Testament*, vol. 1. It is because of the covenant that the salvation and righteousness of God can be so closely linked as to be almost interchangeable in Deutero-Isaiah (e.g. "My salvation is near to come, and my righteousness to be revealed", Isa. 56.1, cf. 45.8, 19-25, 46.13, 51.3-6.) and occasionally in the Psalms (e.g. 98.1-3). Weiser, commenting on this passage, says, "Israel stands out among the nations not as a people who are distinguished from other nations by special superior qualities, and whose election could therefore be regarded as a kind of reward for these superior qualities, but as the people in whose history the divine will to save is continually made manifest."[2] God vindicates his own name among the heathen captors of Israel by espousing the cause of this feeble, oppressed nation which trusts him. His salvation is indeed an expression of his righteousness in the sense of faithfulness to his covenant promise. "Thus it is because God is righteous, not because of any righteousness of her own, that Israel may hope for salvation: Yahweh is 'a just God and a Saviour' (Isa. 45.21)."[3] The extent to

[1] See L. Köhler, *Hebrew Man* (1956), ch. 8.   [2] *The Psalms*, (1962), p. 638.
[3] A. Richardson, *Introduction to the Theology of the New Testament* (1958), p. 80.

which this background influenced Paul's doctrine of justification is debatable, because the situation envisaged in Romans is very different from that of Deutero-Isaiah,[1] but it certainly influenced the action of Jesus the Saviour when he entered Jerusalem in triumph. For the refrain of Isa. 45.21, "a just God and a Saviour" is taken up precisely in the prophecy of Zechariah (9.9) which he fulfilled on that occasion. The coming king of the ideal age is seen by Zechariah as "just and having salvation". He comes to express the character of Yahweh and to continue his work.

Satisfaction

Third, there is often a suggestion of release, freedom and complete well-being, not only in the root meaning of *yasha'* but also in the context in which it appears.

The word itself involves the idea of being wide or spacious. Knight explains it delightfully.[2] "The Israelites, confined to their narrow hills and valleys, always felt danger lurking behind their back. From over the crest of a hill an arrow could fly from a bow sped by an enemy hid from all sight. The Hebrew used to believe that it would be good to live on a flat, open plain, where he could see an enemy from afar. Then he would be able to lie down without fear of molestation." The psalmists spiritualized such a conception and thus we find them writing, "He brought me forth into a large place; he delivered me" (Ps. 18.19, cf. Ps. 31.8 in the light of the "redemption" mentioned in 31.5). This deliverance means peace both from physical enemies and from the spiritual foes which assault the human heart (e.g. Ps. 116.13, Mic. 4.10.) Salvation means nothing less than wholeness of body and mind.

The context often illuminates this strand in *yasha'*. Thus we read, "Save thy people, and bless thine inheritance; feed them also, and lift them up for ever" (Ps. 28.9). Again, "God will save Zion and will build the cities of Judah, that they may dwell there and have it in possession. The seed also of his servants shall inherit it; and they that love his name shall dwell therein (Ps. 69.35f.). Or again, "With long life will I satisfy him, and show him my salvation" (Ps. 91.16) and "Save us, O Lord our God, and gather us from among the heathen, to give thanks unto thy holy name and to triumph in thy praise" (Ps. 106.47).

[1] In Romans he is not thinking so much of God's rescue of a people to which he had bound himself by the ties of covenant, but the entirely unlooked for mercy offered to those who had no claim on him. Furthermore, Paul does not quote Isa. 40-55 in this connection. However, Rom. 3.26 is often taken to support the identification of righteousness and salvation in Paul, although I doubt whether this can really be maintained in the light of Pauline usage and theology.

[2] *Op. cit.*, p. 328.

This is invariably the main emphasis in Zephaniah (3.17, 19) and Zechariah (8.7, 13, 9.16, 10.6, 12.7) and it is often to be found in Isaiah and Jeremiah. God brings a man or a nation into a richer, fuller experience of life when he intervenes to save. In the graphic metaphor of Isa. 12.3, he makes men joyfully to draw water out of the wells of salvation.[1]

Costliness

Fourthly, it is often made very plain that God's salvation is no light and easy thing. Though it costs man nothing, being offered him in sheer grace, it costs God dear. This emphasis on the costliness of salvation is important, and is brought out in a variety of ways, notably in the sixth-century prophets. Sometimes the title "Redeemer" is linked with that of "Saviour" (e.g. "I am thy Saviour and Redeemer, the Mighty One of Jacob", Isa. 49.26, 60.16). Sometimes the two ideas are linked in the context, e.g. "Thus saith the Lord, the Redeemer of Israel . . . In an acceptable time have I heard thee, and in a day of salvation have I helped thee" (Isa. 49.7, 8). Particularly memorable is that hauntingly beautiful passage in Isa. 63.8, 9, "Surely, they are my people, children that will not lie. So he was their Saviour. In all their affliction he was afflicted, and the angel of his presence saved them; in his love and in his pity he redeemed them, and he bare them and carried them all the days of old." What a rich complex of associated concepts we have here! God is their Saviour and Redeemer, he suffers with his people, his presence is in their midst; their salvation issues from his love and pity which constitutes them as his people, the "children" whom he protects and safeguards. But in addition to all this, it is impossible to miss the hint of the costliness of their redemption to God. He identified himself with their situation, in order to rescue them from it.

These, then, are some of the main contents in this idea of salvation as used in the Old Testament. And the last one mentioned, costliness to God, seems to be emphasized in two or three other words which are used to denote deliverance, words which are quite closely related in meaning with *yasha'*. We must pay at least cursory attention to them.

C. GO'EL

Go'el primarily means to act the part of a kinsman. It is a family word. The kinsman vindicates his relative; very often he has the duty

---

[1] Mowinckel thinks the imagery derives from an ancient Canaanite anticipation of the water-drawing ceremony of the Feast of Tabernacles (*op. cit.*, i, p. 131): "The water is to procure 'salvation', i.e. peace and prosperity."

of avenging his blood (see Num. 35.19, 21, 24, Josh. 20.3, 5, 9, etc.); sometimes he buys a member of the family out of slavery (Lev. 25.48f.), or reclaims his field by payment of a price (Ruth 4.4, 6, Lev. 25.26, 32). But whenever this word was used it carried with it the idea of effort on the part of the redeemer in the cause of the relative; effort, and often the payment of a ransom, too.

Frequently God is spoken of as the *go'el*, the great kinsman of his people, in particular when reference is made to his deliverance of Israel from Egypt. "Thou art the God that doest wonders. Thou hast made known thy strength among the peoples. Thou hast with thine arm redeemed thy people" (Ps. 77.14, 15); "I will redeem you with a stretched out arm" (Ex. 6.6). Or again, "Their redeemer is strong; the Lord of hosts is his name: he shall thoroughly plead their cause" (Jer. 50.34). This word is applied to God with great frequency in the latter part of Isaiah. He is seen as the Redeemer from Egypt, the Redeemer from Babylon (Isa. 41.14, 43.14, 44.6, 24, 47.4, etc.) and the Redeemer from sin (Isa. 44.21-23, cf. 63.9). Now in what sense can God be a redeemer or kinsman in this way? Has the idea of payment been entirely lost, and does the word mean no more in Deutero-Isaiah than "deliver"? This is often said. Indeed, Snaith in his *Distinctive Ideas of the Old Testament* regards Isa. 52.3 as regulative for the ideas of *go'el* when applied to God, "Ye shall be redeemed without money."[1] Certainly no crude concept of a ransom price must be applied to God's redeeming work, or we shall find ourselves asking with Origen, to whom God paid the ransom, and wherein it consisted. But nevertheless the idea of the costliness of deliverance is not so lightly to be dismissed. It is present in this very passage of Isa. 52. After describing the joyful return of the exiles, the prophet exclaims (52.10), "The Lord hath made bare his holy arm in the eyes of all the nations; and all the ends of the world shall see the salvation of our God." The redemption of God's people was costly. That, presumably, is why the word was retained. In Leviticus, a priestly book thought to have been written at much the same time as Deutero-Isaiah, the element of costliness to the human kinsman is strongly emphasized, as we have seen. Is the word not likely to have carried much the same connotation when applied to God in Deutero-Isaiah? Indeed, a verse such as Isa. 43.3 (to which we shall be returning later) suggests strongly that the idea of costly purchase was very much present still. "I am the Lord thy God, the Holy One of Israel thy Saviour: I gave Egypt for thy ransom, Ethiopia and Seba for thee." The link between redemption and ransom is too palpable to be avoided.

Surely B. F. Westcott has caught the right nuance of the word when

[1] p. 86.

30

applied to God, "It cannot be said that God paid to the Egyptian oppressor any price for the redemption of his people. On the other hand the idea of the exertion of a mighty force, the idea that the 'redemption' costs much, is everywhere present. The force may be represented by divine might, or love, or self-sacrifice which become finally identical."[1] Certainly the *go'el* metaphor was ascribed to God to stress his kinship with his people Israel and his gracious love to them. But it also emphasizes[2] that the carrying out of the kinsman's function by the Lord cost him as dear as it did the human kinsman who had to pay a ransom price.

D. PADAH

The *padah* root is rather similar in meaning. Basically it means "to acquire by giving something in exchange". It is mainly applied to the redemption of a life by the surrender of another life to die in its stead. Thus "Every firstling of an ass thou shalt redeem with a lamb; and if thou wilt not redeem it, then thou shalt break his neck: and all the firstborn of man among thy children shalt thou redeem" (Ex. 13.13). It was a permanent reminder of the deliverance from Egypt, when the firstborn were all killed by the angel of destruction, except those Hebrews who obeyed the divine instruction to sacrifice a lamb in the place of the firstborn; then the destroying angel passed over that household (Ex. 13.14, 15). The word is essentially substitutionary. And it is used in this way of the redemption of men or animals with considerable freedom in Exodus and Numbers. But God is also made the subject of this verb. Clearly, the idea of substitutionary death requires some modification when applied to him. "When it is a question of God ransoming his people, there is no exchange conceivable; God acts purely from grace and requires nothing in return. It is thus that he saved his people from their bondage in Egypt (Deut. 7.8)."[3] True enough, the idea of substitution goes, when this word is applied to God but the overtones of costliness remain. It was no light matter for God to intervene and rescue his people from Egypt (Deut. 9.26, etc.), from trouble (Ps. 25.22), from sins (Ps. 130.8), from the power of the grave (Ps. 49.15, cf. Hos. 13.14 where *ga'al* is used). It was no light matter to redeem Abraham (Isa. 29.22) or bring the nation back from exile (Isa. 35.10, 51.11). All this was not achieved through a wave of God's hand. It required effort. This is made very clear in

[1] Commentary on *Hebrews* (1892), p. 296.
[2] "When applied to God . . . the emphasis is upon the graciousness of the act rather than its cost, even though the latter is still present", G. A. F. Knight, *op. cit.*, p. 222.
[3] F. Michaeli in *Vocabulary of the Bible* (1958), s.v. "Salvation".

2 Sam. 7.23, "What one nation in the earth is like thy people, even like Israel, whom God went to redeem for a people to himself, and to make him a name, and to do for you great things and terrible, for thy land, before thy people, which thou redeemedst to thee from Egypt, from the nations and their gods? For thou hast confirmed to thyself thy people Israel to be a people unto thee for ever; and thou, Lord, art become their God." Deliverance is costly to God.[1] This point is made very clear by the way in which the LXX translators almost translated it by *lutroō*, "to ransom."[2] As with *go'el*,[3] the biblical writers seem deliberately to have chosen a word which expressed the costliness of deliverance, even though they might leave themselves open to some misunderstanding.

B. KŌPHER

The third word to consider here is *kōpher*. It means a "ransom price". Normally it is paid by a man for his life which has become forfeit, in order that he may go free (so Ex. 21.28ff., 30.12, Prov. 21.18, Job, 36.18). In one important passage this word is used of God's deliverance of his people, Isa. 43.1-4. These verses are particularly significant, for they link together several of these related titles of deliverance; they remind us that the God who created his people loves them and saves them, redeems and rescues them, and will never desert them. "For I am the Lord thy God, the Holy One of Israel, thy Saviour; I gave Egypt for thy ransom, Ethiopia and Seba for thee. Since thou wast precious in my sight thou hast been honourable and I have loved thee; therefore will I give men for thee, and people for thy life." Presumably this means that God, in his counsels, has already assigned to the Persians, as compensation for letting Israel go free, the countries of Egypt, Ethiopia and Seba.[4] This was remarkably fulfilled a few years later when the power of Babylon was overthrown by the Persian Cyrus, and Israel allowed to return to her own land. Shortly afterwards Cambysses invaded Egypt and made it into a Persian province, while the Ethiopians were reduced to a tributary status.[5]

It is surely no accident that three words, *go'el*, *padah* and *kōpher*, which in normal usage denote what can only be called a ransom or substitutionary idea, should be applied to God in his redeeming

---

[1] See also Neh. 1.10, Ps. 78.42f.

[2] See L. Morris, *Apostolic Preaching of the Cross* (1955), p. 17.

[3] Though here the primary meaning in the religious sense appears to be that of protector rather than redeemer (A. R. Johnson, *Supplement to Vetus Testamentum*, i (1953), pp. 67ff.), this does not alter the costliness of the action.

[4] On this passage, see S. H. Hooke, "The Theory and Practice of Substitution," in *Vetus Testamentum* ii, pp. 2ff.

[5] See Herodotus 3.97, 7.69.

activity.[1] As we have seen, nowhere does the Old Testament formulate improper queries as to what the ransom is or to whom it is paid. All such crude ideas are foreign to it. What, however, the use of these words does most forcibly suggest is that God's salvation is a very costly matter to him. Despite the dangers, the writers in both Testaments take the risk of using such language of God, lest we should ever assume about God's salvation, what Renan said of his forgiveness, "*C'est son métier*". It is not God's obligation to deliver us. Salvation springs from costly grace.

[1] T. C. Vriezen says rightly, "Biblical theology cannot do without the idea of substitution, but it is only in the personal sacrifice that it can be found in its fulness, in the mediator's service on behalf of his brethren, and to a God who is personally moved with compassion for sinners" (*An Outline of Old Testament Theology* (1958), p. 301).

CHAPTER 2

The Hope of Salvation in the Old Testament

FINAL SALVATION

The salvation hope of the Old Testament was from the earliest times eschatological.[1] By this we do not mean that it was exclusively concerned with the future and the end of history, but that it was an experience by the nation of Israel of a past intervention by God on their behalf at the Exodus, ratified by the promises and covenant at Sinai, and continued in deliverances throughout her history, of which the greatest was the Return from Exile. Moreover salvation history must issue in the final victory of God in and for his creation, simply because he *is* God, and the future is of a piece with the past under his lordship of time. "There is no divorce or contradiction between the historical and the eschatological, because the former, by becoming active in the present, and no mere past-and-gone event, is the matrix and type of the latter; the eschatological salvation, even now active in the present, is the final realization beyond history of that which the historical redemption foreshadowed and promised. Past, present and future constitute, not three deliverances but one deliverance."[2]

The Jew knew full well that God had acted for him in the past. How could he ever forget it? At every Passover his mind was graphically taken back to the great deliverance from Egypt; the very existence of his nation was grounded in that dramatic rescue. "I brought your armies out of the land of Egypt; therefore ye shall observe this day in your generations by an ordinance for ever" (Ex. 12.17). This Passover ordinance was not seen as a bare memorial of what had once happened in the past. In some way it actualized the past for the worshippers. It is interesting to notice, e.g. in Deut. 26.2-10 and in the later Passover

---

[1] See Eichrodt, *op. cit.*, ch. xi, and the use he makes of H. Gressmann's *Der Ursprung der Israelitisch-jüdischen Eschatologie.*

[2] A. Richardson, "Salvation," in *Interpreter's Dictionary of the Bible*, iv, p. 173.

haggadah, how these salvation-events of long ago are represented as affecting not just our forefathers but *us.* The historical salvation of the past is made contemporary in the cult. The logic of this was inescapable. For God was not dead. He who had saved them once would save them still. How can he scrap what is precious to him, what he has made his own at great cost? When Israel sins and Moses asks God to visit their sin upon himself, God does not do so (Ex. 32.30–35). For he is the God who saves (1 Sam. 14.39). He does not save Israel because she deserves it; rather the reverse. "I do not this for your sakes, O house of Israel, but for mine holy name's sake, which ye have profaned among the heathen. I will sanctify my great name . . . and the heathen shall know that I am the Lord, saith the Lord God, when I shall be sanctified in you before their eyes" (Ezek. 36.22ff.). Ezekiel here sums up much of the emphasis of the historical books. Salvation is "into" the name, the possession, the ownership of Yahweh, and his honour is bound up with the rescue of the people to which he has pledged himself. Thus continually throughout their history, God sends saviours to Israel and delivers them (Judg. 6.14, 2 Kings 14.27, etc.). He is a just God and a Saviour (Isa. 45.21) and can never be untrue to his character.

This fact accounts for the ups and downs of salvation history in Israel. Time and again they became proud, idolatrous, immoral, and in consequence they suffered defeat at the hands of their enemies; for God cannot afford to bless men while they are in such a condition. Then, chastened by defeat or by their loss of the sense of God's presence, they repented, became willing once again to obey God, and turned back to him. In response, he saved them. This was the constantly repeated pattern of events. No wonder the psalmist repeats his cry, "Turn us again, O God . . . and we shall be saved" (Ps. 80.3, 7). It is indeed a marvellous thing that God should stay mindful of his covenant, and faithful to the people who were so often unfaithful to him, and they came to recognize the wonder of it; "thy faithfulness reacheth unto the clouds" (Ps. 36.5). They saw, too, that it was only their misdeeds which robbed them of God's help and strength; that defeat or captivity were his means of humbling their pride and drawing them back to himself, their true and only Saviour. The characteristic interplay of God's constant faithfulness and Israel's fitful response (interspersed with more frequent apostasy), is brilliantly depicted in Neh. 9. It was "because they were disobedient and rebelled against thee . . . therefore thou deliveredst them into the hands of their enemies who vexed them; and in the time of their trouble, when they cried unto thee, thou heardest them from heaven; and according to thy manifold mercies thou gavest them saviours, who saved them out of the hand of

35

their enemies. But after they had rest, they did evil again before thee . . .", and the whole sad process began again. "Therefore thou leftest them in the hand of their enemies, so that they had the dominion over them; yet when they returned and cried unto thee, thou heardest them from heaven; and many times didst thou deliver them according to thy mercies" (9.26-28). And through it all "for many years didst thou forbear them, and . . . for thy great mercy's sake thou didst not utterly consume them nor forsake them; for thou art a gracious and merciful God" (9.30, 31). That was it. God never changes. He is a just God – and therefore he must not overlook wrongdoing; he is also a Saviour – and so great is his mercy and graciousness that he must come to the rescue of his people when once they seek his face again and return to him.

But is there no future element in God's salvation? Indeed there is. And increasingly the prophets laid emphasis upon it. It was the corollary of their conviction that God is the Lord of history. He could not rest content with this constant alternation of rebellion and repentance. He would surely one day complete the salvation of which he had so often given them the foretaste. It is quite impossible in a rapid survey of this kind to assess the eschatological hopes of the Israelites as they developed down the centuries, and I am certainly not competent to do so. The writings of Jacob,[1] Knight,[2] Mowinckel,[3] Rowley,[4] Wheeler Robinson,[5] Vriezen[6] and Lindblom[7] are illuminating but to some extent mutually contradictory.[8] It is important to notice, with Knight, the rich variety of imagery in which God's final purpose for mankind is expressed in different parts of the Old Testament; themes such as the Son of David, the Branch, the Royal Psalms, the Ideal Priest, the Holy City, the Bride of Yahweh, the Prophet like Moses, the Servant, the New Covenant, the Outpouring of the Spirit and many others mark the varying conceptions of the "Day of the Lord". Vriezen presents a useful (rough) *schema* when he divides the eschatological hope into four historical periods.

The first is what he calls, somewhat misleadingly, *pre-eschatological*

[1] E. Jacob, *The Theology of the Old Testament* (E.T. 1958), pp. 317ff.
[2] G. A. F. Knight, *A Christian Theology of the Old Testament* (1959), pp. 294ff.
[3] S. Mowinckel, *He that Cometh* (E.T. 1956), *passim*.
[4] H. H. Rowley, "The Day of the Lord," in *The Faith of Israel* (1956), pp. 177ff. and *The Relevance of Apocalyptic* (1963).
[5] H. Wheeler Robinson, *Inspiration and Revelation in the Old Testament* (1946), pp. 135ff.
[6] T. C. Vriezen, *An Outline of Old Testament Theology* (1958), pp. 343ff.
[7] J. Lindblom, *Prophecy in Ancient Israel* (1962), pp. 360ff.
[8] Thus Lindblom finds very little place for eschatology in the Old Testament prophets, and argues that they were primarily men with a message for their own time.

because it is concerned not so much with the renewal of the world as with the greatness of Israel. To this period, before the rise of the eighth-century prophets, he would assign the popular hopes attacked in Amos 5.18, that the Day of the Lord would be a time of great glory for Israel, a sort of reenactment of the idealized age of David. This political and national hope may be represented in such early parts of the Old Testament as Gen. 49, Num. 23f., Deut. 33, the "blessings" of Jacob, Baalam and Moses.

The second period, which he calls *proto-eschatological*, belongs to the prophets from Amos to Jeremiah, who rebuked the eudaemonism of the popular idea of the "Day of Yahweh", and insisted that it would involve judgement as well as salvation. All that offends God will be punished, whether it be found outside Israel or within. Thus Amos cries, "Woe to you that desire the day of the Lord. To what end is it for you? The day of the Lord is darkness, and not light. As if a man did flee from a lion and a bear met him; or went into the house and leaned his hand on the wall, and a serpent bit him" (5.18ff.), and it is only in the concluding verses of his prophecy that Amos offers any hope of salvation (9.11ff.). For that very reason they have often been attributed to another hand. But this is not necessary. The same hope of salvation beyond judgement is found elsewhere in these early prophets. Joel 2.2 makes it clear that the Day of the Lord will be "a day of darkness and gloom, a day of cloud and thundercloud" which will purge the earth in judgement, but will be followed by Yahweh pouring out his Spirit upon all flesh, and despite the cosmic disasters of the end-time, "It shall come to pass that whosoever shall call upon the name of the Lord shall be delivered" (2.28-32). In the apocalyptic chapters of Isaiah the same pattern holds good. The cosmic disasters associated with God's coming in judgement (24.19ff.) are followed by some of the most exalted language about salvation to be found in the whole of the Old Testament: "He will swallow up death in victory; and the Lord God will wipe away tears from off all faces . . . Lo, this is our God; we have waited for him and he will save us . . . We will be glad and rejoice in his salvation" (Isa. 25.6-8).

It is just the same earlier in the book of Isaiah. The famous passages prophesying universal peace and submission to the Lord, the ultimate days of salvation (Isa. 2 and 11), both follow immediately upon passages stringent in their emphasis on judgement. "By prostrating all human greatness in the dust before the divine Judge the prophets made room for the recreating work of the redeemer. Thus the ingredients of the old picture of hope [i.e. the picture of Paradise] could be applied in a refined and purified form, in so far as they described God's activity . . . in its cosmic significance and its concrete immanence, namely as a

37

renovation both of the world and of the people. But the emphasis was now laid in a different place, and the dominating feature in the foreground became the consummation of God's sovereignty."[1] Thus Hosea anticipates a time when Israel will be for "many days without a king and without a prince and without a sacrifice . . . And afterwards they shall return and seek the Lord their God, and David their king; and shall fear the Lord and his goodness in the latter days" (3.4, 5).

Vriezen's third stage of development in the eschatological hope is found in the prophets of the Exile who look for *salvation in the near future*, or see it in process of being realized. Deutero-Isaiah regards the troubles of the Exile as the womb from which salvation will spring forth (40.1f., 51.17ff.). The redemption of the people is nothing less than a new creation, comparable to the creation of the world and the banishment of primeval chaos, comparable to the miracle of deliverance at the Red Sea when Israel was constituted a people for the Lord (Isa. 43.14-16, 51.9ff.). Though each prophet has unique features, there is a common understanding of salvation running through such passages as Jer. 31.31-34, Ezek. 37.21-28, Zech. 8.7-13 and 2 Isaiah. These men of God looked for a return from captivity, the unification of the two kingdoms, a spiritual revival in the land, a moral reformation of the people with whom God would establish a new covenant, written in men's hearts, so that everyone would know the Lord. This would all take place under a scion of David's line, who would be the shepherd of the people and their prince for ever. The effect of this would be an eternal reign of peace, love and righteousness, where even the hostilities of nature would be reconciled, and where the Gentile nations would be drawn into the relationship with God enjoyed by Israel (Isa. 49.5-13, Hag. 2.4-9, Ps. 96.1ff., Zech. 2.7-13) and perhaps inaugurate a new era of political importance for Israel. Salvation in this sense is particularly common in Deutero-Isaiah. Other prophets before him had looked for the spread of the religion of Israel to the Gentiles, but he sees this as the result of the mission of the people of Israel renewed and reconstituted as the servant of the Lord by their divine deliverance from captivity. "How beautiful upon the mountains are the feet of him that bringeth good tidings of good . . . that publisheth salvation," cries the prophet (52.7); "Look unto me and be ye saved, all the ends of the earth; for I am God, and there is none else" (45.22). Again he cries, "Break forth into joy, sing together ye waste places of Jerusalem, for the Lord hath comforted his people, he hath redeemed Jerusalem. The Lord hath made bare his holy arm in the eyes of all the nations; and the ends of the earth shall see the salvation of our God" (52.9f.). This passage leads directly in to the last

[1] Eichrodt, *op. cit.*, p. 481.

38

and greatest of the Servant Songs. If the author is the same,[1] it would seem that he realized that the longed-for salvation of Israel would only be accomplished through suffering and rejection, indeed through atoning suffering.[2] To this we shall return. But at all events, it is plain that the national ideal of the Return from Exile and the spiritual ideal of the inauguration of the kingdom of God on earth merge. Salvation means something far more than the mere return from Babylon.

As we know, the Return from Babylon did take place, but in very different circumstances and with very different results from those expected by the exiles.[3] The Davidic deliverer did indeed come, some five centuries later, but both his person and his kingdom were very different from what they expected. The consummation of all things, and the universal establishment of the kingly rule of God did not accompany the returning exiles, and over two thousand years later it still lies in the future. It seems a characteristic of prophecy to telescope events separated by perhaps many centuries. Prophecy, in its predictive sense,[4] is not by any means history written in the future sense. The prophet sees the great mountain peaks in the vista ahead, and takes no account of the vast tracts of 'dead ground' that lie between them.[5] Thus, while the full picture sketched on the prophetic canvas has not

[1] And to doubt it is quite arbitrary. Had the prophet spoken only of deliverance, he would have represented no advance on the crude conceptions of the Day of the Lord which Amos set out to destroy. With his deep understanding of the nature of sin, it is incredible that he could have thought of external restoration without inward renewal, of salvation without suffering. See Vriezen, *loc. cit.*, p. 363.

[2] His message appears to have had little effect upon his contemporaries and successors, though there are some traces of it in the character of the humble ruler in Zech. 9 and the theme of Lam. 3.1ff. The message of victory through service and suffering is never a popular one.

[3] Thus Zerubbabel begins by being regarded in an almost messianic light; for Haggai he is Yahweh's "servant", his "chosen one", his "signet-ring" (2.23), and Zechariah's references to the Branch (3.8, 6.12) may well have been occasioned by this Davidic governor of the returned people. But neither then nor later was the longed-for consummation of the Davidic kingdom realized, and the bitter disappointment of this hope prepared the way for the hope of a new heaven and a new earth inaugurated by Yahweh himself, with which the prophecies of Isaiah close (65.17ff).

[4] As a corrective to R. H. Charles's celebrated dictum that "Prophecy is a declaration, a forth-telling of the will of God – not a fore-telling", H. H. Rowley remarks acidly, "That the prophets were not merely preachers of righteousness but foretellers of the future is plain to every reader" (*The Relevance of Apocalyptic*, (1963), p. 38).

[5] This characteristic has often been noted in connection with Mk. 13, where Jesus' eschatological discourse treats now "these things, these days", referring to the forthcoming fall of Jerusalem, which took place in the lifetime of his hearers in A.D. 70; and now "those things, those days", referring to the final coming of the Son of Man in glory and judgement at the end of the age.

been completed, two stages of it have been justified. The return from exile intensified the religious devotion of many Jews, and made possible a people prepared, at least to some degree, for the coming of Jesus. And his coming, as we shall see, brought about a great revolution in the eschatological expectations of believing Jews. In a word, it split into two their "monolithic" conception of salvation as the time when God would visit and redeem his people. As the New Testament writers came to see it, the coming of Jesus had inaugurated God's future reign, but not consummated it. Salvation had indeed come with Christ, but only as a foretaste of what was essentially future.

The prophets, then, held fast to the hope that God would one day recapitulate his saving acts on behalf of his people in one final drama of redemption. Despite spiritual overtones, it was a very earthy hope, related to a human deliverer, David's descendant, in a specifically human situation, a reorganized Jerusalem. This was partly because the prophets were also politicians, and were concerned with the here and now, with taxes, power politics and social injustice. It was therefore natural for them to express in these materialistic terms their convictions about the final victory of God's will in history. How else, in fact, could they have expressed them? The Hebrews had so strong a doctrine of man's bodily existence that they naturally viewed the future in these terms. To the Hebrew, man does not have a soul; that is a Greek idea. Rather, man is an animated body, *nephesh*, and all existence must be bodily. Strange though this conception may seem to us, it is of crucial importance. It safeguards the unity of human existence, it stresses God's involvement in history, and it guards against the divorce of the sacred from the secular and the spiritual from the physical. Furthermore, it prevents the self-centred isolationism of much Western thought which has been concerned with the cultivation of the individual soul, the pursuit of the individual's destiny. To the Hebrew man was a social being. His salvation, past, present and future, was a social matter. Not for him any heaven to which the soul escaped at death; he looked for a reign of God in a redeemed community on earth.

A further reason for what seems to us so materialistic a conception of future salvation was this. It was a long time before Hebrew man came to clear convictions about a future life. It is *implied*, to be sure, in the early chapters of Exodus. God's revelation of himself as the source of life, the self-existent "I am"[1] carries with it the corollary that those he saves will be with him, personal beings in communion with their personal God, after death. If God is *ever* concerned with a man, he is

[1] Ex. 3.6, 14. Perhaps the Hebrew *'ehyeh 'asher 'ehyeh* is better rendered by a future, "I shall become what I become."

always concerned with him. Eternal life is only securely based in relation with the Eternal.[1] And this, of course, was the argument used by Jesus to show the sceptical Sadducees that the doctrine of immortality was not some Persian invention wrongly adopted by the Pharisees, but was inherent in the earliest parts of the Old Testament (Matt. 22.31ff.). But though implied, this doctrine rarely becomes explicit. It may be referred to in such verses as Isa. 25.8, 26.19, Job 19.26, Ps. 16.8-11, 49.14, 15 but it only becomes a clear hope towards the end of the Old Testament period, particularly with the rise of apocalyptic. And to this we must briefly turn.

Apocalyptic introduces us to the fourth stage of the hope of salvation in the Old Testament, which Vriezen calls the *transcendental-eschatological*. He means, of course, the tendency to put off to a new world the salvation which apparently had not come in this. The prominence given to such a hope in the last part of Isaiah seems to reflect disillusionment with the Return and the rebuilding of the temple. The cosmic nature of salvation is accordingly stressed over against the national and political. Because God was God, because he was Saviour, he would surely express his victory again by a new creation, just as the Exodus and the Return had been seen as new creations. He would create a new heaven and a new earth in which the peace of God, the longed for *shalōm*, would be manifested, and from which all evil and sorrow would be banished (Isa. 65.17ff., cf. Isa. 34.4, Ezek. 31.16, Ps. 102.26). This is, of course, picture language. Precisely what it signified, the Old Testament writers themselves would not have been able to tell us. But such language expressed their conviction that redemption was the correlative of creation, that God's saving purpose for the whole of his creation would, one day, be accomplished. It was a view of God and his salvation which did not escape from history but saw beyond it. We are here on the borderline between prophecy and apocalyptic proper.

Broadly speaking, apocalyptic literature arose after prophecy ceased in Israel with the post-exilic prophets.[2] It was historically conditioned. The expected messianic salvation had not appeared. Instead, the country of Palestine was ruled, more often than not, by foreign kings. Under Antiochus Epiphanes in 168 B.C. the temple was desecrated, the Jewish faith proscribed, and its adherents persecuted. What was the godly Jew to make of this situation?

[1] See R. Martin-Achard, *From Death to Life* (1960), p. 206.

[2] It is by no means as easy to distinguish prophecy from apocalyptic as was once thought. That there are apocalyptic features in Isa. 65, and in the so-called Isaiah Apocalypse of Isa. 24-27 is undeniable, but the differences are also considerable. See the discussion, and bibliography, in H. H. Rowley's *The Relevance of Apocalyptic* (1963), pp. 25ff.

He could, of course, side with the resistance movement, which combined national with religious aspirations, and hoped against hope that God's promised kingdom might be introduced by the sword. If he did this, he was in any case modifying the prophetic hope which looked for a divine intervention and not a man-made victory. Clearly there were many loyal Jews who took this course. The War Scroll from Qumran shows that the Covenanters there were waiting with eager anticipation for the final battle of the sons of light against the sons of darkness, through which God's promised salvation would be realized.

But there was another course open to the pious Jew. Faced with the manifestly unsatisfactory nature of the present evil age, he might well despair of it, almost regard it as beyond redemption, and set his hope upon a spiritual goal, the blessings of the age to come. It was this historical impetus that led the apocalyptists to examine anew their inheritance in the sacred Scriptures. They held passionately to the old prophetic conviction that God was in control of history, but expected to see his intervention not so much in the affairs of every day as in the great irruption at the End. They recognized anew the time of suffering and distress that might be expected before such a *dénouement*, and saw oppression and evil as the handiwork of a great cosmic force working against God, Satan or Belial. They did not dream of Utopia; they looked for the advent of the kingdom of God, the place where God's will would perfectly be done, after the travail and pain of the present. And just because they were realists, who believed in God's final victory and the righting of all wrongs, they expected a last Great Assize at the end of history, when men and nations would be brought to the bar of God's judgement. But perhaps their greatest contribution to the development of the hope of salvation lay in their emphasis on the hereafter. Doubtless the influence of the Persian world during the time of Israel's captivity had done something to animate this conviction,[1] but the renewed stress on it by the apocalyptists drew its inspiration not from pagan but from Jewish presuppositions. They had enough experience of God in their own lives to be sure that those who are loyal to God through thick and thin would not be excluded from his kingdom.

The hope of life after death had never been entirely absent from the religion of Israel, but the prospect, as assumed by popular mythology, was not particularly comforting.

The Sheol of popular religion had much in common with the

[1] Eichrodt, Nötscher and Martin-Achard all uphold the originality of the Old Testament belief over against Canaanite or Iranian doctrines. See Martin-Achard, *op. cit.*, p. 206.

Homeric hades, as a shadowy abode of the dead, almost a land of not-being. Almost all the sixty-five references to Sheol in the Old Testament come in poetic contexts, where the popular view is alluded to without being taught as part of the religion of Yahwism. "The grave cannot praise thee, death cannot celebrate thee; they that go down into the pit cannot hope for thy truth" was Hezekiah's feeling about it (Isa. 38.18). And the psalmist cries to "the God of his salvation" and pours out his fears, "I am counted with them that go down into the pit; I am as a man that hath no strength, free among the dead like the slain that lie in the grave, whom thou rememberest no more, and they are cut off from thy hand" (Ps. 88.1, 3-5).

Nevertheless, the very existence of Sheol, even in its most shadowy form, bears testimony to their conviction that death did not mean annihilation. Furthermore, the conviction grew in Israel that Yahweh is Lord even of Sheol.[1] It is within the realm of his sovereignty (Job. 26.6, Prov. 15.11). In Amos 9.2 God says, "Though they dig into sheol, thence shall my hand take them"; metaphorical language, of course, but it shows a belief in a God who holds the issues of death and the hereafter in his hand. The dead matter to God. "If I ascend up into heaven, thou art there," cries the psalmist to his God whom he knows to be everywhere, "if I make my bed in sheol, behold, thou art there" (Ps. 139.8).

What is more, the Jew knows of occasions when God has rescued men out of the clutches of Sheol. Sometimes the deliverance was purely temporary, such as that celebrated in Ps. 30. Sometimes God raises men out of Sheol (1 Kings 17.20ff., 2 Kings 4.16, 33ff.). Sometimes he translates them into his presence without their seeing Sheol (Gen. 5.24, 2 Kings 2.11). Ps. 49.14f. shows the psalmist's hope that after death he will continue to enjoy God. Most important of all, deliverance from Sheol was promised by God to his Messiah (Ps. 16.8-11),[2] a passage made much of by the early Christian preachers (e.g. Acts 2.25ff., 13.35). And, of course, the last of the Servant Songs looks for a posthumous vindication of the Servant.

The Jews had realized at an early date, even if by implication only, that God's sovereign power extends over the voracious monster of this shadowy underworld (Isa. 5.14). But in the last two or three centuries B.C. the hope took on clearer outlines. This may have been partly due to the breakdown of national and ethnic groups under the vast conquests of Alexander the Great, and the increasing sense of personal responsibility and personal destiny throughout the ancient world which

---

[1] The Old Testament belief in the life after death is well expressed and sympathetically treated in Martin-Achard's *From Death to Life*, especially pp. 206-22.
[2] See Weiser, *op. cit.*, pp. 177f., and C. A. and E. G. Briggs, *I.C.C.*, *in loc.*

resulted from these conquests. It was partly due, too, to the destruction of thousands of martyrs in the Maccabaean wars, the *ḥasidim* who had demonstrated their election by Yahweh in their faithfulness to him unto death. How could God's final word to them be one of rejection? There *must* be a dualism about man's final destiny. There must be a differentiation in the after-life: "At that time thy people shall be delivered, every one that shall be found written in thy book" (Dan. 12.1). He is speaking, of course, of the last day and final salvation, and he continues, "And many of them that sleep in the dust of the earth shall awake, some to everlasting life, and some to shame and everlasting contempt." How could it be otherwise if God is just? There *must* be a day of reckoning. Current events made it plain that justice was not to be expected in this life. It must therefore be "at that time", when the Day of the Lord comes, when God himself (Zech. 14.5, Joel 3.16, Isa. 26.21), or his Davidic Messiah (Isa. 9.6, 7, 11.1ff., Jer. 23.5, 6), or the Messenger of the Covenant (Mal. 3.1) or the Son of Man (Dan. 7.13f.), or the Suffering Servant (Isa. 42.1-7, 49.1-6, 50.4-9, 52.13-53.12) intervenes to right all wrongs and bring about the promised salvation of God. Such had long been Israel's hope.

Thus under the pressure of current opposition, with no apparent sign of redress in this life, the emphasis of much Jewish faith about salvation shifted to the world to come. Something of this changed perspective may be seen in the Old Testament itself, but for its later and fuller development we must look to the intertestamental literature. Nevertheless, the Old Testament prophets are not ignorant of a catastrophic judgement which is to fall upon the old order (Isa. 13.9-13, and chs. 24-26), nor of the new heavens and the new earth which will be inaugurated when God rends the heavens and comes quickly down (Isa. 65.17, 66.22, 64.1).

Now it is commonly argued that between prophecy and apocalyptic there is a great gulf fixed; that prophecy looks for a consummation in this life, and apocalyptic in the age to come. This distinction is perhaps valid between prophecy and non-biblical apocalyptic, but it does not entirely hold good for apocalyptic elements within the Old Testament itself.[1] The advent of God envisaged in Isa. 64 is a

---

[1] It will not do simply to assign apocalyptic elements in prophecy to another author. That fails to explain how such a combination of prophetic and apocalyptic strands was deemed possible in the fourth or third century B.C. when, presumably, the book was, on this hypothesis, put into its final shape. If an editor could have combined two such different world views, could not an author? See Rowley, *op. cit.*, p. 25. It is interesting that in a recent *Commentary on Isaiah. 1-39* (1962), J. Mauchline thinks part, at any rate, of the 'Isaiah Apocalypse' "may be genuine Isaianic material" (p. 196).

coming to this earth, which will result in judgement of the wicked (64.2) and the vindication of God's promise to his people. Far from entertaining a vindictive and arrogant attitude to the wicked who do not trust in God, the prophet sees himself and his people as sinful: "We are all as an unclean thing, and all our righteousnesses are as filthy rags" (64.6). Their hope is simply and solely in the mercy of their father, God, "Thou art our father; we are the clay and thou our potter" (64.8). Immediately afterwards the prophet makes it clear that he is looking for the reviving of Zion, which has become a wilderness, and of Jerusalem, which is a desolation. The prophetic and the apocalyptic viewpoints are combined within a single chapter.

Similarly, in Isa. 65.17ff., it is an earthly existence that engrosses the seer's attention. An earthly, corporate existence, in true Hebrew fashion, complete with houses and vineyards and based on Jerusalem, but nevertheless a totally transformed existence; no more injustice, no more fruitless labour, no more sorrow, no more destruction. Once again we find the clear distinction between the saved and the lost that is inherent in the character of a God who is holy love. Whilst "I create Jerusalem a rejoicing and her people a joy", "the sinner being an hundred years old shall be accursed" (65.18, 20).

Again, the "apocalyptic" passage Isa. 24-26 has the same themes. It envisages a visitation of the Lord of unprecedented severity, with repercussions both on earth and in the heavenly bodies (24.23) – another point taken up in New Testament apocalyptic. It sees the Lord reigning in Mt. Zion and Jerusalem, adored, served and trusted by his obedient people; in short, it looks for salvation (26.1-5, cf. 60.18). This advent of the Lord involves final judgement (26.21) for those who have long withstood God's patient pleading (26.9-11). After the birth-pangs of the new age (26.16-18) there will be a resurrection to newness of life (26.19) characterized by persistent trust in the Lord (26.1-4, 13), and an increased and renewed people which glorifies God (26.15). They will be completely satisfied, as though by a banquet (25.6). There will be no more defeat, no more distress, no more death (25.8). Such is the salvation the Lord has in store for those who wait for him (25.9).

It would seem, then, almost impossible to draw a hard-and-fast distinction between the prophetic and apocalyptic hopes of a future salvation in the Old Testament. The prophets tended to see it as continuous with this present order (e.g. Mic. 4.1-5, Isa. 11.1-9). The apocalyptists were far from optimistic about this present age, and tended to see salvation as a characteristic of the age to come when God would redeem men from Sheol and create "a new heaven and a new earth in which dwelleth righteousness". But both took history seriously. Both looked for God, the intervener in history, the Lord of history, to complete his saving work. For both the consummation of God's redemptive work will be the redemption of history itself.

We have hitherto said very little about salvation from sin. This is not the ruling concept in the Old Testament doctrine of salvation, but it is by no means absent, especially in the Psalms and Deutero-Isaiah. In Ps. 119, which speaks much of salvation, it is said to be "far from the wicked who seek not God's statutes" (Ps. 119.155). In contrast, the psalmist calls to God for his tender mercies and his life-giving power (119.156). Again in Ps. 116 it is hard to escape the conclusion that the "cup of salvation" (116.13), which the psalmist takes from God's hand in adoring faith, at least includes this interior and profound sense of personal salvation, in view of verse 8, "Thou hast delivered my soul from death, my eyes from tears, and my feet from falling." It is a significant insight into the inability of man to help himself which drives the writer to answer his rhetorical question, "What shall I *render* to the Lord for all his benefits?" with the reply, "I will *take* the cup of salvation." Rather similar is the understanding of salvation as a garment made by God to clothe the men of his choice (Ps. 132.13-18, cf. 2 Chron. 6.41). Much the same thought underlies Isa. 61.10, an important verse in view of New Testament developments, "I will greatly rejoice in the Lord, my soul shall be joyful in my God; for he hath clothed me with the garments of salvation, he hath covered me with the robe of righteousness." The prophet's meaning comes into even clearer relief when contrasted with his view of our state without God, "We are all as an unclean thing, and all our righteousnesses are as filthy rags; and we all do fade as a leaf, and our iniquities like the wind have taken us away" (64.6). Once more we are brought back to the fact that, at whatever level we consider salvation, it is God's work. Isa. 59 bewails the fact that "we look for judgement, but there is none; for salvation, but it is far off from us" (59.11). The reason is that "our transgressions are multiplied before thee, and our sins testify against us; for our transgressions are with us, and as for our iniquities, we know them; in transgressing and lying against the Lord, and departing from our God" (59.12, 13). "And the Lord saw it, and it displeased him that there was no judgement. And he saw that there was no man, and wondered that there was no intercessor; therefore his own arm brought salvation" (59.15, 16). The passage goes on to deal with the ideas of the Spirit (59.19), redemption, repentance and the new covenant (59.19-21), all of which play an important part in the New Testament doctrine of salvation. Of course, the concept of national deliverance is not absent from this passage. As Ryder Smith makes so plain in his book *The Bible Doctrine of Salvation*,[1] salvation is primarily a societary idea in the Bible, not least in the Old Testament. Nevertheless what one might call the spiritual or trans-historical aspect of salvation is much to the fore in passages like these in the latter part of Isaiah. Salvation is God's rescue of his faithful people in the end-time (Isa. 64.1-5). It is the work of God alone (43.11). It brings with it judgement as well as joy (51.5, 6), and its effects will reach the heathen as well as Israel (52.10, 49.6). It will be a manifestation of God's faithfulness to his people and to his covenant when Israel is saved in the Lord with an everlasting salvation (46.13).[2]

This emphasis is by no means confined to Deutero-Isaiah. For all his preoccupation with the return from exile, salvation from sin is unquestionably Israel's greatest need, according to Ezekiel. They need,

[1] Epworth Press, 1941. See also H. H. Rowley's lecture, "Individual and Community" reprinted in *The Faith of Israel* (1956), as ch. 4, pp. 99ff. The ancient Jew was acutely conscious of his solidarity with his forefathers and his successors in the tribe, and salvation was naturally conceived of as salvation for the whole people and the vindication of God's election of them. The deliverances in the past which provided the patterns of their thought about salvation had been national deliverances. The hope of ultimate salvation which figures largely in Zechariah and Deutero-Isaiah point to a saved and reconstituted *community*, in which God will be glorified (e.g. Zech. 10.6, Isa. 49.8).

On the other hand, as I. G. Matthews (in *The Religious Pilgrimage of Israel*, 1947, p. 14) has expressed it, "Individualism to a marked degree, paradoxical though it seems, went hand in hand with solidarity." The extent of this individualism has been shown by Rowley's article. It was certainly not "invented" by Jeremiah and Ezekiel. The salvation of God-fearing individuals like Enoch and Noah from the midst of a sinful world are as noteworthy upon the pages of the Old Testament as the responsibility of individual sinners like David with Bathsheba or Ahab with Nathan. Many of the psalms are intensely individual, despite their cultic use; they spring from one man's personal relationship with a God who saves. Appeals like, "Save me, O my God", "Save thy servant who trusteth in thee", "I am thine, save me" abound (e.g. Ps. 3.7, 86.2, 119.94). The principle of collective responsibility and collective salvation does not conflict with that of the individual, but rather enhances it. Thus Jeremiah looks to the day when God will make a new covenant with the house of Israel (Jer. 31.31f.). That is to say it will be a corporate, collective thing. But he goes on to stress the principle of personal accountability, of personal relationship with God, within that community of the redeemed. "I will put my law in their inward parts, and write it in their hearts . . . and they shall all know me . . . and I will remember their sin no more." The Old Testament looks both for a redeemed community, and for individuals within that community who are right with God.

[2] Chs. 45, 46 contain many key phrases for the concept of salvation. It is exercised by God himself on behalf of his elect (45.4-8). He is a just God and a Saviour (45.21). His invitation is to all the world; all the ends of the earth may look to him and be saved (45.22). He has sworn it; it is guaranteed by his covenant (45.23). Indeed, salvation is the corollary of God's righteousness (46.13). That is how it is possible for men to be justified *in the Lord* (45.25), saved *in the Lord* (45.17) with a salvation which is as eternal as God himself.

of course, to be brought from among the heathen to their own land (36.24), but even more they need God to save them from all their uncleanness (36.29). When they remember their own evil ways and their doings that were not good, and loathe themselves in their own sight for their iniquities, then God will cleanse them from their iniquities and cause them to dwell in their cities, and the wastes shall be built (36.31-34). Once again we meet the characteristic Hebrew recognition that this salvation both from physical and spiritual ill was not due to their own righteousness but for God's own glory. Once again we find universalist overtones in the wonder of the heathen round about, who shall see all this, "and they shall know that I am the Lord". The same chapter tells the Israelites that this cleansing by God will mean not only forgiveness of the past, but the putting of his Spirit within them.[1] "From all your filthiness and from all your idols will I cleanse you. And I will give you a new heart also, and . . . I will put my spirit within you and cause you to walk in my statutes, and ye shall keep my commandments . . . and ye shall be my people, and I will be your God" (36.25-28). God reveals himself as Saviour of both the nation and the individual. His salvation consists not only in forgiveness for the past, in protection for the future, but in putting his Spirit in the lives of his people so that they can begin to do what was previously impossible, actually *keep* his commandments and behave as his people in the land which he gave to their fathers, and, through the return from exile, confirmed to them. Such is Ezekiel's hope. And he links it with the messianic age of the future, when "my servant David" will come as a prince among them, and save and feed the scattered flock of God (34.22ff.). Much the same thought is present in Zechariah 13.1, though the word salvation is absent: "In that day there shall be a fountain opened to the house of David and to the inhabitants of Jerusalem for sin and for uncleanness." Jeremiah too, is aware that "the heart is deceitful above all things and desperately wicked" (17.9). He knows that the Lord is the hope of Israel, and that if men will turn back to him as the fountain of living waters whom they have forsaken, he will heal them, he will save them (17.13, 14). Salvation is an act of God which can deal with the alienation and the ravages caused by sin.

But it is to the four great songs of the Servant of the Lord that we must turn if we are to find the most detailed and sublime prophetic conviction as to how God would deal with sin and bring in his promised salvation. The ground has been well and often canvassed,

[1] C. F. Whitely, *The Exilic Age* (1957), stresses the importance for "the assurance and enrichment of spiritual life" in "Ezekiel's declaration of the atoning grace of God in effecting the salvation of men" (p. 117).

by North[1] and Robinson,[2] Zimmerli[3] and Hooker[4] and a host of others.[5] We cannot now attempt to go into this vast subject; suffice it to recall that the summons to be the servant of the Lord in the sense both of dedication to him, and service for him among the nations, is addressed in the first instance to Israel as a whole (42.1). Service is the complement of election. And the Spirit of God is offered to Israel to equip them for this service to the unreached multitudes of the heathen. "Behold, my Servant, whom I uphold; mine elect in whom my soul delighteth; I have put my spirit upon him; he shall bring forth judgement to the Gentiles."

But Israel as a whole declined this call (42.19). She saw her election by God as a privilege to treasure, to hold on to, to boast about; not as a responsibility to be shared with the Gentiles. So the call, originally directed to Israel as a whole, now goes out again to a body *within* Israel, who are to fulfil the function that really belongs to Israel as a whole. "And now saith the Lord that formed me from the womb to be his servant, to bring Jacob again to him, Though Israel be not gathered, yet shall I be glorious in the eyes of the Lord, and my God shall be my strength. And he said, It is a light thing that thou shouldest be my servant to raise up the tribes of Jacob, and to restore the preserved of Israel; I will give thee also for a light to the Gentiles, that thou mayest be my salvation unto the end of the earth" (49.5f.). Once again we meet the interwoven themes of God's election and man's responsive service; once again the horizon is not bounded by Israel. In the verses that follow (49.7-12), we meet again the familiar themes of salvation, covenant, deliverance and final blessedness. But no longer is all Israel regarded as the agent in this salvation. They have refused their calling, and a group (or a person?) within Israel stands as their representative. He is commissioned both to bring salvation to the Gentiles and to turn Israel again to God. A further development is noteworthy; salvation and the covenant are both embodied in the Servant. He *is* God's covenant (49.8), he *is* God's salvation (49.6). And there is just a hint of the path of suffering the Servant must tread in order to achieve this longed-for salvation (49.7).

This motif becomes much clearer in the next of the Servant Songs (50.4-9). "The Lord hath opened mine ear" (the metaphor is taken

[1] C. R. North, *The Suffering Servant in Deutero-Isaiah* (2nd Edn. 1956).
[2] H. W. Robinson, *The Cross in the Old Testament* (1926).
[3] W. Zimmerli and J. Jeremias, *The Servant of God* (E.T. 1957).
[4] M. D. Hooker, *Jesus and the Servant* (1959). See also the suggestive little book by A. T. Hanson, *The Church of the Servant* (1962), and *The Pioneer Ministry* (1961).
[5] In particular Whitely, *The Exilic Age* (1957), ch. 6, J. Lindblom, *Prophecy in Ancient Israel* (1962), pp. 379ff.

from the branding of a slave) "and I was not rebellious, neither turned away back. I gave my back to the smiters and my cheeks to them that plucked off the hair; I hid not my face from shame and spitting." In this passage the process of contraction seems to have gone farther, and the Servant shrunk to an individual. As Zimmerli puts it, we are given "a picture of the true Servant of Yahweh which far transcends the personal experience of the prophet. Thus it is not by chance or by ineptitude that Isa. 53 has again and again been understood as alluding to the figure of the one that is to come."[1] It is indeed difficult not to be reminded of the way in which Jesus so perfectly fulfilled the picture sketched here; the perfect obedience, the physical mockery, whipping, shame and spitting; his confidence that God was near to help him, that God would vindicate him, and hence his face set like a flint to go to Jerusalem and to face his adversary.[2]

In the last of the Servant Songs (52.13–53.12), we are again face to face with an individual, so it would seem;[3] a shoot out of the apparently dead stock of Israel, "a man of sorrows and acquainted with (? or 'humbled by') grief". What Israel learns to her amazement is that it is her sorrows and griefs that the Servant is bearing; he is "smitten of God and afflicted" on her account. "He was wounded for our transgression, he was bruised for our iniquities; the chastisement of our peace was upon him; and with his stripes we are healed. All we like sheep have gone astray; we have turned every one to his own way; and the Lord hath laid on him the iniquity of us all" (53.5, 6). Although the word "salvation" is not used in this most moving of all Old Testament prophecies, the thought is certainly present; we have here the climax of the prophetic doctrine of salvation. The servant's vicarious suffering for sin, willingly and gladly borne, is the path to success (53.10). Jehovah's righteous Servant puts many in a right relationship with God, for he bears their iniquities (53.11, 12).[4]

Ryder Smith summarizes the position this: "The three great prophets of the sixth century mark the zenith of the Old Testament teaching on the subject of salvation. Jeremiah saw that salvation means

[1] Op. cit., p. 31. What is true of Isa. 53 is no less true of Isa. 50.

[2] See Jn. 14.30, 31, and for this interpretation of ἄγωμεν ἐντεῦθεν see Dodd, Interpreting the Fourth Gospel, in loc.

[3] Though the Hebrew thought moves easily between the idea of an individual and a society as the Servant. However, the messianic interpretation of this passage was normative for subsequent Judaism; for the first thousand years of the Christian era no definitely non-messianic interpretation is to be found in rabbinic literature. This is truly remarkable in view of the effect on Jewish exegesis of opposition to Christianity since the second century. See Zimmerli, op. cit., pp. 75f.

[4] Indeed, it is Yahweh himself who, as Servant, now bears the sin of Israel and the world (Isa. 43.23, 24). Knight (op. cit., p. 291) shows how it is by this utter self-giving and sin-bearing that Yahweh glorifies himself (Isa. 44.23, 49.3).

salvation from *sinfulness* and that this demands a change of character: Ezekiel declared that this change would be wrought by the *Spirit* of God; Deutero-Isaiah taught that men may be saved, even from sin, by *vicarious suffering*, if it be willingly borne.[1] Even here, however, it is God and not the Servant, who saves; or rather, it is God's good pleasure to save through the Servant. "Behold, *my* servant shall succeed."[2]

Throughout this study it has been apparent that it is God who saves, whether it be a matter of saving a small Semitic tribe from the onslaughts of its neighbours, or of saving God's elect with an everlasting salvation in the "Day of the Lord". The understanding of what salvation meant deepened and became more spiritual throughout the centuries, but its broad outlines remained constant during the whole Old Testament period. Salvation does not depend on man's goodness, but on God's faithfulness (Ps. 40.10). And thus we find the psalmist, conscience-stricken, after grievous sin, praying not that God would restore to him his salvation, but rather, the joy of it. "Restore unto me the joy of thy salvation" (Ps. 51.12). He could never have prayed like that had he deemed salvation to depend on human effort and attainment. The author knew, however, that human sin does not abrogate the covenant mercies of God. He had not lost his salvation by the terrible sins he had committed; only deliberate apostasy can cut the link between God and his people. He had not lost his relationship with the Saviour God, but he had lost his joy in it. Wrongdoing always spoils fellowship with God (cf. 1 Jn. 1.7-9), until it is repented of and put away; but it is never said in Scripture to annul the relationship with him. And so here, he cries out in true repentance, "Wash me thoroughly from mine iniquity, and cleanse me from my sin. For I acknowledge my transgression, and my sin is ever before me. Against thee, thee only have I sinned[3] . . . hide thy face from my sins and blot out all my iniquities" (51.2-4, 9). He knows that his prayer will not be in vain, because of the loving kindness and tender mercies of the Lord (51.1). Deep repentance will be met by deep cleansing; God will give him truth in the inward parts, he will cleanse him with hyssop and he will be clean, he will make him whiter than snow, he will

---

[1] Some of these ruling concepts of the prophets are paralleled in the psalms. Ps. 22 comes very near to the doctrine of salvation by vicarious suffering of Isaiah. Ps. 130, especially verse 8, "He shall redeem Israel from all his iniquities", anticipates salvation from sin, like Jeremiah. And in Ps.51 we find this salvation from sin associated with the Spirit of God as in Ezekiel (Ps. 51.10-12) and with a new heart, as in Jeremiah (Ps. 51.10).

[2] *Op. cit.*, pp. 74f.

[3] It is characteristic of this conviction of sin to see that sin is primarily an offence against *God*.

create in him a new heart, he will put his Holy Spirit within him. The Saviour God will heal his broken bones, and renew a right spirit within him; assuredly he will not cast him away from his presence, but, after cleansing and equipping him, he will send the forgiven sinner forth to proclaim to others the astounding mercy of a God who takes bad men and makes them good. Such is the salvation from sin that God will effect for the man who makes to him what is ultimately the only acceptable sacrifice, a broken and a contrite heart (51.17). God can do something with such a man. And he will.

CONCLUSION: SALVATION IS NOT BY WORKS, NOR BY CULTUS, BUT BY GOD

Two surprising things emerge from this study of salvation in the Old Testament. In the first place, we have seen little enough evidence to justify the popular misconception that salvation is achieved by good works in the Old Testament and by faith in the New.[1] It would be far truer to say that salvation is seen in both covenants as springing from God's free grace,[2] appropriated by faith, and issuing inevitably in a changed life. In both covenants God takes bad men, and in sheer grace treats them with a magnanimity which they could never deserve, a generosity which liberates them from themselves and makes new men of them. This is the salvation which redounds to his eternal credit as he shows what he can do with fallen, sinful men, once they make him the God of their salvation.

The other remarkable thing is the tenuousness of the link between salvation and the sacrificial system of the Old Testament. Two of the three usual Hebrew words to denote the idea of "save" and "redeem" do not occur at all in this connection. The third, *padah*, "to ransom", is used in connection with the cultus, but only in the sense of redeeming the firstborn by the death of an animal (e.g. Ex. 13.13, 34.20, Num. 18.15-17; and even in this connection it is much more frequently used of the substitution of one offering for another in the ritual of the firstborn of animals, not men). There is no suggestion that the firstborn of man or beast had sinned, and therefore needed an expiatory offering

---

[1] There are, of course, passages such as Ps. 86.2 and Isa. 56.1f. that appear to be exceptions to this generalization. But this is not the case. The psalmist who prays "preserve my soul for I am holy" is not making his virtue the occasion for God's salvation. Holy means "dedicated, separated to God". And because he is in this relationship of trust and obedience with God, he can with confidence pray for his salvation. Equally, Isa. 56 makes it perfectly plain that salvation is of the Lord, although making it equally clear that such salvation makes moral demands upon its recipients.

[2] "Since sin is separation from God and an offence against God, it can only be effaced by an act of forgiveness" (Jacob, *op. cit.*, p. 290).

for his salvation. It was simply a graphic way of expressing the truth that all life depends on God and belongs to him. Never is *padah* used in connection with a sin offering or a guilt offering. Never are the Old Testament sacrifices said to save or redeem anyone. The cultus was, of course, part of God's Law to Israel. It had *educative* value,[1] to awaken the Jew to the awareness of God's holiness, and to show him that breaches of God's laws necessitate the death of a ritually clean substitute if the offender is to be reconciled with God. But sacrifice and its rationale was very complex in Israel.[2] The majority of sacrifices had nothing to do even with the removal of ceremonial defilement; moreover, the Law offered no ritual means of expiating deliberate sin. "For the sin-offering and the guilt-offering were not valid for sins committed with a high hand";[3] they were intended to cover unwitting sins, particularly the violation of religious tabus.[4] What is more, nowhere in the Bible is sacrifice represented as having any effect without the proper attitude of penitence and faith in the worshipper. On the contrary, when some really serious sin is mentioned its removal is attributed to God himself, not to sacrifice. Thus Nathan can say to David after the Bathsheba affair, "The Lord hath put away thy sin; thou shalt not die" (2 Sam. 12.13), and the worshipper of Ps. 51 knows that nothing but the sheer forgiveness of God can cleanse him from his defilement; the same is true of Ps. 32.

In addition to the educative value of sacrifice, it had a *sacramental* value.[5] No doubt the pious Jew who took part in the Day of Atonement ritual in obedience to God's command did have a trusting confidence that somehow God would find a way to blot out his offences, just as his ceremonial misdemeanours were, as it were, transferred to the head of the goat for Azazel. The High Priest confessed

[1] R. de Vaux, commenting on this prophetic significance of sacrifice, speaks of its preparation for the New Testament, and points out that Jesus did not condemn sacrifice but fulfilled it. He sees the sacrifice of Christ not only as the fulfilment of the Paschal sacrifice, but as the perfect gift of God, the perfect expiation for sin, and the perfect communion-sacrifice; all because of the unique nature of the sacrifice and his obedient self-offering (*Ancient Israel*, 1961, p. 456).

[2] See particularly H. H. Rowley, "The Meaning of Sacrifice in the Old Testament" in *From Moses to Qumran*, (1963), pp. 67-107.

[3] Rowley, *op. cit.*, p. 93.

[4] Thus a sin offering was made after childbirth (Lev. 12).

[5] Ryder Smith comments on the educative function of the Day of Atonement thus: "On the Day of Atonement two ideas reached a symbolic climax. The ritual . . . was paradoxical, and rightly so. The High Priest cannot look upon God lest he die, yet he draws near. God is so holy that he can have nothing to do with the sinful, yet he is so merciful to Israel that he must have everything to do with them . . . The whole ritual is a culminant symbol of the antinomy of holiness and mercy in the character of God" (*op. cit.*, p. 95).

over the head of the goat, as he laid his hands upon it, "All the iniquities of the children of Israel and all their transgressions, putting them on the head of the goat . . . and shall send him away into the wilderness" (Lev. 16.21). This impressive and meaningful ceremony will certainly have helped many Jews to a sense of divine forgiveness, as the defilement separating them from God was thus symbolically and physically removed. But other Jews were, in fact, repelled by the bloodshed of the sacrifices. This attitude is prominent in various of the prophets (Isa. 1.11-17; Jer. 6.20, 7.21, 22; Hosea 6.6; Amos 5.21-27; Mic. 6.6-8). Such men, while not inveighing against sacrifice itself,[1] saw beyond the holocausts themselves to the attitudes of penitence, obedience and simple faith in God which were far more important. They may have come to realize, as Heb. 10.3, 4 puts it, "In those sacrifices there is a *remembrance*" (but no *removal*) "again made of sins every year. For it is not possible that the blood of bulls and goats should take away sins." That would be arbitrary, irrational and sub-personal, as the writer goes on to argue. No, it is not possible that the blood of bulls and goats should take away sins; and the Old Testament never suggested that the sacrificial system was the ultimate answer to the problem of sinfulness in God's world. Its writers never linked salvation with the sacrifices. Sin is always seen in Scripture as rebellion against God, and ritual atonement does nothing to alter that. Nor, of course, can human repentance repair the ravages of sin. "It was not supposed that man could save himself from his sin either by his penitence or by his sacrifice."[2] Salvation belonged to the Lord. He alone was the Saviour and, in his own good time, he would bring salvation.

God did indeed "make a gate for the righteous to enter". He did indeed "hear them and become their salvation" (Ps. 118.20f.). But it was a paradoxical salvation. For the promised Saviour appeared as a stone which the builders rejected, yet became the headstone of the corner in God's temple of the redeemed (Ps. 118.22).

[1] See de Vaux, *op. cit.*, p. 454; Rowley, *op. cit.*, pp. 87ff.
[2] H. H. Rowley, *op. cit.*, pp. 91.

CHAPTER 3

Salvation in the Jewish World of the First Century

The Jews had not lost their hopes of salvation since the writing of the later books in the Old Testament. Indeed, the hope of salvation increased as the years went by. Within the land of Israel the people of God had to put up with invasion after invasion; Antiochus, Pompey, Herod, followed by direct Roman rule through the Procurators after A.D. 6, were a hard succession of evils to bear.

Life was no easier for the many Jews who had to live outside Palestine, in Rome, for instance, or Alexandria. They always seemed to spark off riots, as the pagan populace jibbed at their peculiar dress and appearance, their refusal to work on the Sabbath and their unwillingness to recognize any of the customary gods. They seemed a very curious people to the ancient world, and they were usually met with a good deal of unpleasantness, even when they were not involved in a pogrom, which was often enough. Both inside Palestine and without, the Jew had to be on the defensive against attitudes ranging from suspicion and dislike to active persecution.

This is the background against which we must examine the Jewish hope for salvation in the last century or so B.C.[1] We find it in the curious world of apocalyptic and pseudepigraphy, some of which is contained in the books of the Apocrypha, and some excluded from any canon. It is impossible to understand the viewpoint of these writers without some appreciation of the times through which they were passing. The three centuries between Antiochus Epiphanes' invasion of Palestine (168 B.C.) and Hadrian's final and bloody "solution of the Jewish problem" (A.D. 135), saw the long fight of the Jews to secure self-determination and freedom from Gentile domination. Their opponents

[1] No attempt will be made in this chapter to trace the various conceptions of salvation through all the intertestamental writings. On this, see W. Foerster in Kittel's *Theologisches Wörterbuch zum Neuen Testament*, vol. 7, p. 981, where he considers σῴζω und σωτηρία im Spätjudentum. Concentration is focussed in this chapter on writings that may be ascribed to the first century B.C., and may shed light on attitudes current in the time of Jesus.

were first the Seleucids, then the Romans. And during these centuries of resistance movements under the Maccabees and the Zealots, in the Great Revolt of A.D. 66-70, and the final struggle under the self-styled Messiah Bar Cochba, the messianic hope of the Old Testament days took on more definite (though diverse) shape, and was closely linked with the hope of salvation.

Of these struggles, the early revolt under the Maccabees proved wonderfully successful. And when, beginning with the death of Herod the Great (4 B.C.) the yoke of Rome began to lie heavily upon Jewish shoulders, might it not have seemed probable that a national leader (an anointed one or Messiah) could perhaps be as successful against the House of Augustus as Judas Maccabaeus had been against the House of Seleucus? Might not Tiberius prove as vulnerable to a Jewish patriotism which depended on God's help as Antiochus had been?

These were undoubtedly the hopes cherished by the common man in first-century Palestine. It seemed to him an intolerable thing that the theocracy of Israel should be desecrated by subordination to a Gentile power. The Gentile poll-tax, the Gentile soldiers, the Gentile appointment (and deposition) of the High Priests were a constant provocation to rebellion. Defence of the cause of Israel, which included both political freedom and religious independence, was the dominant concern of the ordinary patriotic Jew throughout these centuries. He knew that God had intervened on behalf of his nation in the past; he looked for God to do so again. Palestine was a giant box of tinder which the smallest spark would ignite into the flame of open revolt – witness the endless succession of abortive risings before the Great Revolt of A.D. 66, which are mentioned in the pages of the New Testament and Josephus.[1]

The actual form which the expectation of the coming deliverer took varied according to a number of factors, particularly the political situation. Perhaps the most common was the hope for a Davidic ruler who would fulfil the Old Testament prophecies (e.g. 2 Sam. 7.12ff., Ps. 2.7ff. Isa. 7.13ff., 11.1f., etc.). We find this hope expressed in some parts of *The Testaments of the Twelve Patriarchs.*[2] Thus, "Then shall the sceptre of my kingdom shine forth; and from your root shall arise a stem; and from it shall grow a rod of righteousness to the Gentiles, to judge and to save all that call upon the Lord" (*Test. Jud.* 24.5, 6).[3]

[1] E.g. Acts 5.36, 37, 21.38, Josephus *Ant.* 20.5, etc.
[2] The date of this work is much disputed, as is the extent of its Christian interpolation. It probably derives from the late second or early first century B.C.
[3] The salvation hope of the *Testaments* is not confined to Israel. The Gentiles (or the "righteous" among them) are specifically included in *Nap.* 8.2, 3, *Sim.* 7.2(?), *Ash.* 7.3, etc.

Often the House of Levi is associated with the House of Judah in this messianic hope. Thus, for example, we find, "Tell these things to your children, that they honour Judah and Levi, for out of them the Lord will raise up salvation for you" (*Test. Gad.* 8.1). Clearly the superb victories of the Maccabees have influenced the hope at this point in the direction of the House of Levi, to which they themselves belonged. Indeed, there is much more emphasis in the *Testaments* on a deliverer arising from the House of Levi than from any other source. According to R. H. Charles, this figure replaces the Davidic Messiah,[1] but the possibility of extensive interpolation and some special pleading on Charles's part leads Beasley-Murray[2] to the conclusion that there are two Messiahs in the *Testaments*, of whom the deliverer from the House of Judah is subordinate to the Levitical leader. This is just what we find in the writings of Qumran, where the expectation of a priestly, Aaronic Messiah is found alongside that of a kingly, Davidic Messiah (see *The Rule of the Community, passim*). If this hope originated in the descent of the great second-century deliverers of Israel, the Maccabees, from Levi, it faded after a century because their descendants sank as low in morals, religion and statesmanship as their forefathers had risen high.

In the first century B.C. the hope took on a new look, at least in some quarters. The author of 1 Enoch 37-71, known as the *Similitudes* or *Parables of Enoch*, who probably wrote about this time,[3] identified the coming great one with the supernatural Son of Man. This was a messianic development of the conception of Dan. 7. In Daniel the title is a corporate one (7.13, 18) and seems primarily to have envisaged a restored and glorified Israel. But in 1 Enoch this figure is fully personal, and is given three titles which are later taken over by New Testament writers and applied to Jesus. He is called the Christ or Anointed One (48.10),[4] the Righteous One (38.2), the Elect or Chosen One (40.5), as well as Son of Man. In him the righteous are saved (48.7, 50.3, 51.2).

[1] R. H. Charles, *The Testament of the Twelve Patriarchs*, 1908.

[2] *Journal of Theological Studies*, 1947, pp. 1ff.

[3] So Mowinckel, *op. cit.*, pp. 353ff., who adduces the evidence. However the dating is very precarious. R. H. Charles also accepts the first century B.C. (*Apocrypha and Pseudepigrapha*, ii, p. 171), but Milik argues for a date in the first or second century A.D. (*Ten Years of Discovery in the Wilderness of Judaea*, E.T. 1959, p. 33) because of the non-appearance of the *Parables* at Qumran where elements from the rest of Enoch were found. See, however, H. H. Rowley, *op. cit.*, p. 60.

[4] Of course, the Anointed One of Enoch parts company with the Old Testament hope of an earthly ruler. "Here the Anointed One is a purely transcendental figure" (Rowley, *op. cit.*, p. 62).

Preexistent in heaven (39.3-7, 48.6),[1] he appears at the end of time (38.2, 69.29), no longer as an earthly ruler, which was the characteristic messianic hope of the Old Testament, but as a divine figure (46.1-3, 61.8, 62.2), God's own emissary come to judge the world (38.4, 46.1, 54.5f.), rescue the righteous (48.4ff., 62.13, 51.2) and be a light to the Gentiles (48.4). His coming will be decisive in the fate of men, both living and dead. The latter will be raised, and "he shall choose the righteous and the holy from among them for the day has drawn nigh that they should be saved. And the Elect One shall, in those days, sit on My throne" (51.2f.).

The problems posed by this evidence are extremely complex. Not only is the Book of Enoch a composite work, dating from various periods; not only are there several words in the Ethiopic which are translated "Son of Man";[2] but the work seems to have suffered some measure of interpolation at Christian hands.[3] Those who believe that this is the case can draw support from the fact that no part of *The Parables* has appeared in the finds at Qumran, although there are many fragments from other parts of Enoch. Nevertheless, despite all the difficulties in the detailed assessment of 1 Enoch, and doubts about its integrity and date, it is highly probable that expectations such as this did circulate freely in the years before Christ's coming, particularly among the perceptive people who realized the futility of any resort to arms against Rome, and rejected as folly the hopes of the masses which were pinned on another deliverance of the Maccabaean type. The Son of Man is expressly stated to be the Messiah; he is God's fellow, and acts on God's behalf. He is called the Elect One, the Righteous One, the Light of the Gentiles, and this has led some scholars to identify the figure of the Son of Man in Enoch with that of the Suffering Servant in Isaiah.[4] He belongs to the age to come, and

[1] T. W. Manson, in his careful study of this problem, objects to the term *preexistent* and maintains that the Son of Man merely existed in the purpose of God from the beginning of time ("The Son of Man" in *Studies in the Gospels and Epistles* (1962), pp. 132ff.). This appears to do less than justice to the text of Enoch, and has not won wide support. See R. H. Charles, *The Book of Enoch* (1912), p. 93, for a summary of some of the evidence supporting the preexistence and eternal glory of the Son of Man. See also M. Black, "Eschatology of the Similitudes of Enoch" in *J.T.S.*(1952), pp. 1ff. for a criticism of the position adopted by Manson.

[2] So J. Y. Campbell in *J.T.S.* (1947), pp. 145ff.

[3] This is widely held because of the similarity in some respects between this teaching and that of Jesus. However, M. Black (*Expository Times*, lx, 1948-9, pp. 14f. and *J.T.S.*,1952, pp. 1ff.), Mowinckel (*op. cit.*, p. 354) and Rowley (*op. cit.*, pp. 61f.) are by no means convinced that this is the case, and P. Geoltrain, in a forthcoming doctoral thesis, will strongly resist any imputation of interpolation.

[4] So C. R. North, *The Suffering Servant* (1948), pp. 7ff.; J. Jeremias, *Deutsche Theologie*, ii (1929), pp. 106f. Their argument is not, however, conclusive.

will one day break into this age, coming in glory to judge both living and dead. He will raise the dead, save the trusting, and reign in an endless kingdom. All this has such obvious parallels – as well as contrasts – with the teaching of Jesus about himself as Son of Man, that it is difficult to avoid the conclusion that both he and his hearers moved in circles where these ideas were familiar.[1] As far as we can tell, these circles were fairly restricted. The Son of Man does not appear in pre-Christian literature except in Daniel, the Apocalypses of Baruch[2] and Ezra,[3] and 1 Enoch. That is to say, the concept is confined to certain apocalyptic circles, perhaps, as Lohmeyer thinks,[4] to be assigned to Galilee, which was undoubtedly a hotbed of eschatological expectation. At all events, this talk of the Son of Man seems to have been in the air during the lifetime of Jesus, and he chose to make use of it. It could embrace the mystery of his divine-human person, and the eschatological function of his mission which both saved and judged, in a way that the traditional messianic hope of an earthly Davidic ruler was quite unable to match. Perhaps that is one reason why he reinterpreted confessions of his Messiahship in terms of the Son of Man (e.g. Mk. 8.29, 31).

Some interesting supporting evidence for the prominence of this sort of eschatological enthusiasm in the first century is to be found in an unexpected quarter. Philo, that educated Hellenistic Jew of Alexandria, puts forward what looks like a cultured and cautious reinterpretation of the same hope, when he argues for the existence of an ideal, heavenly man, from Gen. 1.27, contrasted with the empirical, earthly man of Gen. 2.7. This ideal, divine prototype of man exists in heaven with God.[5] This, of course, is to claim for the ideal Adam (Gen. 1.27), as opposed to the empirical Adam (Gen. 2.7) all that the oriental religions had to say about the first man, the perfect primordial being.[6] True, Philo does not bring this idea of the heavenly man into relation with the hope of a future Saviour, for he spent his life seeking to fit Jewish theology into a framework of Greek philosophy where such an idea would be totally out of place, but he cannot conceal that he shares the characteristic Jewish hope. Twice[7] he allows himself to

[1] See an interesting article by G. H. P. Thompson (*J.T.S.*, 1961, pp. 203ff.), who argues from the Gospels themselves that the idea of the Son of Man as "a figure associated with God's Final Judgement and his Final Reign" was quite familiar to Jesus' hearers.

[2] Baruch seems to belong to the first or second century A.D.

[3] The unity and date of 4 Ezra are disputed; it probably belongs to the first century A.D. (see Rowley, *op. cit.*, p. 156).

[4] *Galiläa und Jerusalem* (1936).

[5] *Leg. Alleg.* 1.31f.; *de Mundi Opific.*, 134f.

[6] See Jeremias's article ἄνθρωπος in *T.W.N.T.*, i, pp. 365ff., also A. Christensen, *Les types du premier homme et du premier roi dans l'histoire legendaire des Iraniens.*

[7] *de Praem. et Poen.* 15; *de Execr.* 9.

speak of the last things, and makes it plain that he does cherish his nation's hope of salvation – universal peace, the moral and political supremacy of a glorified Israel under the guidance of God's mighty leader who would be endued with God's victorious strength, just as Num. 24.17 foretold; indeed, Philo's rendering of this verse shows where his sympathies lie: "For a man will go forth, who leads to the field, and wages war, and will overcome great and powerful nations, because God himself sends help to his saints."

It is interesting that in contrast to Philo, Josephus leaves no trace in his writings of having shared this common Jewish hope of the coming great one who would bring salvation. Manson suggests that for this there are two reasons. In the first place, Josephus was one of the defeated generals in the disastrous rising of A.D. 66-70, and was completely disillusioned of any messianic hope. Furthermore, he had come to the conclusion that the world government of which the messianic hope spoke had fallen to Rome and not to Israel. "He went so far as to reinterpret at least one messianic prophecy in favour of the Emperor Vespasian."[1] One might add that for one who, like Josephus, attended the Roman court, and sought to rehabilitate the image of Judaism in Roman eyes, it would have been foolish in the extreme to have given vent to any of the nationalistic hopes connected with messianism, even if he had still cherished any.

But with Josephus we have gone beyond the period we are examining. It is time to look at the different ways in which the hope of salvation was viewed in the different parties that characterized Judaism in the time of Christ. Though the Pharisees, Sadducees and Essenes could, between them, hardly have numbered ten per cent of the population of Palestine, if Josephus' figures are correct,[2] yet they had an influence out of all proportion to their numbers. To them and to the Zealots we must now turn.

A. THE SADDUCEES

The Sadducees will not detain us long. For one thing they have left no surviving literature, and all we know of them and their views comes from opponents, such as the Pharisees, Josephus, the Mishnah and the New Testament. For another, they did not believe in any life after death worthy of the name; they seem to have clung to the earliest Hebrew belief in the shadowy, tenuous half-life of Sheol, and rejected the more recent belief, current among the Pharisees, in a future life where men are rewarded or punished according to their behaviour in this life (Matt. 22.23.). They were an aristocratic party of noble

---

[1] T. W. Manson, *The Servant Messiah* (1953), p. 34, on Josephus, *B.J.* 6.312f.
[2] *Antiquities*, 17.2, 4.

priestly and landowning families, comprising most of the wealthy men in Palestine.[1] They generally seem to have had a majority in the Sanhedrin under the Herods and the Romans. They were the hard-headed practical men of affairs, stubborn in their ways and conservative in their temperament – characteristics not unknown among aristocrats and ecclesiastics! So devoted were they to the ritual of the Temple that they disappeared as a party with its destruction in A.D. 70. So involved were they with maintaining the *status quo* (with the retention of political influence in their own hands) that they inevitably co-operated with the Gentile overlords of their country, and so earned general odium as quislings. They were great believers in free-will and self-determination, and had little time for those who waited wistfully for God to intervene on their behalf.[2] Had we asked a Sadducee how Israel was to be saved, he might have answered us something like this. "Salvation for Israel lies in cooperation with the ruling powers. You may not like the Romans, but it is folly to oppose them. Politics is the art of the possible. And so long as we hold power in Israel we shall endeavour to keep her from the madness of revolt which those hot-headed zealots are always urging. If the Pharisees like to dream up hopes of an after-life where the tables are turned and all the righteous saved, good luck to them. We are concerned with the harsh realities of life as it is." It is hardly surprising that this blend of spiritual deadness and political dependence made little appeal to the common people, and had little lasting effect upon the beliefs and behaviour of Judasim. Indeed, something of the scorn and hatred with which they came to be regarded is preserved in the Mishnah. "The daughters of the Sadducees, if they follow after the ways of their fathers, are deemed like the women of the Samaritans." And the women of the Samaritans have just above been stigmatized as unclean from their cradles![3]

B. THE PHARISEES

Unlike the Sadducees, the Pharisees were coming to hold clear views on the subject of salvation. They were a democratic party, and they had the ear of the people. They were, furthermore, a progressive party, and were not afraid either to apply the Law to new circumstances by authoritative pronouncements,[4] or to open their minds to new ideas. For instance, there is reason to believe that their doctrine of the after-life with rewards and punishments, of angels and demons, may

[1] Josephus, *Ant.* 13.10, 6.   [2] Josephus, *B.J.* 2.8, 14.   [3] *Niddah*, 4.1.
[4] They regarded the Oral Tradition as a "fence for the Law", and claimed for their traditions equal authority with the Torah. See Mk.7.13 and *Aboth*, 1.1 where it is claimed that the oral law derived from Moses and was transmitted through the prophets to the men of the Great Synagogue i.e. the "elders" from the days of Ezra to their own.

well have been influenced by Persian thought. They believed passionately that God was in control of history, and they speculated a great deal about the Deliverer who they felt sure would come. A large amount of Pharisaic literature is extant; indeed, to all intents and purposes they were the only party in Judaism after A.D. 70. In fact, as G. F. Moore has put it, "Judaism is the monument of the Pharisees."[1] But if we want a clear view of their doctrine of salvation during the period under discussion, we can hardly do better than turn to the *Psalms of Solomon*, a collection of violently anti-Sadducaean songs written by Pharisees in the mid-first century B.C.

They looked for an anointed one, a Messiah (17.36; 18.6, 8 – perhaps here used as a title for the first time) of Davidic stock (17.23), who would be raised up by God himself (18.6). He would overthrow the Gentile overlords (i.e. the Romans), and the "unjust rulers" and "proud sinners" (i.e. the Sadducees) who had cooperated with them (17.24, 25, 27, 41). He would restore Israel's glory, gather the dispersed of Israel, reign from Jerusalem, and the Gentiles would be won to him (17, *passim*). His rule would be just (17.31), spiritual (17.38), and wise (18.8). Although addressed as "Christ the Lord" in 17.36,[2] he is not, apparently, thought of as a divine being; he is God's vice-regent on earth (17.38, 45). But he is the ideal man, the perfect ruler, merciful (17.38), majestic (17.47), sinless (17.41), "mighty in works and strong in the fear of God, tending the flock of the Lord with faith and righteousness" (17.44, 45). As Ryle and James say, "In this representation of the human Messiah, perfect in holiness and taught of God, free from sin, and wielding only the weapons of spiritual power, we find ourselves brought more nearly than in any other pre-Christian writing to the idealization of the Christ who was born into the world not half a century later."[3]

Now the writer of these *Psalms* makes considerable use of the words "save", "salvation", and "saviour", and it is clear that the picture he sketches in Ps. 17 of the coming Deliverer gives content to his references to salvation. He calls God his "Saviour" (3.7, 17.3, 8.39). He looks for "salvation from the Lord to be upon the house of Israel unto everlasting joy" (10.9, cf. 12.7). This salvation will come, not by man's activity, but by God's intervention, when God, who *is* already king (Ps. 17.1, 4, 38, 51), will, through his anointed one, deliver Israel from the "uncleanness of ungodly enemies" (17.51). Therefore they must

[1] *Judaism* (1927), ii, p. 193.
[2] βασιλεὺς αὐτῶν χριστὸς κύριος. This may perhaps be Christian emendation; more probably it is a mistranslation of the familiar Hebrew phrase "The Lord's anointed". However, the phrase is found in Lk. 2.11, "A Saviour which is Christ, the Lord", so it may have been a rare messianic description.
[3] *Psalms of Solomon* (1891), p. lvii.

be content to wait in patient submission for the Lord to send eternal salvation upon Israel, "The Lord preserve the quiet soul that hateth the unrighteous; and the Lord prosper the man that worketh peace in his house. The salvation of the Lord be upon Israel his servant for ever, and let the sinners be destroyed before the face of the Lord once and for all. And let the saints of the Lord inherit the promise of the Lord" (12.6-8). This is the first place in Jewish literature where the phrase "inherit the promise of the Lord" is made to sum up the assurance of messianic salvation. This sort of language played no small part in New Testament terminology (cf. Heb. 6.12, 11.9, Gal. 3.29). It is plain that salvation means not only deliverance from present evils, but also from the defilement of sin (so also 16.4-7). And the Saviour is God himself (ibid). That is why men must contain their souls in patience, and await his time.

Such, it would seem, was the characteristic Pharisee hope in the last half-century B.C. They looked for a Davidic Messiah, raised up by God himself to act as his representative and reign on this earth from Jerusalem over a restored Israel and Gentile converts. This was to be the work of God their Saviour, and the righteous of Israel (i.e. themselves!) must not attempt to force God's hand by premature action, but must wait his time. A thoroughly materialistic hope, it would seem, not far removed from the crude nationalism of the common people; and yet – the deliverer would be the Lord Christ, it would mean salvation for ever and the deliverance would include forgiveness of sins. In other words, the spiritual and the secular go side by side in these Pharisaic writings, just as they do in the Old Testament. This refusal to separate sacred and secular explains how apocalyptic and "other-worldly" conceptions of salvation, such as 2 Baruch and 4 Ezra, could be accepted in Pharisaic Judaism after the Fall of Jerusalem in A.D. 70, alongside the prophetic and "this-worldly" picture we are given in the *Psalms of Solomon*. Both came from circles of responsible leaders who hated the Romans as much as any of the ordinary people did, but saw the folly of revolt, and contented themselves with a healthy hatred of the enemy, and a firm trust that God is in fact sovereign in his world, and would in his own time vindicate their cause precisely because it was his cause.

In the meantime, while God's salvation of Israel tarried, how was the pious Jew to achieve the personal salvation which was a natural corollary of the Pharisaic doctrine of the judgement and separation of the righteous and unrighteous dead?[1] How was he to be sure of the

[1] It is not surprising that an increasing concern with personal salvation marks this period of national frustration, quite apart from the growing influence on Judaism of the Greek emphasis on the individual.

favourable verdict on the great day? One would expect it to be through living a good life. And so it is. As early as Ben Sirach[1] it is stated that those who fulfil their filial duty in honouring their parents will be saved (3.1ff.). Indeed, it goes on to say that "he that honoureth his father maketh atonement for sins". Again, "benevolence to a father shall not be blotted out, and as a substitute for sin it shall be firmly planted" (3.14). We have here the beginning of the Jewish doctrine of merit, the idea that if you kept the Law, you could put God in your debt. This doctrine develops as the keeping of the Law becomes increasingly the main concern of the Jew. Thus in *Pirqe Aboth* 2.8 it is said, "He that getteth to himself words of Torah has gotten to himself the life of the world to come", and in 6.7, "Great is Torah which gives life to those who practise it, both in this life and in the world to come." Good works are taught as the way of salvation equally explicitly in 4 Ezra,[2] a composite work of the first century A.D. "The righteous who have many works laid up with thee shall out of their own deeds receive their reward" in contrast to "those who have no works of righteousness" (8.33-39). But even in these verses there seems to be some recognition that no "works" can constitute a claim on God. The creature cannot, as of right, make demands on his Creator, for "there is none on earth that hath not dealt wickedly". In consequence the author is cast back upon God's mercy as the real ground of his confidence. God is called "the gracious one". He will save.[3] The position of such a writer is, of course, quite illogical. If acceptance by God is due to merit alone, then mercy is irrelevant. But illogicality of this sort shows the writer to be a more religious man than his sentiments would warrant. In spite of his emphasis on works as the means of salvation (a view which at least shows the depth of his understanding of the ethical demands of God), he knows very well in his heart of hearts that good works are never good enough, even if he failed to see with St. Paul that such an approach to God is in itself essentially irreligious.

Of course, if you really believe in a doctrine of merit to win God's

[1] Early second century B.C.

[2] See the similar emphasis on "works" in Baruch, 51.7, "But those who have been saved by their works, and to whom the Law has been a hope . . . they will behold a world which is now invisible to them."

[3] *The Assumption of Moses* (c. A.D. 25 ?), ch. 12, stresses that Israel will not be saved because of her godliness. As in the Old Testament, the covenant relationship between God and Israel was grounded not in human merit but in divine grace (v. 8). Nevertheless the writer is quick to point out (vv. 10-12) that good works will characterize God's people, and those who "sin and set at nought the commandments shall be without the blessings before mentioned, and they shall be punished with many torments".

64

favourable verdict on the day of judgement, you must recognize that, in all probability, there will be few enough who pass the test! There is reason to believe that the question, "Are there few that be saved?" (Lk. 13.23) was debated with interest in rabbinic circles. The more rigid your doctrine of merit, the gloomier became your estimate of the number of the saved. So while the *Apocalypse of Baruch*,[1] a book which is, at any rate in places, marked by a generous and genial tone, asserts that "not a few will be saved" (21.11), 4 Ezra, which belongs to much the same date, but has a very much stricter doctrine of merit, is in no doubt that the saved will be few. "Many have been created, but few shall be saved." (8.3) This view, of course, involves the corollary, which the writer does not shrink from drawing, of a ghastly doctrine of God. 'Ezra' represents him as saying, "I will rejoice over the few that shall be saved" (7.60), and "I will not concern myself about the creation of those who have sinned, or their death, judgement or perdition. But I will rejoice, rather, over the creation of the righteous, over their pilgrimage also and their salvation and their reward" (8.38, 39). And that, of course, is the logical – though intolerable – outcome of the doctrine of merit. You only gain a credible doctrine of salvation at the expense of an ethical doctrine of God.

Much more could be said about the Pharisaic eschatological hope, and the doctrine of salvation that went with it. But perhaps enough has been said in these brief extracts from their surviving writings to make the New Testament story a little more intelligible, and to illuminate the deeply held prejudices over this concept of salvation with which Jesus, and St. Paul after him, had to contend.

C. THE ESSENES

It is time now to glance at the salvation doctrines of the third great party in first-century Palestine, the Essenes. A fairly cursory examination will suffice, for the obvious reason that, as the Essenes withdrew from public life, and went to live in their monasteries in the desert, they naturally exercised little influence on the turn of events and on popular opinion. It is interesting to notice that, for all the possible links that have recently been suggested between the New Testament writers and the Essenes, the fact remains that no overt reference is made to these people anywhere in the New Testament, while the Sadducees and Pharisees figure prominently upon the stage of the gospel story.

In days gone by, it would have been impossible to speak with any confidence about the views of the Essenes, for we relied only on second-

---

[1] Another composite work, usually dated to the first century A.D.

hand information from Philo, Josephus and Pliny the Elder.[1] However, since the discovery of the Dead Sea Scrolls and the settlement at Qumran which is almost certainly Essene, we are better placed to assess not only their views about salvation, but the possible influence they may have had on some of the earliest Christian disciples.[2]

The covenanters of Qumran are very probably the descendants of the *Hasidim*, the "holy ones" who retired into the wilderness of South Judaea in the days of the godless persecutor, Antiochus Epiphanes (175-163 B.C.). Under the leadership of the "Teacher of Righteousness", they dedicated themselves wholly to the Lord, as the righteous remnant of his Israel. They would have nothing to do with the new Hasmonean dynasty which, although not descended from Aaron's priestly line, had seized not only civil power, but control of the Temple and high priesthood as well.

And so, in protest against the iniquities of this present evil age, the adherents of the ancient line of Zadok prepared themselves in the desert for the age to come when wrongs would be righted, the true priesthood and leadership restored to Israel, and the holy ones, the children of light (i.e. themselves) would resume control of the Temple and its sacrifices once again.

This coming deliverance for which they waited with such passionate longing was associated in their minds with three eschatological figures, an anointed priest of Aaron's line (1QSa 2.11-22), an anointed king of David's line (1QSb 5.20ff., CD 9.8-10, etc.) and the prophet like Moses (e.g. 1QS 9.11 and 4Q *Testimonia*). The prophet, priest and king of Old Testament hopes are not united in a single figure here, as they were to be in Jesus. The Davidic Anointed One or Messiah would be a great warrior prince, and lead them to victory over the "sons of darkness". He would be subordinate to the Aaronic Anointed One or Messiah, as the king always was subordinate to the High Priest in Jewish thought.[3] And the prophet like Moses (cf. Deut. 18.18) would teach men the will of God in the age to come, just as Moses had done for the men of his day.

The covenanters of Qumran were remarkable for the way in which they interpreted Scripture as applying to themselves, and being fulfilled in their situation. Most significantly, they saw themselves as the Voice crying in the wilderness, "Prepare ye the way of the Lord."[4] They believed that they would have a crucial role to play in the great

---

[1] Philo, *Quod omnis probus liber sit*, 12, 13; *Hypothetica*, 11.1-18. Cf. his references to the closely associated Therapeutae in *de Vita Contemplativa, passim*; Pliny *N.H.*, 5.15; Josephus, *Bellum Judaicum*, 2.8.2-13; *Antiquities*, 13.5.9 and 18.1.5.
[2] See *The Scrolls and the New Testament*, ed. K. Stendahl (1960), *passim*.
[3] See Ezek. 40-48.   [4] 1QS 8.14ff.

eschatological battle between the sons of light and the sons of darkness. Indeed, it seems probable that, in the tradition of the Maccabaean heroes (1 Macc. 2.31-38), they accepted suffering and martyrdom gladly, and saw themselves in the light of the Suffering Servant of Isa. 53. In 1QH 2.8 we read, "I became healing for all that turned from transgression" (cf. Isa. 53.4, 5), and the language of Isa. 53 is freely used of the sufferings of the covenanters in 1QH 9, "Thou hast put supplication in the mouth of thy servant, and hast not rebuked my life. My sacrifices hast thou not rejected, and hast not abandoned my hope . . . For thou art my God . . . thou wilt plead my controversy, for in the mystery of thy wisdom thou hast chastised me . . . And thy chastisement was for me joy and gladness, and my wounds were for healing . . . And the contempt of mine adversaries became a crown of glory, my misfortunes an eternal triumph. In thy glory did my light shine forth, for a light out of darkness hast thou caused to shine" (10-12, 23-27).[1]

This is noble writing. It teaches the redemptive power of patient suffering. But nevertheless it is not brought into any connection with the hope of salvation, nor with cleansing from sin. It is noteworthy that the verses in Isaiah which speak most clearly of the sinbearing of the Servant are omitted by the sectaries of Qumran when they apply it to themselves. They pinned their hopes for the future on separation from sinners, a more thoroughgoing separation even than that of the Pharisees. They were not in the least interested in the salvation of sinners. Indeed, they wanted nothing more than to kill them! This is one of the places where the theology of the men of Qumran is so strikingly different from that of the New Testament. Their bloodthirstiness and the egocentric and esoteric ethos of their way of life are in violent contrast to the love and catholicity of the early church. W. F. Albright summarizes it in this way. "Christ came to save sinners, not (merely) the elect . . . Christ taught the gospel of love, not merely the gospel of righteousness."[2] Despite their love of its language, the covenanters never got to the heart of the message of Isa. 53, as did the man who, though separate from sinners (Heb. 7.26), was the friend of sinners (Matt. 11.19) and bare away the sin of the world (Jn. 1.29).

But perhaps we ought to see this refusal of the men of Qumran to accept the role of sinbearer not so much as a defect in their understanding of the theology of the Servant, but rather a faithfulness to the essential position of Israel. Like the other strands in Judaism, they

[1] See M. Black, *The Scrolls and Christian Origins* (1961), pp. 143ff., whose translation appears above.
[2] *The Background of the New Testament and its Eschatology*, ed. Davies and Daube (1956), p. 170.

knew full well that salvation is of the Lord. No one else can forgive sin but God alone. And in a moving passage this conviction is clearly stated. It could almost have been written by St. Paul. "As for me, I belong to an evil humanity, and to the company of wicked flesh . . . For a man's way is not his own, a man cannot direct his steps. But to God belongs justification, and from his hand is perfection of way. All things come to pass by his knowledge. He establishes all things by his design, and without him nothing is done. As for me, if I stumble, the mercies of God shall be my eternal salvation. If I stumble in sins of the flesh, my justification shall be by the righteousness of God which endures for ever . . . Even from the pit will he draw forth my soul, and will direct my steps in the way. In his grace he will draw me near, and in his mercy he will bring my justification. In his steadfast righteousness will he justify me, and in the greatness of his goodness he will atone for all my iniquities. Through his righteousness he will cleanse, me from man's impurity . . . that I may confess to God his goodness."[1]

The language and the thought here, at first so reminiscent of Romans and Paul's doctrine of justification,[2] are in fact rooted in the prophets and psalms of the Old Testament. It is repeatedly asserted by the most profound thinkers in the Old Testament that man has no righteousness of his own, but is saved by trusting in the sovereign mercy of God.[3] Such is the message of the Old Testament as well as the New. It is characteristic also, as even this cursory summary has shown, of the best of the intertestamental literature as well. Salvation is of the Lord.

From all this evidence it is clear that Palestine in the time of Christ was, with the significant exception of the Sadducees, throbbing with the hope of some sort of a messianic deliverer. How far the common people were impressed by the various tenets of the different intellectual circles in Judaism may be doubted. The man in the street knew that his Old Testament had promised him a great deliverer who would save God's people. Most Jews probably saw him as a leader of Davidic descent who would triumph over the hated Roman occupying forces, and establish Israel not only in independence, peace, and prosperity, but in some position of leadership of the nations of the world. Most of the people, most of the time, were persuaded by the quietism of the Pharisees (not to mention the troops of the Romans) that they should bide their time – or rather, await God's time – and not risk armed revolt.

[1] 1QS 11.10ff.
[2] H. Kosmala is so impressed by this that he thinks the New Testament doctrine of salvation is based on that of the Essenes (*Hebräer – Essener – Christer*, 1959, esp. pp. 135ff.). The differences, however, are even greater than the similarities.
[3] Isa. 45.21, 46.13, 51.5, Mic. 7.9, Ps. 71.2, 98.2, and cf. Isa. 64.6 with 61.10.

D. THE ZEALOTS

But there were always the Zealots. They were the hotheads who were all for stirring up rebellion when they could; and when no such prospects opened up, they became cloak-and-dagger men, brigands who hid in the hills, and robbed and killed any of the cursed foreigners who had the misfortune to fall into their clutches.

They became identified as a party[1] within Judaism under Judas the Galilean in the revolt of A.D. 6,[2] when Rome took over Judaea as a province of the empire because of the misgovernment of Herod Archelaus who had held it as a tetrarchy. It is clear that the Zealot temper had never died in Israel. Ever since the stirring days of the Maccabaean resistance[3] to Antiochus Epiphanes and his attempts to stamp out the worship of Jehovah, there had been loyal patriots who would die rather than acquiesce in foreign domination of their soil and heathen domination of their religion. "War to the death" was their motto. Such men cherished a genuine theocratic ideal; the state of Israel should be governed by the congregation of Israel, under God. The difference between the Zealots and the masses was not in their theory but in their practice. The Zealots, so called from their zeal for the Law, had the courage of their convictions; that was the only difference. They took violent action in A.D. 6 when the Romans tried to take a census of the people of God. The revolt was crushed (as Luke notes in Acts 5.36, 37), but not the Zealot movement. They preached a holy war; they prepared for it and, whenever opportunity offered, they organized resistance movements and uprisings. There was the revolt of the Egyptian Zealot leader (Acts. 21.38) with his four thousand followers; Josephus tells us that two of the sons of Judas the Galilean were crucified in A.D. 46 for sedition,[4] while a third, Manahem, took a leading part in the great revolt of A.D. 66-70.[5] The abortive risings of many more of these Zealots are noted in the pages of Josephus. It is very likely that the Galileans whose blood Pilate mixed with their sacrifices (Lk. 13.1) were Zealots too. At all events, they were as popular a party with the masses as such resistance movements always are. This is what made their capture so difficult. That, no doubt, is why the authorities were so elated when they captured the Zealot leader, Barabbas and two of his men; that is why they were determined to

[1] The situation in Palestine during the Roman administration must have been somewhat similar to that in Cyprus under the British rule in the 1950s. The actual terrorist outbreaks were restricted to a comparatively small minority of fervent and intrepid patriots; but the people were behind them. That is why the imperial government was never able to make much progress in the country as a whole.

[2] Josephus, *Ant.* 20.5.1, 2; 18.1.1, 6.   [3] 1 Macc. 2.24-27.
[4] Josephus, *Ant.* 20.5.2.   [5] Josephus, *B.J.* 2.17.8f.

make a public example of them; and that is why Barabbas was so popular with the crowd that they clamoured for his release in preference to their erstwhile idol, Jesus the Nazarene. We may go farther. This sudden *volte-face* in the attitude of the crowd to Jesus is most readily explicable on the assumption that they had Zealot sympathies. Their support for Jesus in his triumphal entry into Jerusalem was support for the one who came in the name of the Lord to usher in the kingdom of David which had been so long awaited (Mk. 11.9, 10). It was support for the King of Israel riding in triumph into his capital (Jn. 12.13). That is why they raised the festal cry of "*hosanna*", "save now". When such a gesture came to nothing, when it became clear that no military *coup* was in Jesus' mind, their enthusiasm fell as fast as it had risen. It gave way to revulsion, in fact. He was, it appeared, a bogus Messiah, not the man they had hoped for. Let him die. Particularly if thereby they could get the great Barabbas back – there were no half-measures about him. And so took place one of the most tragic ironies of history. Jesus, who had repudiated the way of political and military force advocated by the Zealots, was crucified as a Zealot, a dangerous political rebel (the title on his cross proclaimed as much, "The King of the Jews") whilst Barabbas, who was in fact a character of just this description, was allowed to go free!

Earlier in his ministry, Jesus had appealed considerably to this Zealot party; several of his followers seem to have belonged to it. Simon the Zealot clearly did, and others may well have done so. Judas' surname, Iscariot, rendered *skarioth* in some MSS., may well be a retranslation into Aramaic of the Roman word for "Zealot", *sicarius*,[1] It is possible, too, that Peter's name Barjonah (Matt. 16.17) may not be a patronymic at all, but an Accadian word meaning "bandit". Certainly a connection with the Zealot party would fit well with his violent and rugged temperament. His desire to turn Jesus away from his interpretation of Messiahship in terms of suffering (Mk. 8.29-33) to Peter's own interpretation of it in terms of earthly dominion would be readily explicable on this view. So would his defence of Jesus with a sword in the Garden of Gethsemane. If this is so, his denial might well, like Judas' treachery, have sprung from bitter disappointment.

It is possible, moreover, that James and John, "sons of thunder" as Jesus called them, had sympathies with this movement. At all events they were particularly interested in the question of top positions in the coming kingdom (Mk. 10.35f.). And their desire to call down fire from heaven upon the Samaritan village which refused to give them shelter (Lk. 9.52ff.) would be very much in character for Zealots. It is,

---

[1] If so, this would explain his betrayal of Jesus. It would be due not so much to greed as to disillusionment at Jesus' failure to capitalize on his Triumphal Entry.

therefore, by no means unreasonable to see Zealot sympathies among the followers of Jesus himself.

Although, then, they have left no written remains, it is clear that the Zealots were an important element in Judaism at the time of Christ, and continued to be, even after the fall of Jerusalem, until they had helped to embroil their country in the final *débâcle* of the Bar Cochba rising under Hadrian. And Bar Cochba was, interestingly enough, both a Zealot and a self-styled Messiah.

Their views on salvation are easy enough to imagine. Salvation, they would say, belonged to the age to come, when God's Messiah had arisen, driven the Romans from the Holy Land, and ruled in peace and justice from Jerusalem. This, of course, was the characteristic messianic belief (if one may generalize) of first-century Palestine, except for the Sadducean collaborators who repudiated all such hopes. The Zealots shared it, but believed it would be brought about by their own resistance, culminating in a general revolt. The common people shared it, but were too fearful of their skins to join actively with the Zealots. The Pharisees shared it, but believed that only disaster could come from revolt; they must patiently wait God's time for intervention. The Essenes shared it, but believed that the best preparation for the longed-for day of salvation lay in separation from the wicked world, and the cultivation of the spiritual life in desert communities, until the day when "salvation shall come for the people of God, an age of dominion for all the members of his company, and of everlasting destruction for all the company of Satan . . . The dominion of the Kittim [i.e. Romans] shall come to an end, and iniquity shall be vanquished, leaving no remnant."[1] They, like the Pharisees, advocated non-aggression until this great day should dawn; then they would fight. In all probability they mistook the Jewish War for the last great battle, and joined forces with the Zealots, only to call down on themselves the full might of Rome and suffer complete extermination.

It remained for Jesus to reinterpret and fulfil this all but universal longing for salvation. We shall see in ch. 6 that what he offered was not political or cultic freedom, not an earthly kingdom, not a military operation, but something far better, far more profound and lasting, and something entirely unexpected.

But before we examine the treatment in the Gospels of this great theme of salvation, we might profitably glance at the pagan religions of the day. They, too, were a *praeparatio evangelica*. They, too, were haunted with the search for salvation.

[1] 1QM 1.4ff.

71

CHAPTER 4

Salvation in the Graeco-Roman World
of the First Century

At the time of Jesus's birth, there was a deep longing for salvation throughout the length and breadth of the ancient world. The politician, the thinker, the man of religion, the man in the street, and supremely the Jew, all alike were looking for "salvation". Indeed, W. M. Ramsay takes special note of the vast numbers of inscriptions from this period in different parts of the Mediterranean world recording prayers ὑπὲρ σωτηρίας, for salvation.[1]

Of course, it meant different things to different people, and in different circumstances. To a great many it carried political overtones, and without some understanding of the political history of the major world power of the day, Rome, it will be impossible to understand the enthusiasm for salvation which is so characteristic of the first century.

THE IMPERIAL CULT

The world political scene was scarcely less troubled then than it is now. By the first century B.C. the senatorial aristocracy of Rome had lost grip on events, and their foolish refusal to meet the appeal of the Italians for the franchise led to a disastrous war. The outcome of this was an equally disastrous personal rivalry between two of the successful Roman generals, Marius and Sulla. Sulla marched on Rome in 88 B.C., and his *coup d'état* set a precedent which led to a series of military coups and half a century of civil war. The dictatorships of Marius, Sulla, Cinna and Carbo, then the wars of Lucullus, Pompey and Crassus, then of Crassus, Pompey and Caesar, shook the very foundations of the civilized world. Out of the turmoil, Julius Caesar emerged as sole ruler of the Roman world – only to be struck down by an assassin's dagger. With great speed and presence of mind his grand-nephew, Octavian, claimed his name, secured the allegiance of his legions, and there began the uneasy triumvirate between this stripling of

[1] *The Teaching of Paul in Terms of the Present Day* (1914), p. 10.

eighteen, and the two seasoned generals, Mark Antony and Lepidus. Antony and Octavian ousted Lepidus, and then fell out among themselves, and a further gruelling civil war, embracing the whole *imperium Romanum*, ensued. Finally, in 31 B.C. the Battle of Actium left Octavian the undisputed master of the world. The wars were over. Peace had come at last.

Octavian was presented by a grateful Senate with the title "Augustus", a word with numinous overtones, because, as the coins of the period tell us, he had brought *salutem* to the people.[1] So many religious honours were heaped upon him that, says Tacitus, many people thought that there were none left for the worship of the heavenly gods![2] Is it altogether surprising that after nearly a century of wars, the world was thirsty for rescue, for salvation? Is it surprising that when Augustus brought in what he proudly called the *Pax Romana*,[3] he should be regarded as the Saviour of the State? In Rome a great archway was erected in his honour, inscribed with the legend *re publica conservata*.[4] In the East he was regularly given titles which associated him with the gods, and called *Sōtēr* as well as *pontifex maximus* and *divi filius*; "saviour", "high priest", "son of god" – this is how the titles of Augustus and of succeeding emperors would have sounded to Eastern ears. The poets sang of the return of the golden age, and were utterly sincere about it. Augustus himself issues "a coin with a Janus head, composed of the heads of Julius Caesar and his adopted son, and the inscription 'The divine Caesar – and the son of god'. On the reverse appeared the chariot of Saturn, the primeval king of paradise."[5] When the 23-year-old Augustus officially proclaims himself as "king of paradise", it is hardly surprising that Virgil should take the cue; *redeunt Saturnia regna*.[6] As an inscription found at Philae on the Nile put it, more than twenty years after his great victory at Actium, "The emperor is the ruler of oceans and continents, the divine father among men, who bears the same name as his heavenly father – Liberator, the marvellous star of the Greek world, shining in the brilliance of the heavenly Saviour."[7] This is how the achievement of Augustus was viewed by a war-weary world. He was "Saviour of the Universe", "Saviour of the World".[8] This divine man (how could he

[1] *Civibus servatis* or *ob civis servatos* figures prominently on coins celebrating the conclusion of the Civil War. H. Mattingley, *Coins of the Roman Empire*, i, p. 29 (nos. 136, 137, 139, 140, etc.).
[2] *Annals*, 1.10.   [3] *Res Gestae*, 13.   [4] *Inscriptiones Latinae Selectae*, no. 81.
[5] E. Stauffer, *Christ and the Caesars* (1955), p. 95. "Paradise" is, of course, Stauffer's Christian gloss on *Saturnia regna*!
[6] *Ecl.* 4.6.   [7] *Orientis Graeci Inscriptiones Selectae*, no. 458.
[8] See A. Deissmann, *Light from the Ancient East* (1910), p. 369, for examples of σωτήρ τῆς οἰκουμένης, σωτήρ τοῦ κόσμου, etc.

be less?) had shackled the evil demon of war, so long unleashed. He had closed the Temple of Janus, in token of universal peace, for the first time for two centuries. The *Ara Pacis Augustae*, one of the loveliest pieces of sculpture from Roman antiquity, was set up in honour of this astonishing man who had so enlarged the Roman sway that it comprised everything between the Rhine and the Euphrates, and had brought peace throughout the whole world. Surely this was the son of god, the prince of peace, the saviour of the world?[1]

Such was the general climate of opinion in the Roman Empire at the time of Christ. Yet everything in the garden was not so lovely as it seemed. Despite all the propaganda of the coins and the inscriptions, the long-lived Augustus was not immortal. What would happen when he died, as he did in A.D. 14? The dangers inherent in autocratic rule became increasingly evident under the next two emperors, the suspicious Tiberius and the megalomaniac Gaius Caligula. The latent powers of the mammoth Roman armies raised their ugly head when they secured the succession of Claudius in A.D. 41; still worse was to come when, in the year A.D. 68-69, they made and unmade no less than four emperors! Even on a political level, Augustus's salvation was proving imperfect enough.

On deeper levels, it was even less adequate. As Epictetus was to observe, "Caesar can give peace from war, but he cannot give peace from sorrow." And on a moral level, there was much to cause concern. *In Tiberim defluxit Orontes*; the East disgorged its filth into Rome, and immorality began to sap the stoic virtue of this once rustic people. On the religious plane, the picture was even more confusing. Augustus made it his plan to extend the pantheon by the simple process of addition, or else syncretism;[2] thus the Roman Mars was equated with the Greek Ares as the god of war, Diana with Artemis as the chaste huntress goddess, Venus with Aphrodite as the goddess of love, and so forth. Man in the first century was faced with a positively bewildering variety of claimants on his worship and many of them were clearly unworthy of it, if the poets were to be believed; for the gods, as they depicted them, were immoral, selfish, cruel human beings writ large.

There was, it is true, the beginnings of the Imperial Cult to provide a focus for his loyalty and worship. This was the very reason why Augustus founded it; it was to be a bond of unity among the varied peoples of his far-flung empire. In the East he allowed himself to be

[1] Thus a coin minted in Rome in A.D. 22 has this simple but significant legend on its reverse, *salus Augusta* (Mattingley, *op. cit.*, p. 131, no. 81).

[2] This, of course, had begun long before Augustus. He merely accelerated the process.

worshipped as God and Saviour.[1] This was nothing new; all great conquerors had for centuries been treated in this way by their Eastern subjects. Not only the Seleucids, but the Ptolemies in the three centuries before Christ took the title of saviour and god,[2] so it was no innovation, but sober realism for Augustus to take over this focus of devotion unchanged.

In the West he had to be more circumspect. They were not in the habit of worshipping any living man. So Augustus authorized and encouraged the worship of *Roma et Augustus*, thus allying himself with the tutelary goddess of his country. He went farther, and allowed the worship of the *genius Augusti*, i.e. the fortunate and fortune-bringing spirit which animated him. Indeed many temples were built to carry out this new worship. Thus, although he did not allow worship of himself personally in the West, he went as far as he dared in that direction, and had his adoptive father Julius Caesar declared divine by decree of the Senate, so that he could call himself with every propriety *divi filius*, "the son of a god".

It is clear that the Imperial Cult was as much political as religious. It grew out of the jubilation and gratitude felt by the West for a return to settled times, and it quite naturally took over the current liturgical terminology in the East. Dressed, as it was, in the garments of religion, its main purpose was political, to promote harmony and loyalty throughout a singularly diverse conglomerate of peoples. But it could not, and did not, satisfy the hunger of the human heart for salvation, or its instinct for worship.

How, then, did the citizen of the empire react to this situation? Where did he look for salvation?

"RELIGIO" AND "SUPERSTITIO"

It is as well to begin by differentiating between *religio* and *superstitio* in Roman eyes. *Religio* was the state religion. It stemmed from an

[1] Thus we find inscriptions such as *Augusto deo* at Thinissut in Africa (*Inscr. Lat. Sel.* no. 9495), and Θεῷ Σεβάστῳ at Ancyra (*Or. Gr. Inscr. Sel.* no. 533). See Wendland's article on *Sōtēr* in *Zeitschrift für die neutestamentliches Wissenschaft* (1904), pp. 342ff., and L. R. Taylor, *The Divinity of the Roman Emperor* (1931), pp. 267-83.

[2] So Ptolemy *Sōtēr* in the late fourth century B.C., after which it became common. Antiochus the First in that same century called himself *Sōtēr*, Antiochus the Second, his son, took the surname "god" (*Theos*), whilst Antiochus the Fourth called himself *Epiphanes*, "god made manifest". Inscriptions are extant addressing these rulers as Saviour and God, e.g., Πτολεμάιου τοῦ σωτῆρος καὶ θεοῦ (*Collection of Ancient Greek Inscriptions in the British Museum*, vol. iv, 1.906). It was, therefore, quite in character when, as early as 166 B.C. Prusias the Second of Bithynia addressed the Roman Senate as "saviour gods" (θεοὶ σωτῆρες Polyb., *Hist.* xxx.16). This was the way in which the Easterns addressed their rulers, and Augustus astutely made capital of it.

agreement between the king of the gods, Jupiter, and the first king of Rome, Numa. It was, in fact, a contract between the state and the gods, whereby the gods undertook to protect and further the nation provided its peoples observed them, and offered regular sacrifices to them. On the proper performance of the cult depended the *salus populi Romani*, "the salvation of the people of Rome". It did not matter whether or not one happened to believe in the pantheon of the gods. As a matter of fact, most educated Romans of the first century had ceased to believe in them, and had adopted a scepticism which we meet among the Greeks as early as the fifth century B.C. in men like Xenophanes, Euripides and Plato. Belief was unimportant; it was the state religious ceremonial that mattered. Once leave off those sacrifices, and disaster could overtake you. Indeed, Horace was voicing common sentiment when he put down the disasters at the end of the Republic to the deserted altars of the gods, and when he attached great importance for the success of the early empire to Augustus's repair of the temples of the gods and his reemphasis on their worship.[1] Augustus himself was at pains to emphasize his virtues as a builder and restorer of temples (*Res Gestae*, 19-21, etc.).

The Roman Empire was very broadminded and tolerant in religious matters. She was continually enlarging the boundaries of her pantheon to accommodate the deities of captured races. But what she would not brook was an exclusive religion which precluded its devotees from worshipping the traditional gods of the state. This was seen not only as an affront to whatever gods there be, but as an act of sinister political disloyalty to the empire. Celsus in the second century A.D. felt this strongly.[2] So did Pliny, and he records with satisfaction in his letter

[1] See particularly *Od.* 3.6.1ff.

> Delicta maiorum immeritus lues,
> Romane, donec templa refeceris
> aedesque labentes deorum et
> foeda nigro simulacra fumo.
>
> dis te minorem quod geris, imperas;
> hinc omne principium, huc refer exitum,
> di multa neglecti dederunt
> Hesperiae mala luctuosae.

Virgil, too, congratulates Augustus on the restoration of three hundred temples (*maxima tercentum totam delubra per urbem, Aen.* 6.716), and Ovid calls him *templorum positor, templorum sancte repositor, Fasti* 2.63. So, too, Suetonius (*Augustus* 30), *aedes sacras conlapsas aut incendio consumptas refecit.* It was widely felt that because the gods had been neglected, they refused their favours to the arms of Rome in the chaotic years at the end of the Republic.

[2] Indeed, the main burden of Celsus's *True Discourse* seems to have been an appeal for Christian cooperation; if men withdrew their worship, they were endangering the defence of the world against the encircling hordes of barbarians.

to the emperor about Christians that since his prompt action in arresting them, "Temples which had been almost deserted begin now to be frequented, and the sacred festivals, after long neglect, are revived while there is a general demand for sacrificial animals, which, for some time past, have met with few purchasers."[1] That is why, for the next three centuries, we find persecution of Christians going hand in hand with renewed dedication to the gods of the state; it was so with Julian, so with Decius,[2] and when in A.D. 410 Rome was sacked by the Huns, there were plenty who brought a *crimen laesae religionis Romanae*, and attributed this crowning disaster to apostasy from the gods of Rome brought about by Christianity.

Alongside your *religio*, then, which for most men was a mere formality devoid of what we could call religious content, you were free to hold what private beliefs you liked. These, if not Roman, were called *superstitiones*, and there were many of them, all competing with one another to capture that basic religious instinct in man which the formal state religion did little to satisfy. Their astonishing success is due to the hunger in men's hearts for wholeness, emotional release, security, in a word for salvation in this world and the next. This salvation is what the *superstitiones* offered. Indeed, the very instability of the times helped to make men conscious of their needs and ready for a religion that would save them from the emptiness and insecurity of life.

The directions in which they turned were, broadly speaking, two. Salvation was sought either through cultus, or else through knowledge. The first method comprised magic, astrology, mystery cults, and appealed particularly to the ignorant masses; the second comprised philosophy and gnosticism, and appealed to the more sophisticated.

A. SALVATION BY CULTUS

(i) *Mystery cults*

The mystery religions of the first century, comprising a fusion of Greek and Oriental elements, were, as far as ritual goes, the successors of the Eleusinian Mysteries, and the precursors of the Masons. They grew out of the age-old fertility cult and nature worship. Men were fascinated by the successive rise, flowering, fall and rebirth of the seasons of the year. Renewal of life was at the heart of the mystery

---

[1] Pliny, *Ep.* 10.96.

[2] Indeed Decius matched his persecution of the Christians by issuing a command that the whole population of the Roman world should attest its devotion to the gods of Rome by sacrifice. Many such certificates have been found in Egypt dating from June and July A.D. 250.

religions. And as sex is intimately connected with regeneration, many revolting obscenities became part of the mystery religions. But this was incidental to the main object of the worshipper, which was to seek for divine aid to intensify and enrich his life here and now, and to assure him of immortality hereafter. All the mysteries, therefore, held out to their initiates the hope of salvation. And salvation meant primarily deliverance from the tyranny of an oppressive and capricious Fate which could quench life at a moment's notice; it meant the promise of a better life beyond the grave – and this was singularly attractive to the slaves, the maimed and the unfortunate who had an unsatisfactory present existence. Many of the cults initiated their worshippers into this experience of salvation through a sacramental ritual by which they were said to die and to be born again. A man who has been through the *taurobolium* of Mithras and thus achieved salvation is described in the inscriptions as *renatus in aeternum*, "born again to eternal life". Salvation, in fact, was secured, as Cumont says, "by the exact performance of sacred ceremonies".[1] Dionysus, chief god of the Orphic cult, together with Serapis, Mithras and other cult deities were given the title of "Lord and Saviour", and the worshippers sought union with their god through sacramental acts, including baptism in water and a sacred meal! This notion of salvation, of course, was for the most part both irrational and non-ethical. There was no theology, no rationale in this supposed salvation. Nobody attempted to show *how* the death of a bull, or castration, or the Bacchic frenzy of Orphism could make a man sure of salvation. Nobody expected the worshipper to live a better life as a result. The salvation of which they spoke had no necessary connection with morality – indeed, normally the very reverse was true. Although Apuleius, after his conversion to the worship of Isis and Osiris at the end of his highly immoral adventures recorded in *The Golden Ass*, fears that he will have to be more chaste in future, the dictum of Gardner remains true. "We have no reason to think that those who claimed salvation through Isis or Mithras were much better than their neighbours. They felt secure of the help of their patron deity in the affairs of life in the future world, but they did not therefore live at a higher level."[2]

There are, of course, similarities between Christianity and some of these mystery religions. Unquestionably there are parallels of a sort between the Gospel miracles and those of Apollonius of Tyana; without doubt much of the teaching of Jesus was not new, but could be found, albeit hidden in heaps of rubbish, among the innumerable rabbinic pronouncements. There are indeed parallels between Christian

[1] F. Cumont, *Les Religions Orientales* (1906), p. xxii.
[2] P. Gardner, *Religious Experience of St. Paul*, p. 87.

and heathen cultus.[1] But if we regard Christianity as a mere product of its religious environment and analogous to the mystery religions, it is very difficult to see why it should have succeeded where they failed. Why did Christianity become the greatest single influence in subsequent history, while the very names of many of the mystery religions have been lost? Christians *knew* they were different, both from Jews and from pagans.[2] They were a third race, a *tertium genus*. And their opponents recognized it too. That is why Christians were regarded as such sinister people during the first two hundred years of their history. They were acknowledged as different. And the ancient world suspected what it could not understand. The difference between Christianity and the mystery religions was really quite simple. It lay in the person of the Saviour. Unlike Sabazius, Demeter and the rest, Jesus was a recent historical figure. Unlike them, he was alive, and manifestly at work in his people. And he proved it by the moral transformation he constantly effected in the lives of those who came to him for salvation. In Christianity there was not only a ritual side to salvation, as in the mysteries, but both an ethical and a truly religious side. The Christians could explain how and why the death of Jesus could save people from the consequences of their wrongdoing. They could attribute the revolution in their lives and characters to the work of the risen Saviour in their hearts; and in view of their changed behaviour it was hard to deny it. In other words, the Christians could provide a *rationale* of salvation, and this was something entirely new in the history of religions. The altered lives, and changed aspirations of the Christians afforded to the ancient world solid ground for believing in the future reality of a salvation whose foretaste had proved so impressive.

(ii) *Magic*

Magic was very popular in this age when the spiritually cold, intellectually discredited, and morally unedifying state religion could not satisfy the religious instincts of mankind. In magic the aim was to get control of the demonic forces that control the world by getting to know their name. This gave one a lever over them. Indeed, people who practised magic believed that one could gain salvation, access to

[1] The danger of overemphasizing the parallels between Christianity and the mystery religions in terms of cultus had been stressed by H. A. A. Kennedy. "It is vain," he writes, "to endeavour to find points of contact between Paul and the Mystery-cults on the side of ritual" (*St. Paul and the Mystery Religions* (1913), p. 282).

[2] Thus Kennedy (*op. cit.*, p. 282) can say, "We were able to show that the central conceptions of the Mystery-Religions belong to a different atmosphere from that in which the Apostle habitually moves."

the celestial regions, by knowing and uttering the correct password. Preisendanz has made a collection of magical papyri found in Egypt, *Papyri Graecae magicae*, and there are graphic accounts of magic in Homer, Lucan, Apuleius and Petronius. Furthermore, some magical papyri have come down to us from the second and third centuries A.D., and they show an astonishing mixture of Egyptian, Jewish and third-hand Christian elements. Practitioners of magic were essentially syncretistic; they were prepared to use any name or formula that sounded impressive or appeared effective. In the Paris Magical Papyrus, for example, the writer adjures the demons by various charms, gibberish like 'Elo Aeo Eu Jiibaech, Abarnas' on the one hand; and on the other, familiar names like the God of Sabbaoth, Moses, Jeremiah – and Jesus! We are reminded of the Jewish exorcists in Acts (19.13ff.), who tried to use the name of Jesus in their spells, and got a shock. The same chapter speaks also of many who had practised magic coming to give it up and to burn their books of spells and incantations, once they had been converted to Christianity. A valuable bonfire it must have been; for the spells and other paraphernalia cost 50,000 pieces of silver (19.19). "So mightily grew the word of God and prevailed", comments Luke dryly.

(iii) *Astrology*

Astrology, too, exercised a fatal fascination. There had been long centuries of supposed divination by means of the stars both in Rome and the East. With the decline of religion, astrology came into its own, as it commonly does; this is one of the disturbing elements in the contemporary British scene. God is deposed, blind Fate is enthroned, and a right reading of the stars which govern human destiny will, it is hoped, unlock the secrets of the future. C. K. Barrett cites a fragment of an astrological work from the second century, *P. Tebt.* 276, "Saturn in triangular relation to Mars signifies bad fortune. If Jupiter, Mercury and Venus are in conjunction, they cause glories and empires and great prosperity; and if the conjunction takes place at the morning rising (of Venus) they cause prosperity from youth upwards."[1]

As an example of the hopes of salvation this sort of thing could engender, we need look no farther than the heavenly portents which were held to signify Vespasian's coming greatness. They had an immense currency, and are recorded independently in Josephus, Tacitus and Suetonius.[2] Similar portents in the skies foretold the rise of Alexander[3] and Augustus.[4] Indeed, most of the "saviours" of

---

[1] *The New Testament Background, Selected Documents* (1956), p. 35.
[2] Josephus, *B.J.* 6.5, 4; Suetonius *Vespasian*, 4; Tacitus, *Hist.* 5.13.
[3] Cicero, *de Divin.* 1.47.   [4] Virgil, *Ecl.* 4.

antiquity had their star![1] It would have occasioned nobody any surprise, therefore, when Magi from the East came to Jerusalem saying, "Where is he that is born king of the Jews? For we have seen his star at its rising" (Matt. 2.2.). The "star" in question may well have been the very bright light effected by the triple conjunction of Jupiter and Saturn in Pisces, a very rare conjunction which occurs only once in every 794 years. This took place in 7 B.C., and evidence from the Star Almanac of Sippar on the Euphrates shows that it was eagerly awaited by the astronomers of the day, who predicted the precise days in the year when the conjunction would be visible.[2] When we recall that Jupiter was the royal star belonging to the Father of gods and men, and that Saturn was the star of Israel (Tacitus calls Saturn the god of the Jews!)[3] it is hardly surprising that the Magi made their way to Jerusalem. It would seem that even so inadequate a manifestation of the religious instinct as astrology was used as a *praeparatio evangelica* under the sovereign hand of a God who saves.

Magic and astrology have brought us to the lower reaches of that

[1] Indeed the association of stars with "saviour" emperors as denoting their deity became current practice in the Empire. The reason for this is the curious coincidence in the case of Julius Caesar which made an immense impression on Roman society. Julius had decreed Games in his honour to be held in the July of 44 B.C. But he was assassinated in the March of that year. Nevertheless the Games were held, and at them appeared a completely unscheduled comet in the sky. This could be none other than Julius, now divine, presiding at his Games! And from then onwards the formal deification by the Senate of deceased emperors was preceded by someone who testified that he had seen the *genius* of the dead emperor ascend to the skies from his funeral pyre and become a star. This was proof of his divinity.

[2] The significance of this conjunction heralding Christ's birth is all the more notable in view of the meaning commonly attributed to Pisces, *viz. the last days* (see Billerbeck, vol. 4, p. 1046, and *The Book of the Zodiac*, ed. E. S. Drower, 1949). It meant, then, that the world ruler would appear in Palestine in the last days. Hence the remarks of Suetonius and Tacitus referred to above. Suetonius says, "An ancient and persistent idea was circulated throughout the whole East, that it was fated that at that time [c. A.D. 70] the rulers of the world should arise from Judea." And Tacitus remarks, "Most Jews were persuaded that according to their ancient scriptures, at that very time the Orient should get the upper hand, and from Judea should come rulers of the world." Doubtless these accounts are garbled, but they make it abundantly clear how wise men from the Orient could have come to Jerusalem to seek the newly born world ruler.

This date 7 B.C. had been calculated by Kepler in the seventeenth century, and he drew attention to it in a series of publications between 1603 and 1614. His calculations were confirmed by the publication in 1925 by P. Schnabel of clay tablets from the Observatory of Sippar. The Star Almanac contains calculations of the movements of the heavenly bodies in the year 7 B.C., and the positions of Jupiter and Saturn in the constellation of Pisces are worked out over a period of five months. See Schnabel's article in *Zeitschrift für Assyriologie* for 1925, pp. 66ff.

[3] Tacitus, *Hist.* 5.2.4.

other method of ascent to God adopted by the ancient world, salvation by knowledge. It is impossible to separate too precisely the cultic and the gnostic way of salvation. A direct line joins knowledge of the right password by which to escape the attentions of the evil stars and attain the heavenly realms, to that higher knowledge of the good, or of God, which the more sophisticated and earnest-minded hoped would produce the same happy result.

B. SALVATION BY KNOWLEDGE

(i) *Gnosis*

It is, of course, much debated among scholars as to whether there was a pre-Christian gnosticism or not. The answer may depend largely on how we define the word "gnosticism".[1] In the second century A.D. the main features common to a variety of associated but rival gnostic cults were:

(a) A claim to have an immediate knowledge of God. It was this knowledge that brought salvation.

(b) A dualistic view of the universe, which saw the body as evil, created by an inferior deity, and regarded the spirit as good, created by the supreme God.

(c) A consequent disregard for the body. What mattered was the soul. This writing off, as it were, of bodily existence led to one of two opposite extremes. It produced either asceticism – the attempt to mortify the body so that the soul might the more readily be saved; or else licence – based upon the assumption that nothing a man did with his body could possibly affect the heavenly destiny of his eternal soul.

(d) A highly developed angelology with an emphasis on a hierarchy of aeons, or "principalities and powers" of ever decreasing spirituality. This was necessary to the theory, in order to explain how a good spiritual God could have any relations with an evil physical world.

(e) A doctrine, derived ultimately from Plato, which taught the immortality of the soul when released by death from the confines of the body. This, needless to say, was promised to the *élite*, those who had *gnosis*. Here again was a debt to Plato who had virtually equated goodness with knowledge.

The whole gnostic system tended to foster an emphasis on knowledge unrelated to morality, and a sectarian exclusiveness, which

[1] See C. K. Barrett, "The Theological Vocabulary of the Fourth Gospel and the Gospel of Truth," in *Current Issues in New Testament Interpretation* (1962), pp. 210ff.

formed a striking contrast to the catholicity and real sanctity of primitive Christianity. It is not difficult to understand its appeal, nor the violence of the patristic assaults upon it. Whether or not we give it the name of "gnosticism" in the first century is unimportant;[1] the origins of the movement meet us plainly in the pages of the New Testament, particularly the Corinthian Epistles, 1 John and Revelation, together with Colossians and the Pastorals, where the "knowledge" is emphatically associated with a form of Judaism, which certainly seems to suggest a pre-Christian origin. In all these New Testament books the dangers of this attempt to gain salvation through knowledge are ruthlessly exposed. Indeed, it is *a priori* probable, in any case, that the attempt to fit Jewish doctrine into Hellenistic conceptions of salvation had been made some time before the birth of our Lord. As Goodenough has shewn,[2] from his survey of Jewish funerary art of this era, Hellenism had penetrated to the heart even of conservative Judaism. I remember being very struck by a bas-relief of the Sun god upon the very walls of the synagogue at Chorazin! If pagan symbols could be tolerated on a synagogue wall, it is not surprising if the characteristically Greek idea of the salvation of the soul from the prison-house of the body made inroads into the Hebrew conviction of embodied existence (both in this life and the next) long before the second century A.D. At all events, as we shall see when we come to the New Testament doctrine of salvation, its writers had to contend, against teachers of the gnostic type, that Christian salvation is not merely an individual but a corporate experience; not the emancipation of the soul alone but of the whole man; not the perquisite of an exclusive coterie, but open to all men; and most emphatically it does not exempt men from the claims of either morality or charity.

(ii) *The Hermetica*

Perhaps the highest example of what may broadly be called gnostic thought is to be found in the *Hermetica*.[3] These treatises about *Hermes Trismegistus* (thrice-greatest Hermes), *alias* the Egyptian Thoth, have come down to us from the end of the second century A.D., but there is little doubt that this written form of the material is the fruit of a long line of oral tradition stretching back perhaps to pre-Christian times. In the majority of these eighteen tractates Hermes discloses to his disciples (i.e. gnostics) the truth about God, man, the world,

---

[1] For a recent consideration of this issue, see J. Munck, "The New Testament and Gnosticism," in *Current Issues in New Testament Interpretation*, ed. Klassen and Snyder (1962), pp. 224-38.
[2] E. R. Goodenough, *Jewish Symbols in the Graeco-Roman Period* (1953-).
[3] See C. H. Dodd, *The Bible and the Greeks* (1935).

and salvation. In many ways they provide a striking preparation for Christian truth. They lay great emphasis on individual repentance and enlightenment. A man's salvation is secured by receiving the knowledge of God that Hermes has to bring. In order to do this, he must "repent", and leave "the way of the flesh"; he must "be born again" and "partake of immortality" by "receiving the knowledge of God".[1] Nobody can be saved before that. Indeed, the first paragraph of the treatise On Rebirth actually says, "Nobody can be saved before he is born again." Pagan though the framework of the Hermetica is, it has been strongly influenced by the noble theology of Judaism, particularly in its emphasis on a single Creator God, who is moreover a God of mercy. The Hermetic writers were ready to learn by drawing from the riches of Judaism, just as philosophically-minded Jews like Philo were prepared to reverse the process, and interpret Jewish thought in pagan philosophical terminology. There was an inextricable intertwining of philosophy and religion in the Levant of the first century; and it was by no means a one-way traffic.

(iii) Philosophy

By the first century A.D. even the classical schools of philosophy were becoming religious. Plato, of course, had taught the immortality of the soul when saved from the grip of life on this earth; after numerous reincarnations, depending upon the quality of the life lived in the previous existence, the soul would be reunited with the good God.[2] To him, and many of his followers, salvation[3] lay in absorption. Posidonius,[4] whose own most influential philosophical system owed something to his teacher Panaetius (whose Stoicism was combined with elements drawn from both Plato and Aristotle), and owed a good deal more to the fact that he lived in the period when the Roman Empire was being created, is also basically dualistic in outlook. Heroes and "daemons" act as intermediaries between man and God, and such salvation as he can contemplate is essentially physical (deliverance from the shackles of the material) not moral (deliverance from the guilt

---

[1] The Greek words used, μετανοεῖν, ἀναγεννᾶσθαι, γνῶσις τοῦ θεοῦ, σωθῆναι are very reminiscent of the New Testament terminology, although used with very different meaning. Clearly, however, the early Christian missionaries had to hand a ready-made vocabulary which they could take over and fill with new significance.

[2] See, particularly, the Phaedo and Timaeus.

[3] It is interesting to notice how Dio Chrysostom more than once refers to the philosophers as saviours. "These men are the saviours of such as can be saved" (Or. 32.18). The making of philosophers of this quality he attributes to two things, training and reason (Or. 32.3).

[4] He lived from about 135 B.C. until 50 B.C.

of sin). That was a subject upon which ancient Roman thinkers had very little to say. They found the whole subject of guilt and cleansing, with which such Oriental cults as Isis worship were so concerned, rather unhealthy and alien to the Roman spirit. The Roman prided himself on being a practical man of affairs, unconcerned with introspective matters of this sort. His religion was a cold unemotional affair; a matter of respect to his household gods and ancestors, a matter of ceremonial observances which were designed to securing various practical benefits – a safe journey, a good crop, and so forth. But despite this brave façade, there must have been a hunger for something more lurking in many a Roman breast. Otherwise the Romans would not have fallen so easy a prey to every foreign cult which offered salvation, nor to the diluted Platonism which, now more a religion than a philosophy, was concerned with much the same thing.

The Stoics at once spring to mind as the exceptions to this tendency to hanker after salvation. They understood by salvation, not so much deliverance of any sort, least of all in a spiritual sense, for they did not believe in immortality; but rather the maintenance of order and harmony, the conservation of the universe and prosperity. They taught that there is a divine spark in every man. Peace lay in retiring within yourself; salvation for the individual lay in the suppression of the passions and a stern devotion to duty.[1] In the first century A.D. popular work of Cebes called the *Picture*, people are encouraged to repent and enter on the good life of (stoic) philosophy. Such a man becomes "master of all things and superior to all that formerly distressed him" (ch. 3). There must be no distraction with the liberal arts and other trivialities; salvation (and Cebes uses the word nine times in his short treatise) lies in devotion to the dictates of philosophy. It cannot be denied that Stoicism produced some of the most admirable characters in antiquity, but it had no hope in it. And thus we find even so representative a Stoic as Seneca showing his dissatisfaction with his philosophy on two counts, towards the end of his life. In the first place, he became increasingly dissatisfied with his ethical attainments (not without some reason!).[2] He came to see that evil was not to be so easily exorcized by mere dutiful obedience as he had hoped. Evil "has its seat within us, in our inward part".[3] He began to see himself not even as a *homo tolerabilis*, let alone a good man.[4] In other words, as

---

[1] The duty envisaged is that of accepting things as they come, conforming one's life to the position which Universal Reason has assigned one in the natural order. Pleasure is to be avoided; it is ephemeral. Desire is to be repressed; it is likely to be disappointed. Duty is the all-important thing.

[2] See J. B. Lightfoot's essay on "St. Paul and Seneca" (*Commentary on Philippians* (1868), p. 310), for an assessment of Seneca's character.

[3] *Ep.* 50.4.   [4] *Ep.* 57.3.

T. R. Glover has put it, "in their contempt for the passions the Stoics underestimated their strength".[1] As a greater contemporary of Seneca found to his chagrin, "When I would do good, evil is present with me" (Rom. 7.21). Stoicism had too shallow and glib a doctrine of human nature.

Its other great weakness was that it left no room for immortality. There might or might not be a limited duration of the soul after death. On this point Stoics were not agreed.[2] But at the great conflagration which would periodically envelop the universe, according to their theories, the souls of men would share in the general dissolution. In his later years Seneca tentatively, timorously reaches out in the direction of the immortality of the soul of which Plato had spoken. At the crisis, the vaunted Stoic *autarkeia* failed. Man was not so self-sufficient after all. "It pleased me," he writes to his friend Lucilius, "to enquire into the eternity of souls, or rather, I should say, to trust in it . . . I surrendered myself to that great hope . . . I was beginning to be weary of myself, to despise the remaining fragments of a broken life . . ."[3] There was not, it would seem, so very much difference between the ignorant devotees of the mysteries, and the educated, wealthy philosopher, when it came to the ultimate issue of life and death. Like Epictetus after him, Seneca began to see the philosophers' school no longer as an intellectual and moral *corps d'élite*, but as a hospital; not for the glad but for the sorry. "That man," writes Epictetus of the philosophical enquirer, "that man is looking for salvation."[4]

CONCLUSION

We have glanced, albeit cursorily, at some of the main expectations, both pagan and Jewish, concerning salvation at the dawn of Christianity. The two approaches are very different. The Graeco-Roman view of the world is anthropocentric; the Jewish, theocentric. For the Jews the land of bliss and salvation lay in the future of God's promise; hence their ever-growing expectancy and hope for deliverance. For the Graeco-Romans the Golden Age lay in the past; hence their conception of history as gradual degeneration from the ideal, or at best, an ever-repeating cycle. The Jew recognized the transcendence of God, his

---

[1] *The Conflict of Religions in the Early Roman Empire* (1909), p. 67.

[2] *Diog. Laert.* 7.157; Seneca *ad Marc.* 26; *ad Polyb.* 1.20; Epictetus *Dissert.* 3.24. It would be very interesting to know how much the fear of the after-life entered into the thoughts of the ordinary man in the pagan world of this period. No doubt the answer would be as diverse then as now. To judge by the writings of Lucretius, one would think that fear of the hereafter played a very big part in the Rome of his day. To judge by the First Book of Cicero's *Tusculan Disputations* one would think that it played very little.

[3] *Ep.* 102.   [4] *Dissert.* 3.23.

holiness; to the Greeks and Romans "the divine" was not far away from any one of us, but rather congenial to us.[1] The Jew was impressed by the creatureliness of man, his sinfulness and inability to save himself. The Greek or Roman was impressed by the dignity and ability of man; he was, for the most part, unconscious of or indifferent to the ravages of sin within. If saviour were needed, he would be his own saviour by means of his magic, his knowledge, his philosophy. But for some, as we saw earlier, no personal salvation was to be thought of; had not the great Augustus proved the saviour of the Roman world? This, of course, was only another expression of the anthropocentric; it was merely transferred from the individual to the emperor.

What, we may ask, contributed to the breakdown of the Roman self-sufficiency? Partly, no doubt, the sense of sin induced, and catered for, by some of the mystery-religions. Partly, as the century wore on, a growing political and social disillusionment: one has only to contrast the bright hopes of Livy, Horace and Virgil at the beginning of Augustus's principate with the bitter disillusionment evident, say, in the first two chapters of Tacitus's *Histories* to take the point. Partly the growing religious emphasis in philosophy, accentuated by the absence of any real religious feeling in Roman institutional religion. But certainly one of the contributory factors in preparing the world for the spread of Christianity was the ever-widening circle of Jewish influence. Wherever there was the opportunity for trade, in the wake of Roman conquest, there you would find Jews – in Asia, in Egypt, and in Rome itself, where the ghetto occupied no small part of the city. Their monotheism, their morality, their earnestness, their Scriptures in the Septuagint translation, their synagogues, each with its circle of interested God-fearers, began to make a great impression on the Roman world. And wherever they went, they carried with them the eschatological hopes and messianic expectancy of late Judaism. In both East and West at this period there were, as we have seen, great expectations of a coming deliverer, an ideal ruler. These hopes were by no means confined to the Jews; Horace in his *Carmen Saeculare* hails the new epoch of justice and peace. Virgil in his Fourth Eclogue prophesies the birth of a wonderful child of heavenly origin, destined to usher in a new age. Indeed, as Conway puts it, "It can hardly be denied that in both the *Georgics* and the *Aeneid* we continually meet with a conception which is in many ways parallel to the Jewish expectation of a Messiah;

[1] When Paul on the Areopagus (Acts. 17.22 ff.) addresses the philosophers in their own language, he says, "God is not far from any one of us; for in him we live and move and have our being . . . for we are his offspring." This phrase is a quotation from a Stoic poet Aratus (*Phaenomena*, 5), and although Paul meant by it something very different from the Stoic pantheism of Aratus, the language would be readily understood.

that is to say, the conception of a national hero and ruler, divinely inspired, and sent to deliver not his own nation only, but mankind, raising them up to a new and higher existence."[1] As was pointed out above, at the time of the Jewish War of A.D. 66-70 there were still rumours of Jewish ascendency circulating in Roman ears. But in addition to the witness of Tacitus, Josephus[2] and Suetonius, we find Orosius saying that the reason why the Jews revolted in A.D. 66 was that certain prophecies emanated from Mt. Carmel saying that the Jews would become controllers of world affairs.[3] And the idea must have been given a very wide public through the so-called Sibylline Oracles, most of which were written by Jews in the last two centuries B.C. and the first A.D. under the name of the inspired Sibyl of Cumae. The express purpose of these Jewish additions to the collection of sacred utterances of the pagan prophetess was to commend their faith to an apparently gullible Roman public. A typical example of this propaganda is, "Let thy spirit within thy breast no longer be vexed, thou blessed one, child of God, excellent in wealth, well favoured Judaea, fair city inspired in hymns. No longer shall the unclean foot of the Greeks run riot in thy land."[4] In such (disreputable) ways the idea of the messianic age and its salvation was made familiar to a large and avid readership.

All these factors combined to turn the eyes of the ancient world towards the East. It was unwittingly looking for the arrival of the "Desire of all Nations".

---

[1] *Virgil's Messianic Eclogue*, p. 31.

[2] See p. 81, n. 2. Josephus, who became court historian to the Flavians, not unnaturally says that the ambiguous oracle that the rulers of the world should arise from Judaea referred to Vespasian and Titus (*B.J.* 6.5, 4). But he is severely taken to task by Hegesippus (*Excid. Hierosolym.* 5.44) and Eusebius (*H.E.* 3.8), who point out that Vespasian became ruler of the Empire only, not of the world! At all events, this shows the prevalence of the idea.

[3] Orosius, 7.9.2.   [4] *Sib. Orac.* 5.260ff.

CHAPTER 5

Salvation in the Preaching of John the Baptist

"When the fulness of the time was come, God sent forth his Son . . . to redeem" (Gal. 4.4). So Paul sums up the situation; and subsequent ages have only been able to admit that he was right. For Jesus was born at the one time in history when all civilized nations in the world were united within a single empire, linked by excellent communications, divided by no customs barriers. A single peace, the *Pax Augusta*, reigned from France to the Euphrates; a single language, Greek, could be understood throughout practically all the diverse nations which together made up the Roman Empire. There was, as we have seen, a widespread longing for saviours; there was a growing movement towards monotheism. Such was the world into which Jesus made his obscure entry, probably in the year 7 B.C. "The Incarnation of the Desire of all nations," wrote S. Angus,[1] "answered the universal question of Seneca, '*Ubi enim istum invenies quem tot saeculis quaerimus?*'"[2] Jesus was the answer to that inchoate longing for salvation; Jesus came to seek and to save the lost (Lk. 19.10). He was rightly given the ancient name Jesus ("God the Saviour"); for he was to save his people from their sins (Matt. 1.21).

But we must begin at the beginning. And the beginning of the gospel of Jesus Christ is the work of John the Baptist, so the New Testament writers make plain (Mk. 1.1ff., Acts 1.22). John the Baptist was very much concerned with salvation (Lk. 3.6). What did he mean by it?

If we are to believe St. Luke, and scholars are increasingly recognizing the primitive nature of his birth stories, John grew up in a home impregnated with the hope of salvation as understood by the end of the Old Testament. In contrast to the pessimism of contemporary paganism,[3] and the varieties of Jewish expectation outlined in ch. 3, godly

[1] *The Environment of Early Christianity* (1914), p. 226.
[2] "Where, pray, will you find him whom we have been seeking for so many centuries?"
[3] Gilbert Murray, *Five Stages of Greek Religion* (1925), ch. 4.

priests like Zacharias were quietly trusting that God would remember his mercy, and deliver his people Israel. They were looking for salvation. Simeon was one such man; he was "waiting for the consolation of Israel" (Lk. 2.25).[1] So was the prophetess Anna, who served God so assiduously in the temple (2.36). When she saw the child Jesus, she gave thanks to God and told all those who were waiting for redemption in Jerusalem (2.38) of her conviction that the promised redeemer had come. "Redemption"[2] spoke volumes to a pious Jew, being the regular LXX translation for *padah*, which, as we have seen, played quite an important part in the Old Testament doctrine of salvation. Simeon also interpreted the person and future achievements of the baby Jesus in Old Testament categories. He identified him with the Servant of the Lord (2.32, cf. Isa. 42.6 and 49.6); he described his work as the messianic salvation (2.30f.) promised in Isa. 52.10, 40.5. Indeed, the short hymn we call the *Nunc Dimittis* is steeped in the thoughts and language of Deutero-Isaiah. The child would bring in God's eschatological salvation; he would be the glory of Israel and the light of the Gentiles; and he would come as the Servant of the Lord. This was evidently the circle of ideas in which Simeon felt at home.

Much the same is true of John's father, Zacharias. In his short hymn he mentions "salvation" no less than three times (1.69, 71, 77); the thought of it is central to the *Benedictus*. Like Simeon, Zacharias speaks of God visiting and redeeming his people, but he is more specific than that; for he assigns that redemption to the "horn of salvation" raised up by God in the house of David – a characteristic Old Testament and inter-testamental belief. The content he gives to this salvation combines the main strands of Old Testament expectation – deliverance from enemies (1.71, cf. Ps. 106.10, 47), faithfulness to the covenant (1.72), and lifelong service of God in holiness and righteousness (1.75). All this is due to the gracious deliverance afforded by God himself. (1.68). Zacharias then goes on to speak of the infant John as the messenger of the Lord, and, by a bold reinterpretation of Mal. 3.1. (1.76), as the one who would prepare the way of the Lord (1.76, cf. Isa. 40.3) and tell men of the coming salvation (1.77). That salvation

---

[1] This word was used in a messianic sense, in view of Isa. 40.1, 49.13, 51.3, 61.2, 66.13. The "horn" metaphor was derived from the wild ox (wrongly translated "unicorn" in the A.V.) which was famous for its strength (e.g. Num. 24.8, Deut. 33.17). The phrase was probably widely used of the Messiah; as early as Ps. 132.16, 17 the "horn of David" is associated with salvation in this sense. But in Ps.18.2 God himself is called "the horn of my salvation". We may possibly have another messianic metaphor in *anatolē*, verse 78, if, as Jacoby argued, it means shoot or sprout in the sense of Zech. 3.8 and Isa. 11.1. (*Zeitschrift für neutestamentliches Wissenschaft* (1921), pp. 205ff.).

[2] Cf. Lk. 24.21. This was clearly current language in first-century Judaism.

would include forgiveness of sins, as Jeremiah had foretold (1.77, cf. Jer. 31.34), and it would apparently embrace the Gentiles too (1.79 refers to Isa. 60.1f. and 42.6, 7, both of which passages include the Gentiles). As Isa. 9.1-7 prophesies, Galilee of the nations (i.e. Gentiles) will be among the people who "walked in darkness and saw a great light; for unto us a child is born . . ."

If this is the way Zacharias used the prophetic Scriptures, and there is no *a priori* reason to doubt it,[1] it gives us some insight into the background in which John was brought up. How long he lived in such a home we cannot even speculate. Luke tells us, however, that "he was in the deserts until the day of his shewing unto Israel" (1.80), and by the "deserts" he must mean the wilderness of Judaea near the Dead Sea. In this case, he would have lived for some time, perhaps for many years, at no great distance from the covenanters of Qumran. He must have known of them. He may even have been a member of their community for a while. If this were so, and it is a possibility being increasingly canvassed among New Testament scholars,[2] it would help to explain a good deal about this enigmatic figure John which was obscure before the discovery of the Scrolls.

Take, for example, his insistence, recorded in all four Gospels, that he is "the voice of one crying in the wilderness, 'Make straight the way of the Lord.' " Now the *Community Rule* shows that the men of Qumran, whose community, like John's, was almost certainly entered by baptism,[3] were in the habit of applying this very Scripture to *their* sojourn in the desert, as they studied the Law, and waited for God to reward their virtue by sending to them the prophet like Moses (Deut. 18.18) or the Messiahs of Israel and Aaron,[4] who would lead them into the messianic kingdom.[5] Did John react against this interpretation of the prophet Isaiah? Did he see *himself*, and not the covenanters of Qumran, as God's true preparation of Isaiah for the coming of the Messiah? Is it because the covenanters were selfishly interested only in their own salvation, and blind to any responsibility to the nation

---

[1] Indeed, the divergence in style and technique of Old Testament quotation in the *Benedictus, Nunc Dimittis* and *Magnificat* from Luke's normal pattern makes the possibility that he himself composed the songs remote, and lends colour to the view that they represent good primitive tradition, which persisted in Baptist circles.

[2] See, e.g. W. H. Brownlee, "John the Baptist in the light of the Ancient Scrolls," in *Interpretation* (1955), pp. 71-90, and J. A. T. Robinson in *Twelve New Testament Studies* (1962), pp. 11-27.

[3] 1QS 5.13, "to enter the water" is probably to be associated with 5.8 "to enter the covenant", cf. 6.14ff.

[4] 1QS 9.11.   [5] 1QS 8.13-16.

as a whole, that John came out from their midst, and began to address the whole nation and, it would seem, the Samaritans, too?[1] John agreed with the covenanters[2] in seeing the Jewish society as corrupt and sinful (Lk. 3.7); he agreed with them in his stinging denunciation of the official priesthood (Matt. 3.7), but, unlike them, he saw that the whole people could be within the scope of God's salvation, if only they would repent. And that, surely, is why he continued the quotation of Isa. 40 farther than they did, so as to include verse 5 (LXX), "and all flesh shall see the salvation of God" (Lk. 3.6).

In addition to their common location, asceticism, ethical insistence, eschatological expectation and scathing critique of contemporary piety, John and the men of Qumran had another striking feature in common, namely baptism as a symbol of repentance. But it is clear that while they indulged in repeated washings,[3] John's baptism was unique and unrepeatable. What did it mean? If we can understand that, we shall know what he meant by salvation.

It has long been argued, inconclusively, that John's baptism was unique because it extended to Jews the baptism customarily administered to proselytes on joining Israel. It would mean, on this view, that the Jews could not rely on their membership of the physical Israel to save them, but must, like the proselyte, be "born again" through the washing away of uncleanness.[4] This would accord well with John's stern insistence that Jewish parentage would not save anybody (Lk. 3.8). Men must repent and change their attitude of arrogant self-satisfaction for one of humble dependence upon God, who is about to set his axe to the root of the trees, and to make the final separation between the wheat and the chaff (Lk. 3.9, 17). They must prove the genuineness of this changed attitude by a changed life, "fruits worthy of repentance" (3.8).

However, even if proselyte baptism was carried out at this period,[5] it provides a very inexact parallel for John's baptism. As opposed to proselyte baptism, John's rite was administered to Jews, in running water, and in an eschatological setting; moreover it was not, like proselyte baptism, self-administered. This is leading many scholars to

[1] He preached at Aenon, near Salim, in Samaritan territory, and baptized there (Jn. 3.23). Furthermore, the disciples are said to enter into the labours of other men in the Samaritan scene (Jn. 4.38), which points in the same direction.

[2] Cf. 1QH 5.27.   [3] Cf. 1QS 5.13ff.

[4] "The proselyte in his conversion is like a new-born child," b. Yeb. 48b. See the whole discussion in Jeremias, *Infant Baptism in the First Four Centuries* (1960), pp. 24ff.

[5] This is probable, but not demonstrable at present. See Jeremias, *op. cit.*, p. 29, n. 1 for bibliography of those who accept it; see Robinson, *op. cit.*, p. 16, n. 1 for some of those who remain unconvinced.

set John's baptism against the background of Qumran. And this undeniably presents some important points of comparison. As J. A. T. Robinson pointed out, while baptismal cults were common in the Levant at that time, the baptisms of John and Qumran have a unique feature in common.[1] Both regard the washing with water as merely a preparatory rite; the great cleansing lies in the future. John spoke of the coming one who would baptize with the Holy Spirit (Mk. 1.8, Jn. 1.33, Acts 1.5), or with the Holy Spirit and fire (Matt. 3.11, Lk. 3.16). "The covenanters, too, regarded the dispensation of water . . . as being merely provisional till the coming of the messianic age (1QS 9.10f.; CDC 15.4), when it would be superseded by the new dispensation of Holy Spirit."[2]

We may, indeed, be able to get closer to the meaning of John's baptism if we examine the reference to fire with which he said men would be baptized. This, presumably, is related to the eschatological fire of judgement of which he spoke (Lk. 3.17). Some years ago, C. H. Kraeling suggested that this conception might owe something to Zoroastrian religion. "In Persian eschatology, the mountains, which are made of metal, melt at the end of the world, and the molten metal passes over the earth like a river. All men pass into this river of molten metal, and in so doing are either purified or destroyed."[3] This, he thought, accounted for the river of fire proceeding from the throne of God in Dan. 7.10, itself an eschatological passage. All this, of course, was prior to the assessment of the contents of the Scrolls. When these were read, however, what should turn up in one of the Qumran hymns but an actual description of this river of fire which will break in at the last day![4] If this sort of thinking does indeed supply the background of John's preaching, then the meaning of his proclamation of the kingdom and the coming mighty one will be something like this. "The day of crisis is at hand; God is about to break into history in the person of the Mighty One.[5] He will come as the reaper, to destroy the wicked with the breath of his mouth, however impeccable their Jewish credentials, while gathering the wheat of the truly penitent into his eternal barn. He will come as the Servant of the Lord to carry away the

[1] *Op. cit.*, p. 19. [2] *Op. cit.*, p. 20. On the Spirit, see also 1QS 4.21.
[3] *John the Baptist* (1951), p. 117. [4] 1QH 3.28ff.
[5] The one whom John calls "mightier than I" is clearly not to be taken as God, as used frequently to be assumed, to the discredit of the Fourth Gospel, where John the Baptist makes it plain that Jesus is the one for whom he was looking (1.30, 32f.). It is perfectly obvious that God is greater than John, and we are surely right in taking the title to refer to the Messiah. Kraeling links it with "the Mighty God" as a messianic title in Isa. 9.6, and suggests, plausibly, that the title is used here, as in the LXX of Isa. 9.6, to denote a supernatural Messiah without compromising Jewish monotheism.

sins of the world.[1] He will give men the gift of the Holy Spirit, the long-expected mark of the age to come,[2] to enable them to live the sort of life pleasing to God." John may well have meant something like this by his preaching and his baptism. Indeed, this view has the support of Origen,[3] who sees in the running water of the river a symbol of the fiery river of God's wrath at the end of the age. Those who were prepared to submit to the severity of God in accepting the symbol, in an attitude of true repentance, would be saved from having to undergo the awful reality on the Judgement Day. This view would account well for the eschatological setting of the baptism, the running water, the emphasis on repentance, and the uniqueness of it all.

On the other hand, it is dangerous to overstress the coincidences between John's rite and that of Qumran. There is always a temptation to see in the latest discoveries long-awaited light on difficult problems of biblical exegesis! Certainly, if John had ever been a member of the community of Qumran, he had come out from among them, and the word of the Lord which came to him in the wilderness (Lk. 3.2) transformed all he may have learnt with the covenanters. From henceforth, he was in direct line of descent from the ancient prophets of Israel. Is that why he dressed in a way reminiscent of Elijah, and, like him, lived in the deserts? Is that why, as Elisha had been instrumental in the cleansing of Naaman in the river Jordan, John saw that same river as the natural place for the washing of those who repented of their sins? It may, as Flemington has argued, be a piece of prophetic symbolism that John was enacting. "Just as Isaiah or Jeremiah expressed their prophetic insight . . . by performing a symbolic act, so John gathered up his conviction about divine judgement and the need for 'turning' to God, in this 'baptism of repentance unto remission of sins'. Further, as a Hebrew prophet saw his act not only as expressive, but also in some way effective, of the divine purpose, so John summoned men to submit to baptism, convinced that thereby they became equipped, as it were, and made bold to face the Day of the Lord."[4] One might add that John could well have got the basic justification for his novel action

---

[1] That John could have spoken of Jesus as the Lamb (or Servant; see commentaries) of God is no longer inconceivable; Brownlee shows (*op. cit.*, pp. 50f.) how "the Suffering Servant motif is one of wide application among the Qumran covenanters." He shows how 1QH 8.10f., "But a holy branch shoots forth, as a planting of sacred truth; in not being esteemed and in not being known, is the seal of its secret," would be a characterization of the Messiah precisely in line with Isa. 53.2, 3 and also with the Baptist's teaching in Jn. 1.26, 33. Whether or not the community applied the prophecy to themselves or the Messiah is unimportant; it is quite clear how John used it.

[2] Ezek. 36.27; Joel 2.28, etc.   [3] *Hom. in Luc.* 3.16.
[4] *The New Testament Doctrine of Baptism* (1953), p. 22.

from the Old Testament itself. Such verses as Zech. 13.1 and Ezek. 36.25 would open the way for the association of cleansing from sin with cleansing of the body in water; and such verses as Isa. 44.3 and, less clearly, Ezek. 39.29 connect the Spirit with this cleansing. If this is the background to John's work, there will still be a value in the parallels we have adduced from Qumran. Even if John had no direct links at any time with the desert community, their writings enable us to do justice to the portrait of John contained both in the synoptic and Johannine accounts. They enable us to see how he could have been both a prophet of the coming age and also a witness to Jesus once he had appeared. It is no longer difficult to imagine John speaking of Jesus in terms of the Suffering Servant; it is not difficult to imagine his having grasped the significance of Jesus's own baptism as a commissioning both as Son (Ps. 2.7) and as Servant of God (Isa. 42.1).[1] It is not hard to see how he would have recognized endowment with the Spirit as the mark of the Messiah, since his Old Testament Scriptures made that perfectly plain (Isa. 11.2, 42.1, etc.). And the hope that the messianic age would mean endowment with the Spirit for all the elect people of God was Jewish orthodoxy itself (Joel 2.28, Ezek. 37.1-14), quite apart from its possible reiteration at Qumran (e.g. CDC 2.10, "And through his Messiah he shall make them know his holy Spirit").[2]

John's doctrine of salvation, then, is in proper succession to that of the Old Testament. Like the prophets, he knows salvation is the work of God, yet he sees it will be accomplished through an intermediary. Like them, he sees clearly that salvation for the trustful and obedient goes hand in hand with destruction for the disobedient. Like them, he knows salvation belongs to the last day, the Day of the Lord. He makes some advance, perhaps in his insistence that religious pedigree by itself is no guarantee of acceptance with God, and that individual repentance and openness to God's future were the only acceptable preparations that could be made against that dread Day of the Lord. To him, salvation is eschatological, moral, and fully individual. But the really new thing we meet in the teaching of John which marks an advance both on the Old Testament and the contemporary movement at Qumran is just this. John taught that the eschatological crisis was imminent, at the very doors. Hence the urgency of his appeal for repentance. For there would be no other way into the coming kingly rule of God (Matt. 3.2).

[1] This is what the combination of the two texts in the voice at the Baptism is meant to signify (Matt. 3.17, Mk. 1.11, Lk. 3.22).

[2] This translation, or rather emendation by R. H. Charles has been powerfully challenged by Y. Yadin, and must be held to be most precarious. The tense appears to be past not future, and to refer to a completed not a coming act. Apart from this, there is, as yet, no decisive evidence, so far as I know, to show that Qumran expected a Messiah to come and baptize with the Holy Spirit.

CHAPTER 6

Salvation in the Teaching of Jesus

It is not particularly easy to approach the teaching of Jesus on any subject, because of the diversities of opinion on the extent to which the Gospel material gives us a reliable account of his words. Estimates vary from the very conservative[1] to the completely agnostic; indeed Bultmann regards the whole quest for the historical Jesus as not only hopeless ("I do indeed think that we can know almost nothing concerning the life and personality of Jesus")[2] but irrelevant ("The Jesus of history is not *kerygma*, any more than my book on Jesus was").[3] Even his own pupils, however, are reacting against this quite unnecessary and unwarranted scepticism. After all, what gave rise to the "Christ of faith" if not the "Jesus of his history"?[4]

It is universally recognized today that however far you penetrate back into the oral stage that preceded the writing of our Gospels, you cannot find the non-supernatural Jesus so long and so fruitlessly sought by Liberal scholarship. Wherever we probe, it is a supernatural Jesus that we find, a Jesus who works miracles, a Jesus who makes claims that would be madness if not true. The Gospels, of course, were the products of a believing community. They are not *disinterested* history (some theologians talk as if such a thing were possible). They were written by believers to give evidence on the strength of which others might come to faith in the One they had found to be the Saviour of the

[1] E.g. B. Weiss, *Manual of Introduction to the N.T.* (1888), T. Zahn, *Introduction to the New Testament* (E.T. 1909), and more recently E. Stauffer, *Jesus and His Story* (1960).

[2] *Jesus and the Word* (E.T. 1962), p. 14.

[3] *Kerygma and Myth* (E.T. 1953), p. 117.

[4] On some recent attempts to deal with this problem, see H. Zahrnt, *The Historical Jesus* (1963), G. Hebert, *The Christ of Faith and the Jesus of History* (1962), and the extremely balanced and well written *The Birth of the New Testament* by C. F. D. Moule (1962). Among Bultmann's pupils reacting against his position is G. Bornkamm, *Jesus of Nazareth* (E.T. 1960), H. Conzelmann, *The Theology of St. Luke* (E.T. 1960), E. Käsemann, *Das Problem des historischen Jesus* (1954, now included in his *Essays on New Testament Themes*, 1964). On the whole subject of the place and significance of history, see A. Richardson, *History Sacred and Profane* (1964).

world (Jn. 20.31). But that does not mean that they are *dishonest* history. Because they selected the events which would be useful in the church situation, this does not mean that it had no place in the life of Jesus, but that they made it up instead! Indeed, it is interesting to notice down the history of Gospel criticism that the most conservative estimates of its reliability are taken by the *historians*[1] and the most sceptical estimates are made by those *theologians* who sit loose to history because of Hegelian or existentialist presuppositions.

There will always be a diversity of opinion about the interrelation of history and interpretation in the Gospels. The present writer is of the opinion that their historical reliability is great, and the interpretative element is small. This is not the place to argue the point, one of the most difficult in biblical studies, but the following points may indicate some of the grounds for confidence in the reliability of the Gospel tradition. The date of the Gospels is now almost universally assigned to between A.D. 65 and 95, and there is an increasing willingness to recognize the early date of St. John, or at least of the material his Gospel contains. There is as good reason as ever to connect Mark's gospel with the preaching of Peter; and there is a strong possibility that in the lost source Q, which contained sayings of Jesus and was used by the author of Matthew and Luke, we have an apostolic document, the famous Logia which Matthew composed in the Hebrew tongue (and in the early days "every man translated them as he was able"). Despite the current attempt to show his theological interests, the historical accuracy of Luke stands as high as ever.[2] When the Gospel material can be controlled by external evidence, it is seen to be reliable, and when it cannot, there is encouragement to be derived from the fact that although the evangelists alter the setting of the sayings of Jesus with some freedom, they pay meticulous respect to the words themselves, and treat them with considerable conservatism. It is hard to suppose that evangelists who behaved in this way could have invented sayings[3] freely and put them into the mouth of their Master. This conservatism is particularly notable in Mark, with his bad

[1] See most recently A. N. Sherwin-White, *Roman Society and Roman Law in the New Testament* (1963).

[2] See C. K. Barrett, *Luke the Historian in Recent Study* (1961), H. J. Cadbury, *The Book of Acts in History* (1954) and F. V. Filson, *Three Crucial Decades* (1964).

[3] Indeed, it is argued, by H. Riesenfeld, *The Gospel Tradition and its Beginnings* (1957), and in more detail by B. Gerhardsson in *Memory and Manuscript* (1961), that we are in very close touch indeed with the *ipsissima verba* of Jesus in the canonical Gospels, because he taught his disciples to memorize his words, like the rabbis. See the careful assessment of this thesis by W. D. Davies in *Neotestamentica et Patristica* (1962), pp. 14ff., and Gerhardsson's reply in *Tradition and Transmission in Early Christianity* (1964).

Greek, full of Aramaisms both above and below the surface, and in Luke who, although possessed of one of the best classical Greek styles in the New Testament (see Lk. 1.1-4) sacrifices it in the main part of the Gospel and the Acts, apparently in order to remain true to his sources.

Furthermore, it is remarkable how absent from the pages of the Gospels are the burning questions of the apostolic church; the Gentile mission, the circumcision issue, the Jew–Gentile relationship, the Church, the Holy Spirit, and a developed doctrine of the atonement, are barely hinted at. There is great restraint in calling Jesus "Lord", particularly in Mark, though his Lordship was the deep-seated conviction of the early Christian who wrote the New Testament documents.

All this gives us at least a starting point. We shall approach the New Testament accounts of Jesus' teaching and work with the initial assumption that they are honest attempts to show what Jesus really said and did, unless they can be proved to be otherwise. If we find that his teaching about salvation has demonstrable roots in the Old Testament, if it contains new features such as bespeak the originality of a great man, if, finally, it is in several respects less developed than the doctrine of salvation which the early Christians came to hold for themselves after the cross and resurrection, that will all be corroborating evidence of the basic reliability of the picture which the evangelists place before us.[1]

John the Baptist belonged to the old order. He was the last of the prophets and the greatest of them all, because of his unique and immediate relation to Jesus (Matt. 11.10, 11). Jesus went to great pains to stress his solidarity with the Baptist. He was baptized by him: he came preaching exactly the same message (Matt. 3.3, 4.17); and he made his own authority coordinate with that of John (Mk. 11.27-33). It would not therefore, be surprising if his doctrine of salvation were an extension of his forerunner's. But to our surprise we find that it is not so. John had looked for what we might call a unitary eschatological crisis. The Coming One would save and would destroy; he would gather his wheat and burn his chaff. His coming would be final and conclusive.

But it did not turn out like that. In the early days when Jesus joined John in preaching repentance in view of the coming kingdom, and when his disciples joined in the work of baptizing (Jn. 4.1, 2), the Bap-

[1] See further F. F. Bruce, *The New Testament Documents; are they reliable?* (1960), H. E. W. Turner, *Historicity and the Gospels* (1963), C. H. Dodd, *The Apostolic Preaching and its Development* (1944), and T. W. Manson, *Studies in the Gospels*, ed. M. Black (1962), also a valuable and powerful assessment in J. A. Baird, *The Justice of God in the Teaching of Jesus* (1963), pp. 17-34.

tist will have felt that all was proceeding according to plan. Particularly will this have been the case if the chronology of the Fourth Gospel is correct in placing the cleansing of the Temple at the outset of the Ministry. This would have seemed right and desirable to John. The messenger of the covenant comes to his Temple to judge and to refine, just as Malachi had said he would (Mal. 3.1, 2). John from his prison would have no grounds, as yet, for doubting the correctness of his unified eschatology. But then the days and months pass and, instead of judgement, he hears that Jesus offers men mercy and forgiveness, and is meek and gentle. He begins to doubt whether this can possibly be the one to whom he had been led to point (Lk. 7.18-23, Matt. 11.2-6). Jesus' reply to these honest doubts of John takes the Baptist back to the prophecies Isaiah had given of the messianic age. He alludes to Isa. 35.4, 5, "God will come and save you. Then the eyes of the blind shall be opened, and the ears of the deaf shall be unstopped. Then shall the lame man leap as an hart, and the tongue of the dumb shall sing", and 61.1, "The Spirit of the Lord God is upon me; because the Lord hath anointed me to preach good tidings unto the meek; he hath sent me to bind up the brokenhearted, to proclaim liberty to the captives, and the opening of the prison to them that are bound; to proclaim the acceptable year of the Lord." Jesus points out, in effect, that he is indeed fulfilling the prophetic picture of the Coming One. But in citing Isa. 61.2 he stops short with the phrase before, "and the day of vengeance of our God". He is reported as having broken off at the identical point, midway through the verse, in Lk. 4.18, 19, when he uses the same passage of Scripture in the synagogue at Nazareth at the outset of his ministry, and claims that the Scripture is fulfilled in their ears. This stopping point is not accidental, but highly significant. Jesus is pioneering the way that the rest of the New Testament writers were all to follow. He splits the unified eschatological crisis, the Day of the Lord, into two. From now on, his followers will come to see that the last days were indeed *inaugurated* with the coming of Jesus. But they were not *consummated* then. The end is not yet; the "day of vengeance" belongs to the future. For the present, he takes upon him the role of the Servant (Mk. 10.45), the task that was assigned him at his baptism. But John did not understand this split in the Day of the Lord, this inaugurated eschatology, of Jesus. How could he? He could not appreciate the mystery of a suffering Messiah, and it is little wonder. That is why, for all John's greatness, he belonged to the old order; that is why "he that is least in the kingdom is greater" than John (Lk. 7.28). For to John the central mystery of the gospel remained a stumbling-block (7.23).

Jesus, then, came preaching a salvation different from that which

John looked for; different, too, from the expectations of the other parties in Judaism. That, no doubt, is at least part of the reason why he did not welcome the title of Messiah. It was much too liable to be confused with an earthly, militaristic and unspiritual ideal. Instead, he came preaching the kingdom of God, and the title he affected for himself was the Son of Man. Both these concepts are indivisible from his doctrine of salvation, and will take us to the heart of its significance.

A. SALVATION IS EQUATED WITH THE KINGDOM OF GOD

More than once in the Gospels it is made plain that the eschatological salvation promised by the prophets and the kingdom of God preached by Jesus are one and the same thing (e.g. Lk. 8.10, 12.) In one important passage recorded in all three synoptic Gospels, the kingdom of God, salvation, and eternal life[1] are all equated with each other, and related to following Jesus (Mk. 10.17, 21, 24, 26). What, then, did Jesus teach about the kingdom of God and the conditions of its entry

This is an immense subject, and it will only be touched on here.[2] Basically, both the Semitic and Greek words translated "kingdom" have a primary reference to the "kingly rule" of God, not to a specific kingdom. Indeed, in less than one-sixth of the references to the kingdom in the Gospels is the thought of a community at all prominent; elsewhere the main emphasis is on the rule of God. But God's reign is no abstraction. It is manifested on earth in the community of those who accept it. It is, in fact, the standing claim of God on man's loyalty and obedience. It has, in the teaching of Jesus, both a present manifestation in the lives of those who, like children, receive the kingdom of God (Mk. 10.15), and a future consummation, when God's kingly rule will be undisputed (Lk. 22.30, Matt. 13.41, 43). There is, then, a progressive unfolding of the kingdom; not, of course, of the kingdom as the kingly rule of God, which is always seen as supreme in Scripture, but as the company of those who accept it and live by it. And this steady growth of the kingdom seems to be the point of such verses as Mk. 4.30. The kingdom drew near in the preaching of John the Baptist (Matt. 3.2.). It dawned in the person of Jesus, and it was proclaimed as a present reality in his preaching. He tells us that the kingdom has been eagerly besieged by throngs of people since John's preaching awoke them to the realities of the situation (Lk. 16.16).[3] A scribe is told that he is not far from it (Mk. 12.34).

[1] This phrase is preferred in St. John, although "kingdom of God" does appear. And his preference for "eternal life" over "salvation" is all the more understandable since "life" and "salvation" are the same in Aramaic, ḥayyē.

[2] See, among most recent literature, W. G. Kümmel, *Promise and Fulfilment* (E.T. 1957), and Norman Perrin, *The Kingdom of God in the Teaching of Jesus* (1963).

[3] I take this to be the meaning of this difficult verse; but it is *varie tentatus*.

The disciples already have the kingdom among (or "in") them (Lk. 17.21). Discussion has often centred on whether the incarnation, the atonement, or the coming of the Spirit should be thought of as the inauguration of the kingdom. But surely the question is wrongly put. God has never abdicated his kingly rule, and there have always been those who accepted it. Needless to say, the coming of Jesus marked a new era in God's kingly rule, and it is interesting to see how the three main characteristics of Old Testament kingship are revealed in connection with him. They are clearly delineated in the portrait of the Son of Man in Dan. 7.13, 14, 22 – the themes of power, glory and judgement. A little reflection will show that all three are associated with what the New Testament records of the birth of Jesus, his death, and his second coming; whilst individually the strands of power, glory and judgement characterize Jesus's baptism, transfiguration, and temptation, and are similarly present in the events of Pentecost, the ascension, and the destruction of Jerusalem respectively.[1]

If this is the progressive unfolding of the kingdom of God, what are the human conditions for its entry? Jesus clearly taught that this was dependent on the response men made to its moral demands; ultimately, this came down to the response men made to the person of Jesus himself. The reason for this was twofold. On the one hand, he was the *perfect* representative of God the king, as the kings of Israel *imperfectly* were in Old Testament days. On the other, in him alone, the Servant of the Lord, did the rule of God find complete response in an ideal subject. He is thus both the founder and the embodiment of the kingdom, which men enter by relationship to him. That explains how, in the Acts, the proclamation of Jesus by the apostles can aptly be summarized as the preaching of the kingdom of God (8.12, 19.8, 20.25, 28.23, 31). The message of the kingdom was rightly integrated with the person of the king. Their message to repent and believe in Jesus, though formally different, was substantially identical with his appeal for repentance and belief in the good news of the advent of the kingdom (Mk. 1.15f.).

It becomes plain, therefore, that the synoptic association of salvation with entering the kingdom and commitment to Jesus is far from arbitrary. Indeed, this equation enables Jesus to integrate the diverse approaches of the Old Testament prophets and apocalyptists to salvation. The prophets had, for the most part, seen God as immanent,

[1] I owe this extension of T. W. Manson's view to R. E. Nixon, who further points out in conversation that such *cruces interpretum* as Mk. 9.1, 14.62 and Matt. 10.23 may well refer to different moments in the coming of the kingdom; the first to its coming in power at Pentecost, the second to its coming in glory at the ascension, and the third to its coming in judgement in A.D. 70 with the fall of Jerusalem.

intimately concerned with his world and in the righting of its wrongs. The apocalyptists, on the other hand, had been so impressed with the transcendence of God that they tended to think of him as remote and disinterested in this world and primarily concerned with the age to come. The prophets had looked for salvation *in* this world, the apocalyptists for salvation *from* it. What Jesus did was to agree in the apocalyptists in his emphasis on the transcendence and heavenly nature of the kingdom. But he agreed with the prophets in stressing its immanence (Lk. 17.20f.), shown by the present concern and love of the heavenly Father who gives good gifts to his children (Matt. 7.11), and who cares so much for his creation that not one sparrow falls to the ground without his notice (Matt. 10.29). That is why salvation is both present and future in the teaching of Jesus. It means submitting to the kingly rule of, and, indeed, sharing in the very life of, God who is both immanent and transcendent. It is entered on here and now as men enter (Mk. 9.47), or receive (Lk. 8.17), or inherit (Matt. 25.34) the kingdom. It is to be fulfilled hereafter (Lk. 20.34-36). And for the meantime, life in the kingdom is characterized by humility (Lk. 6.20), the assurance of answered prayer (Matt. 7.7), the confidence of forgiven sins (Matt. 6.10-12), the experience of God's power (Lk. 11.20), the understanding of God's plan (Lk. 8.10), single-hearted obedience to God's will (Matt. 6.23, 24) and an implicit trust in his protection (Matt. 6.31-34). It is a foretaste of the life of heaven.

Such was the revolutionary conception introduced by Jesus's splitting of the eschatological event. In so doing, he shifted the ultimate crisis in man's destiny from death to conversion, from concern over the future life to commitment here and now to God's messenger of the kingdom. Salvation had become a present reality in the light of Jesus's teaching about the kingdom of God.

B. SALVATION IS ACHIEVED BY THE SON OF MAN

It is clear from the most cursory glance at the Gospels, that this was Jesus's favourite name for himself. A closer look reveals two interesting points. Nowhere in the Gospels does anyone else refer to Jesus in'this way, and it was not a title used to describe him in the early church.[1] This, incidentally, argues strongly for the reliability of the evangelists. They knew that while they did not refer to Jesus in this way, he himself had done so.

Now the Son of Man is unambiguously linked with salvation in the teaching of Jesus, notably in Lk. 19.10, a verse which seemed to be of such importance to the early Christians that it was introduced in two

---

[1] The one exception is Stephen's use of the phrase at his death, Acts 7.56. It is distinct from the title in Revelation "one like unto a son of man".

other places in the Gospels.[1] It is important, then, to discover what Jesus meant when he spoke of the Son of Man coming to seek and to save the lost. The antecedents of the Son of Man doctrine lie far back in the Old Testament.[2]

They probably go back, indeed, to the original man, man as he was intended to be, subordinate to God, but in authority over God's world. This is how the phrase Son of Man is used in Ps. 8.3-8, where it is a synonym for *man* and refers clearly to Adam. Adam, of course, failed in this twofold function. Was Jesus quietly suggesting, by the use of this title, that he came as the second Adam to fulfil the proper destiny of man? Indeed, in Ps. 80.17-19, God's salvation is expressly associated with the man of God's right hand, "the Son of Man whom thou madest so strong for thyself". This could well supply part of the background for the term in the teaching of Jesus.

The title comes frequently in Ezekiel, where the prophet is repeatedly called Son of Man, and is bidden to judge both Israel and the nations. Sidebottom[3] thinks that this is where we should look for a background to Jesus's function of judging Israel and the nations (e.g. Matt. 25.31-46). He shows what a great influence this prophet had on Jesus. Thus it is Ezekiel as Son of Man (Ezek. 34.1) who proclaims the word of the Lord which underlies Jesus's words in Lk. 19.10, "I will seek that which is lost" (34.16).

Nevertheless Dan. 7 remains the most likely quarry for Jesus's thought. The Son of Man here is at any rate to some extent seen as a corporate figure, the embodiment of "the people of the saints of the Most High" (compare 7.13 and 18); and, in the teaching of Jesus, the Son of Man sometimes has corporate overtones (e.g. Mk. 2.28 in its context). Furthermore, the Son of Man in Dan. 7, if not divine, is at least on God's side against the world and sin; and this is clearly implied in Jesus's use of the phrase (e.g. Mk. 2.10). What is more, he is an eschatological figure, sent to exercise God's kingly rule with power and glory and judgement in the last days (Dan. 7.14). This again finds parallels in some of Jesus's words about his future coming in glory to judge mankind (Mk. 13.26, 27, 14.62).

There are, of course, other sources from which Jesus might have drawn. There was, perhaps already in the world of Christ's day, a great deal of speculation in pagan religions about the original man. Iranian mythology told of a heavenly man who came to save mankind

---

[1] Added by some MSS. to Lk. 9.56, Matt. 18.11.
[2] The literature on the subject is enormous. The latest massive treatment of it is by A. J. B. Higgins, entitled *Jesus and the Son of Man* (1964). His conclusions appear to me to be most improbable.
[3] *Expository Times*, May 1957.

and lead them to their original destiny. It used to be suggested[1] that Jesus might have been influenced by this widespread speculation on the original and ideal man. This, however, is now seen as most unlikely. For one thing, it is quite uncertain that this sort of language was pre-Christian. When we meet it, it is in the gnostic works of the second century. For another, the nature of this heavenly redeemer is as uncertain as that of the salvation he came to bring, and the destiny he is supposed to have won for men! Furthermore, the dualism of these religions, which regarded all matter as evil, would make it impossible for them ever to contemplate an *incarnation* of the Ideal Man.[2]

However, the *Similitudes of Enoch*, as we saw in ch. 3, do seem to provide close parallels to the teaching of Jesus on the Son of Man. This, of course, assumes that they are in fact pre-Christian, that Jesus knew them and that he would have given a non-canonical book so normative a role in his conception of his mission, which he bases fairly and squarely on the Old Testament.[3] In Enoch the Son of Man is equated with the Anointed One; he is preexistent, and comes as God's personal representative. His origin is hidden, as Jesus's was, "The Son of Man was hidden from the beginning, and the Most High has preserved him and revealed him to the elect" (62.7). He comes as a staff to the righteous and a light to the Gentiles (48.4). All judgement is committed to the Son of Man (69.27-29) in the last day at the resurrection of the dead (51.1-3, 61.8). Then the mighty will suffer awful pangs "when they see the Son of Man sitting on the throne of his glory" (62.2-5). All this is a development of what we found in Daniel. And it would seem that Daniel's picture, with or without the additional features of Enoch, supplies the most likely background for a great deal of Jesus's teaching on the Son of Man. It represented the form of messianic expectation least compromised by nationalistic hopes. It suggested his supernatural origin while accounting for his humble station in life. It pointed to his judicial function and his cosmic significance, to those who had eyes to see. To others it could appear, as in Ezekiel, a mere synonym for "I".[4]

---

[1] E.g. by R. Reitzenstein, *Das iranische Erlösungmysterium* (1921).

[2] See O. Cullmann, *The Christology of the New Testament* (1959), p. 143.

[3] It is difficult to be sure how much weight the supposed analogies in *Enoch* will bear. It is a conglomerate work composed of diverse strands. The identification of the Son of Man with the Messiah is only made twice, and moreover, several different Ethiopic words are used for the Son of Man.

[4] J. Y. Campbell, writing in the *J.T.S.* (1947), argued that the Greek phrase, ὁ υἱὸς τοῦ ἀνθρώπου is an over-literal rendering of the Aramaic *bar nash* "a man". Like ὅδε ὁ ἀνήρ or the French *l'on*, it could be used by a speaker to refer to himself. He thinks that the phrase, used only by Jesus (of himself) has nothing to do with Dan. 7 or *Enoch*, but was simply a self-designation to stress his solidarity with mankind. This view, however, has not won general support. It is particularly unconvincing on such verses as Mk. 13.26, 14.62.

If this was the varied background of the term inherited by Jesus, it is not surprising to find him using it in a number of ways. First of all there are the passages where it is a simple equivalent for "I", such as Matt. 8.20, 11.19, and perhaps 12.32. Indeed, by comparing Matt. 16.13 with the parallel in Mk. 8.27, Matt. 16.21 with its parallel in Mk. 8.31, and Matt. 10.32 with Lk. 12.8 it is clear that at least in some contexts the evangelists felt free to introduce it or omit it at their discretion. They knew it to be an equivalent of Jesus.

A second group of sayings may perhaps be corporate in nature, notably Mk. 2.10 and 28. Indeed, these are the only two that can plausibly belong to this class, but they were sufficient to lead T. W. Manson to suppose that the Son of Man was always regarded by the disciples as a corporate body until the Last Supper, when Jesus unambiguously equated this figure with himself (Mk. 14.18, 21).

The third and fourth groups of verses say that the Son of Man must suffer (e.g. Mk. 8.31, 9.31, 10.33, 45, 14.21, 41, and parallels) and that he is to come again in glory (e.g. Mk. 8.38, 13.26, 14.62 and parallels). It is in these two categories that Jesus made such startling innovations. He identified himself, a poor wandering peasant carpenter, with the heavenly Son of Man! This whole idea of the incarnation of the divine (or semi-divine) figure of the Son of Man must have been shattering to his hearers and to the whole apocalyptic tradition in which they were reared, which emphatically did *not* expect this eschatological judge to come as a man among men. But such a conception fitted very well with the background of the Psalms and Ezekiel. Once again, Jesus has combined prophetic and apocalyptic expectations.

As if this was not revolutionary enough, Jesus united the functions of the Suffering Servant and of the Son of Man, though not apparently in his public teaching, for no trace of this identification exists in Q, the sayings-material common to Luke and Matthew. This, of course, is a commonplace. What is not so often remarked is that the Q material never speaks of the saving work of Jesus either. Perhaps this may be attributable to the fact that it *is* a sayings source, largely devoid of contexts for the sayings, and salvation is essentially a matter of action, not talk. The sayings of Jesus that do concern salvation are all spoken in concrete situations with individuals or a community in mind. However that may be, the uniting of the functions of the Son of Man and the Suffering Servant is crucial in the doctrine of salvation. "Son of Man represents the highest conceivable declaration of exaltation in Judaism; ʿebed Yahweh (the Servant of the Lord) is the expression of the deepest humiliation," writes Cullmann. "This is the unheard-of new act of Jesus, that he united these two apparently contradictory tasks in his self-consciousness, and that he expressed that union in his life and teaching."[1]

It is important to notice the pattern of this identification in Mark. Only after Peter's confession at Caesaraea Philippi that Jesus is the Messiah does the figure of the *suffering* Son of Man appear; Jesus immediately corrects Peter's "Messiah" to "Son of Man", and then tells him that the Son of Man must suffer, a conclusion so alien to all Jews that it is hardly surprising that Peter remonstrated with Jesus about it. Jesus told him straight that to attempt to turn him away from this dual function was satanic.[2] The Son of Man must suffer (Mk. 8.27-33). There are numerous places where Jesus alludes to his work as the Suffering Servant, quite apart from his explicit quotation of Isa. 53.12 at the Last Supper (Lk. 22.37). They occupy a whole page in Jeremias' book, *The Servant of God*.[3] The three passion predictions in Mk. 8, 9, and 10 lead up to the tremendous assertion of 10.45 that the Son of Man came not to be ministered unto (as in the traditional picture of the glorious Son of Man), but *"diakonēsai*, to act the Servant", and give his life a ransom in the place of many (*lutron anti pollōn*). Despite the hesitations of some scholars,[4] it is hard to escape the conclusion that this verse goes back to Isa. 53.5, 6, 11, 12. It is important not to miss the substitutionary element in the *anti*. It is the constant teaching of the Bible that sin makes man's life forfeit (e.g. Rom. 6.23, and in another idiom, Gen. 3.24). And "no man can by any means redeem his brother, nor give to God a ransom for him ... that he should live and not see corruption" (Ps. 49.7, 9). What no man could do for his brother, the Suffering Servant was to do for the many. "He was wounded for our iniquities ... and the Lord hath laid on him the iniquity of us all ... for the transgression of my people was he stricken ... he shall justify many, for he shall bear their iniquities ... he hath poured out his soul unto death ... and he bare the sin of many."

It is with this Servant of the Lord that the Son of Man identifies himself in Mk. 10.45. Again, Jesus at the Last Supper says that "the Son of Man goeth, as it is written of him ... this is my blood of the new testament which is shed *for many*". (Mk. 14.21-24, Matt. 26.24-28, Lk. 22.20, 1 Cor. 11.24). Now the four accounts of the institution of

[1] *Op. cit.*, p. 161.

[2] The very fact that this complex of sayings calling Peter "Satan" was preserved in the early Church of which he was undisputed leader, is sufficient guarantee of the authenticity of Jesus's logion equating the Son of Man with the Suffering Servant.

[3] Zimmerli and Jeremias, *The Servant of God* (1957), pp. 98, 99.

[4] E.g. M. D. Hooker, *Jesus and the Servant* (1959), C. K. Barrett, "The Background of Mark 10.45" in *New Testament Essays*, ed. A. J. B. Higgins (1959), and R. Bultmann, *Geschichte der synoptischen Tradition* (1931), p. 154.

the Lord's Supper differ considerably, which makes all the more notable their agreement in representing his death as being "for many", as in Isa. 53.12. As Jeremias has shown,[1] the separate mention of his body given and his blood shed indicate violent death, almost certainly as a sacrifice. This is confirmed by the "for many" – those for whom the sacrifice avails. The Isa. 53 background is stressed again by the reference to the (new) covenant which is sealed in his blood – another feature common to all four accounts. This, of course, recalls Ex. 24.8, the "blood of the covenant" at Sinai, but it also brings to mind the function of the Servant in Isa. 42.6 and 49.8, not only to reestablish the covenant, but actually to embody it. Thus Matthew's (doubtless interpretative) addition to the words of institution, "for the remission of sins", almost certainly preserves Jesus's meaning, once given his ideas of representative sacrifice and covenant. It would seem that Matthew is thinking of the new covenant promised in Jer. 31.31-34, the surprising feature of which (on comparison with the rest of the Old Testament) is the absence of any mention of blood to dedicate the covenant. Perhaps Matthew saw that, centuries later, Jesus's death had completed the picture. The sacrificial blood which dedicated the new covenant was *his own*, and it achieved the forgiveness of sins to which Jeremiah had looked longingly forward.[2]

This recognition of the importance of vicarious suffering in the role of the Son of Man should not blind us to the teaching of Jesus on the glorious future awaiting him. Each time the sufferings of the Son of Man are mentioned in the Marcan passion predictions, the glorious outcome of those sufferings is mentioned too (8.31, 9.31, 10.34). In this case, the resurrection is the glorious future referred to, and this may well owe something to the prophecies of the resurrection or at least vindication of the Suffering Servant (Isa. 52.13, 53.10, 11). In other passages the glory of the Son of Man is given a less restricted meaning. Take, for example, the Transfiguration. There can be little doubt that the unique time reference ("after six days", Mk. 9.2) linking it with the first passion prediction is meant to draw attention to the connection between the two. The glory of the Son of Man is thus

[1] *The Eucharistic Words of Jesus* (1955), pp. 140ff. He compares Heb. 13.11, "The *bodies* of those beasts whose *blood* is brought into the sanctuary . . ."
[2] In Jn. 3.13-16 the heavenly Son of Man is identified with Jesus as usual, and interpreted in terms of another expiatory symbol, the brazen serpent (Num. 21.6-9), which was made like the poisonous snakes that were troubling Israel, but was not itself poisonous. Instead, when erected on a pole it became a healing remedy for those poisoned by snakebite who looked to it in faith. Rom. 8.3, 4 is perhaps the most apt theological commentary on this analogy. The point to note here, however, is that yet another soteriological symbol of the Old Testament is used to explain the saving work of Jesus, the Son of Man.

related to his suffering. St. John's account strengthens the link between the suffering and the glory, and indeed synchronizes the two. The Son of Man will be glorified *by his passion* (12.23, 13.31). Finally, there are many passages in the Gospels which refer to the return of the Son of Man in the glory traditionally associated with his coming (Mk. 8.38, 13.26, 14.62, Lk. 17.24, Matt. 19.28). Only then will his saving work be completed, for he will gather his elect and they will be saved for ever (Mk. 13.20, 27). In one sense, the judgement which the Son of Man was always expected to exercise belongs to this final coming of of the Son of Man (e.g. Matt. 24.37-42, 25.10-13, 31). But in another sense, as St. John saw, the judgement of men is already anticipated in their reaction to the Son of Man who mingles with them as a man amongst men. The Son of Man who was raised up on a cross is the one who inevitably judges men, although that is incidental to his saving purpose (Jn. 3.13-18). He *already has* from God the authority to exercise all judgement, and to raise the dead, *because* he is the Son of Man (Jn. 5.21, 22, 26, 27).

Jesus, then, in his doctrine of the Son of Man who was to seek and to save the lost, made two astonishing advances on anything that had gone before. He was the first to identify the eschatological Son of Man with an obscure human being, himself; and he was the first to show that the work of judging involved the Son of Man in that of sin-bearing. Once again the prophetic and the apocalyptic pictures meet in the person of Jesus. In him the divine antinomy of wrath and mercy is resolved. He both vigorously asserts and vicariously bears the judgement of God upon sin. The heavenly Judge is the Suffering Servant. The lost are indeed judged in righteousness, but called in grace. The judge of human hearts will be one who has shared our nature, one who bore our sin. He is not wholly other than ourselves; the Son of Man is one with us, both to judge and to save. That is the main point of the parable of the sheep and goats (Matt. 25.31-46).

Just as the unitary concept of the kingdom of God had been split by the coming of Jesus, so is the unified view of the person and functions of the Son of Man. That explains how he could apply concepts proper to the end-time to his own person and work. In him the end-time had dawned; in him the kingdom had been inaugurated; in him, therefore, the salvation, which was integrally associated with both, had become a present reality.

This naturally leads on to the third characteristic of Jesus's teaching.

C. SALVATION CENTRES ON FORGIVENESS OF SINS

What had been peripheral to the Old Testament doctrine of salvation becomes crucial to the New. Forgiveness is a primary part of salvation to the New Testament writers, and in this they clearly follow Jesus himself, who came, not to call the righteous, but sinners (Mk. 2.17).

This spelt revolution in Judaism. There had been nothing like it since the individualism of the psalmists, and their patient trust in God to save them despite their sins. No rabbi in Israel addressed himself to the common people, the 'Am-ha'arets. They were *ex hypothesi*, beyond the pale, not only because of the moral and social odium accorded respectively to the harlots and the tax-gatherers, but because righteousness in later Judaism was beyond the reach of the poor and the ignorant.[1] How could the poor afford the sacrifices and the elaborate ritual that was proper for the "righteous"? How could the ignorant masses acquire that knowledge of the Law which led to "righteousness"? The Jewish leaders for the most part despised "the people of the land". This is particularly noticeable in the tractate *Demai* and elsewhere in the Mishnah. "An 'Am-ha'arets cannot be saintly", was Hillel's conclusion (*P. Aboth*, 2.6), and it was widespread. The attitude of the Pharisees in the time of Christ is doubtless fairly reflected in Jn. 7.49, "This multitude which knoweth not the Law is accursed."[2]

Now it was precisely to this company of outcasts that Jesus directed his appeal. "The whole have no need of a physician," he pointed out, "but the sick" (Mk. 2.17). Accordingly, it was with the morally and socially sick that he constantly mingled, to the chagrin of the Pharisees. They complained that he ate with tax-gatherers and sinners (Mk. 2.16), or that he was friends with them (Lk. 7.34). In their pride they adopted an attitude of superiority which made it impossible for Jesus to help them. In their shallow and external view of sin,[3] they failed to see that hypocrisy, pride, envy, uncharitableness and so forth are every bit as bad as crude and flagrant vice.[4] They were in precisely the same need of forgiveness as the notorious evil-doers whom they despised. It is a sad commentary on a paradoxical situation that when Jesus goes to his death, a death engineered by these self-righteous men who despised sinners,[5] he says, "The Son of Man is betrayed into the hands of

[1] See Holzmann's *Neutest. Theol.*, I.132ff.

[2] See also 2 Es. 7.51, 52, 59ff. Needless to say, the dislike of the scholars for the common people was returned with interest. *Pesahim* 49b recalls a saying of R. Akiba, which refers to the time when he was an 'Am-ha'arets. He used to say, "I wish I had one of those scholars, and I would bite him like an ass." His disciples said, "You mean, like a dog?" He replied, "An ass's bite breaks the bone; a dog's does not."

[3] See Lk. 7.39; Mk. 7.1-23.   [4] See Matt. 23.

[5] Thus they can plot the death of Jesus on the Sabbath without a twinge of conscience. But if he heals a man on the Sabbath, they fly to the defence of their broken tradition concerning what may and what may not be done on the Sabbath (Mk. 3.1-6).

sinners" (Matt. 26.45, Mk. 14.41, Lk. 24.7). St. John's way of bringing out the same truth is the drama of Ch. 9. Jesus has healed the blind man. The Pharisees say he could not possibly have done so. Since he had not been to one of the scribal schools of theology he was by definition an 'Am-ha'arets (quite apart from the fact that he had done this reputed cure on the Sabbath). God does not hear sinners; therefore he could not have heard Jesus, and healed in answer to his prayer. Q.E.D.! A superb example of the aphorism, "The dogma must conquer history." Jesus concluded the incident by telling the Pharisees that if they were blind (i.e. to spiritual truth), they would not be accounted as sinners: but because they said, "We see", therefore their sin remained (9.41). Because they claimed to be the instructed members of the community, they regarded their own insight as sufficient, and refused to respond to the light brought by one who was concerned to break out of the privileged circle, and reach those who admitted their need of salvation.

This attitude of Jesus was maintained throughout his ministry. The three parables of Lk. 15, the lost sheep, the lost coin, and the lost son, are placed in the illuminating context of 15.1, 2, which make their main thrust inescapable. They describe Jesus's attitude, in contrast to that of the Pharisees;[1] it is simply this, to save the lost (see the refrain in 15.7, 10, 32). Thus we find him holding conversation with the *respectable* sinner, Nicodemus, and showing him his need of a radical rebirth (Jn. 3); we find him speaking with a *brazen* sinner (and she a hated Samaritan) and offering her the lasting satisfaction she had sought so long but in vain (Jn. 4). We find him seeking out Zacchaeus, the *financial* crook, and offering what such a social outcast would never have dared to hope, that the great teacher would "be guest with a man that is a sinner" (Lk. 19.7). He confronted the *sexual* sinner, and instead of joining the Pharisees in hounding her to death,[2] he first quietly but forcefully indicated their own sinfulness to such effect that they shrank away ashamed, and then told that woman that she was not to think of herself as condemned, but to go and sin no more (Jn. 8.1-11). He had come to save sinners. And thus when a *sick* sinner was presented to him, he went straight to the man's deepest needs, and

[1] The latter are content if some of the sheep are in the fold; Jesus is not willing for a single one to be lost.

[2] Whether or not the Jews at this time had the right to inflict the death penalty, or whether it would have been administered for adultery, is much debated. Jews were certainly allowed to inflict the death penalty on any Gentile who entered the inner court of the Temple, and, whether allowed to or not, they killed Stephen and James, though in both instances these were mob killings rather than judicial executions. However, the point here is the contrast in *attitude* between Jesus and the Pharisees to the adulterous woman.

said, "Your sins are forgiven" (Mk. 2.5). In so doing, of course, he incurred a charge of blasphemy from the Pharisees. Forthwith he vindicated his claim to have God's authority to forgive sins, by showing that he had God's power to heal – to the amazement of them all.

It is not, of course, surprising that the attitude Jesus adopted to sinners appeared to the Pharisees as not merely indecent but positively blasphemous. They could not recognize the relation of the kingdom to salvation, nor the link that bound the Son of Man to the Suffering Servant, and both to the person of Jesus. It was only in virtue of what he would do in *bearing* the sin of the world that Jesus could *remit* it with such confidence and authority. Needless to say, the common people did not understand all this either, but they did respond in faith to what they sensed was the authentic voice of God speaking through this peasant teacher.[1] That is why they thronged to hear him (Lk. 15.1) while the Pharisees stood aside and murmured. That is why the harlots and tax-gatherers pressed into the kingdom of God before the Pharisees (Matt. 21.31). The messianic banquet would not be short of guests; if those originally invited made excuses, and were unwilling to come on terms of acceptance by grace alone, then the '*Am-ha'arets*, the poor, the lame, the blind and the needy would throng in from the highways and hedges (Matt. 22.1-14).[2]

"The issue," says Professor Richardson, "was whether salvation was by the righteousness of God, or by men's own righteousness; it is stated by Jesus with devastating lucidity in the parable of the Pharisee and the publican (Lk. 18.10-14). The man who acknowledged that he was a sinner in need of God's mercy went down to his house justified, rather than the man who boasted of his genuinely good works."[3] This story, in fact, emphasizes several of the points we have been considering, and, incidentally, links the teaching of Jesus very closely with that of St. Paul. There is Jesus's interest in the individual sinner, however disreputable he may be. There is the stress on the sense of sin that this publican has, and the recognition that he must repent. His acceptance of unmerited mercy stands out in strong contrast to the self-sufficiency of the Pharisee, who clearly thinks there is nothing God need do for him. And the story ends with the striking paradox, reminiscent

[1] Thus they had responded to the preaching of repentance by John the Baptist, while the Pharisees had kept clear of it (Jn. 1.19-28), no doubt with a bad conscience (Mk. 11.30-32). Those who do not accept the water-baptism of repentance cannot have the Spirit-baptism of the kingdom (Jn. 3.5).

[2] The current tendency to regard verses 11-14 as disconnected with 1-10 springs, I think, from failure to recognize the *Sitz-im Leben Jesu* of the parable, where the crying issue was the free grace offered to sinners, and repudiated by self-righteous Pharisees.

[3] Article, "Salvation" in the *Interpreter's Bible Dictionary*.

of Rom. 4.5, of God justifying the ungodly, while the Pharisee, being ignorant of God's righteousness, and going about to establish his own righteousness, has not submitted himself to the righteousness of God (Rom. 10.3). Salvation is the gift of God.

D. SALVATION IS CONCERNED WITH THE WHOLE MAN

We suffer today from a false distinction between the secular and the sacred, the physical and the spiritual. The Christian Church has sometimes behaved as though only the spiritual element in man was the subject of God's concern. The actions of Jesus as recorded in the Gospels give the lie to this, and show that God's salvation concerns the whole man (Mk. 3.4). Indeed, the word is used most frequently in the Gospels with reference to the healing of disease. Both Matthew and Mark summarize Jesus's healing ministry thus: "As many as touched him were saved" (Mk. 6.56, Matt. 14.36. Indeed, Matthew uses a compound, *diesōthēsan* to emphasize his point). Blind Bartimaeus was "saved" (Mk. 10.52), so was the Samaritan leper (Lk. 17.19), the man with a withered hand (Mk. 3.4, 5) and a host of others. Jesus showed concern for the whole man. The Gospels speak a good deal of the compassion of Jesus (e.g. Matt. 9.36, 20.34, Lk. 7.13). In every instance we are told that the *cause* of this compassion was the sight of human need, perhaps a hungry crowd, or a diseased body; in every instance it is made clear that the *effect* of this compassion was the alleviation of that need. In Mk. 1.41 the strange reading *orgistheis* ("was angry") appears to be original, especially in view of the *embrimēsamenos* in 1.43, another word denoting anger. The sight of marred humanity filled Jesus with profound and passionate emotion against the forces of evil which had wrought this damage. The same concern for the wholeness of the human personality can be seen in Jesus's exorcisms. Thus Lk. 8.36 tells how a man who had been demon-possessed was "saved". Furthermore, the accounts of Jesus's deliverance of the disciples in the storm (Matt. 8.25) and Peter from sinking into the water (Matt. 14.30) use the same term, "save"; this is yet another example of his concern for the whole man.

Nevertheless, when this has been said, we must beware of supposing that the mighty deeds of Jesus are simply philanthropic works of mercy.[1] They are nothing of the sort. They are tangible evidence of the presence of the kingdom of God in the person of the Son of Man

---

[1] On some occasions, indeed, Jesus deliberately withdraws from situations where the healing ministry was occupying too much of his time (Mk. 1.34, 37, 38); on others he refuses to perform a "sign" (Mk. 8.12), and on yet others he bewails the hardness and blindness of heart which remains satisfied with the miracle without penetrating to its meaning (Mk. 8.14-21; Jn. 6.26, 27).

(Matt. 12.28). St. John calls them "signs" rather than "mighty works"; the healings are not complete in themselves. They point to spiritual realities. Quite apart from the individual parabolic meaning of particular miracles (brought out in each of the seven signs John selects), supremely they *all* point to Jesus being the Servant of the Lord. Isa. 32.2-4, 35.5, 6, 42.7, 61.1 speak of the lame walking, the blind seeing and so forth, in the days of salvation. This is exactly how Jesus described what was happening in his work (Matt. 11.5).[1] He was bringing in the days of salvation, and the main purpose of the miracles was to indicate this to those who had eyes to see (Jn. 10.37, 38).

At this point it is important to notice the ambiguity in the Greek word *sōzein*, for the evangelists make effective play with it. The word can mean both "to heal" and "to save". It is impossible to doubt that there is deliberate ambiguity about its use in Mk. 5.34 and parallels. This story of the woman with a haemorrhage is recorded in all the synoptics. It was basic early Christian tradition about Jesus. The Form Critics have taught us to look for a *Sitz-im-Leben Kirche* as well as a *Sitz-im-Leben Jesu* for any event recorded in the Gospels. What particular usefulness did such a story have for church work which led to its incorporation in the Gospel? Here the answer can hardly admit of doubt. The story, like so many in Mark, is plain *kerygma*, and makes a marvellous sermon illustration for evangelistic preaching. Here is a woman with a disease which makes her ceremonially impure and increasingly weak physically. She has tried all the remedies that she knows, and was nothing bettered but rather grew worse.[2] She hears of Jesus; she comes to Jesus; she touches Jesus in simple (if superstitious) faith that he can cure her, or, as Matthew and Mark put it, that she could be "saved" (Mk. 5.28, Matt. 9.21). She was assured by Jesus that her faith had "saved" her, and she went out into a new life of peace and wholeness. We have here a paradigm of Christian conversion in the apostolic church.

The same ambivalence in the term *sōzein* is useful in Mk. 10.52 and its Lucan counterpart. Bartimaeus was in a sorry plight, blind and destitute. He heard of Jesus; he called to Jesus; he came to Jesus, throwing away all that impeded him. He laid his request before Jesus. Immediately he received his sight from Jesus, and followed Jesus in

---

[1] Not all healings are messianic; these ones are. See A. Farrer, *A Study in Mark* (1951), p. 223. See also the connection Matthew makes between the healing of a man both blind and dumb and the fulfilment of the prophecy of the Servant (Isa. 42.1-4) recorded in the words immediately preceding (12.17-22), not to mention his view that the healings are the fulfilment of Isa. 53.4 (Matt. 8.17).

[2] A phrase which Luke the physician cannot bring himself to use; he softens it into the professional verdict "her case was incurable" (Lk. 8.43 Greek).

the way.[1] Here again the statement, "Thy faith hath saved thee", shows the kerygmatic importance of the healing. It spoke of the complete and instantaneous righting of that wrong relationship with God induced by sin,[2] which comes about when a man recognizes his need, hears of Jesus, and comes to him in simple trust. There is an interesting play on the word in Jn. 11.12, which is deliberately ambiguous to cover both the healing of Lazarus who is physically asleep (as the disciples thought), and also the ultimate salvation of Christians who "sleep in Jesus" (cf. 1 Thess. 4.13, 14).[3] St. Luke brings out this parabolic significance of the healing miracles very strongly, which is interesting, since he is the evangelist who is most interested in their medical side.[4] Thus he records Jesus as saying, "Thy faith hath saved thee; go in peace" (7.50) to a sinful woman whose sins he had declared forgiven (7.48). It is Luke, too, who records Jesus as using the same phrase, "Thy faith hath saved thee", to a healed leper (17.19); this is significant, because leprosy throughout the Bible is illustrative of sin.[5]

We have already remarked on the most striking example of all (Mk. 2.1-12 and parallels), where the declaration that the sufferer's sins are forgiven is proved by Jesus's ability to make the palsied man get up and walk. The healings, in short, are messianic. They are designed to illustrate that supreme gift of the age to come, forgiveness of sins, and show that it is a present possibility simply because the age to come is a present reality in the person of Jesus.

Two further points must be made about the healings of Jesus. It will have been noted that these healings are normally granted in response to faith. "Thy faith hath saved thee" is, as we have seen, a constant refrain.[6] Surely this is significant. The early Christians will

[1] Both these words are loaded. Following Jesus is used of the Christian life (Mk. 1.18, Jn. 1.37), and the Way is an early name for Christianity (Acts. 9.2, 19.23, 24.14).

[2] The way in which disease is made an illustration of sin in the Gospels must not, of course, mislead us into supposing that Jesus shared the common belief that all suffering was the result of specific sin. This is expressly repudiated in Lk. 13. 1-5, Jn. 9.2, 3—without denying that some illness may be due to previous and particular sin.

[3] See C. H. Dodd, The Interpretion of the Fourth Gospel (1953), in loc.

[4] See A. von Harnack, Luke the Physician (1907), for the sanest summary of the evidence.

[5] Unlike any other disease, leprosy is cleansed. Is that why Mark puts the healing of the leper right at the start of his Gospel, to make plain that Jesus came to save from sin? "The cleansing of a leper," says Richardson, "since leprosy was defilement requiring priestly absolution, bore a significance which it is hard for us today to understand" (Theological Wordbook of the Bible, s.v. 'Heal').

[6] See also Mk. 9.23, 11.24, Lk. 8.50.

have used such sayings to show that the ultimate salvation, God's salvation which Christ came to bring, is entered by faith alone,[1] and not by "the works of the Law" as the Pharisees held. This takes us back to the strand of vindication which we saw in the Old Testament doctrine of salvation. Salvation is of the Lord, and must be accepted in simple trusting faith, if it is to be enjoyed at all.

Secondly, these healings are bound up with the person of Jesus. It is Jesus who heals, just as it is Jesus who forgives sins. Renan's famous aphorism, "*Il ne prêche pas ses opinions, mais lui-même*", applies as much to the healing as to the preaching work of Jesus. All aspects of salvation are Christocentric. It is by his words (Jn. 5.34), by his person (Jn. 10.9), by his total mission (Jn. 12.47) that men can be saved. Salvation is inseparable from the person and work of Jesus, and that is why there is more about it in the Epistles than in the Gospels.[2]

These two points are nowhere more clearly brought out than in the story of Zacchaeus. In Lk. 19.5, 6 it is said that *Jesus* came to his house. In 19.9 Jesus declares that *salvation* has come to his house. Why? Because he has shewn by his trusting faith, and the obedience that followed it (19.8) that, although a great sinner, he is a true son of Abraham,[3] the man who believed and obeyed God.[4] He was lost; he has now been saved, through his relationship with the Son of Man who not only came to bring but actually himself constitutes salvation. It may have taken two thousand years before Martin Buber formulated the I-Thou relationship,[5] and the existentialists laid such emphasis on personal encounter. But all the time it had been plainly there for all to see in the New Testament records.

Like the healings, the exorcisms performed by Jesus must be seen as having a dual function. Jesus had no more doubts about the reality of demon possession than modern missionaries who work in primitive areas have. There can be no doubt at all that he did exorcize demons.[6]

---

[1] This is not by any means the same as modern "faith-healing", or the influence of mind over matter. It is the one in whom faith is placed, Jesus, who heals. Faith is particularly linked with salvation in Lk. 8.12, a point not made by the other evangelists at that juncture.

[2] One of the remarkable things about the Gospels is how little they record of the characteristic doctrine of salvation of the early Christians. This suggests that they are either an example of conscious archaism unparalleled in antiquity, or else a remarkably faithful record of the actions and sayings of Jesus on this and other subjects.

[3] Cf. Gal. 3.29 and Rom. 4 *in toto*.   [4] Gen. 15.6, 22.16-18.

[5] M. Buber, *I and Thou* (E.T. 1937).

[6] The evidence from the New Testament is hard to contravene; e.g. Acts 2.22 (part of the *kerygma*), Mk. 3.22, Jn. 11.47. And there is plenty of rabbinic evidence to support it, e.g. "Jesus practised magic and misled Israel" (*Sanh.* 43a, 107b). See E. Stauffer, *Jesus and his Story* (1960), pp. 19f. for further evidence. He

And he taught that his exorcisms showed that the kingdom of God had come (Matt. 12.28 and parallels), and from henceforth the kingdom of Satan was doomed. The religious authorities, who could not deny the fact of these exorcisms, attempted to attribute them to satanic power, only to be met with the unanswerable argument that if Satan were to cast out Satan, his house would be divided against itself, and could not stand. Satan's power was real enough, as both Jesus and his opponents agreed; "the strong man" still "kept his house"; but Jesus's authority over demons showed that "stronger than the strong" had come to bind the strong man, and spoil his goods (Mk. 3.27). The exorcisms presaged the crucial victory over Satan on the Cross (Jn. 12.31). Their significance was this: while the healings were related to the forgiveness of sins inherent in salvation, the exorcisms spoke of power over evil impulse which Christ can exercise in those who have tasted of salvation. They set forth Jesus in his role of conqueror,[1] and thus they are related to another important strand in the Old Testament doctrine of salvation, that of victory. Since the coming of Jesus, man is no longer helpless under the domination of sin (Jn. 8.34, 36), Satan (Lk. 13.16) and his powers of evil. The salvation of the Gadarene demoniac was not only a matter of healing a distraught mind and integrating a split personality. That man tasted the powers of the age to come (cf. Heb. 6.5) when he came face to face with Jesus and had his needs met. He was not only healed, but saved (Lk. 8.36).

In the same way, Jesus's saving of the disciples in the storm and of Peter on the water are parables of his ability "to keep you from falling" (Jude 24), and must have been used in this way in the preaching of the early Church. Why else should the stories have been treasured and recorded? Thus it would seem that even the most physical and secular uses of "salvation" in the Gospels carry spiritual overtones which are complementary to the natural (and doubtless primary) meaning of the words.

But even deliverance from sin's guilt and power are inadequate as a summary of salvation. They do not exhaust the ancient prophetic hope; they are no more than a foretaste here and now of what lies ahead in the goodness of God. "Eye hath not seen," writes Paul, "nor ear heard, neither have entered into the heart of man the things which

concludes, "the polemics of the rabbis completely assume and admit the brute fact that Jesus worked miracles". Indeed, it would seem that exorcisms were relatively common in the Hellenistic world (Acts 19.13, Just. *Dial.* 85, Iren. *A.H.* 2.6.2, and, of course, the *Life of Apollonius of Tyana, passim*). The crucial differentia in the case of Jesus was that they took place in the context and in substantiation of his messianic claims.

[1] See G. Aulen, *Christus Victor* (1931), p. 77; H. Schlier, *Principalities and Powers* (1961), pp. 40ff.

God hath prepared for them that love him" (1 Cor. 2.9). And so we find in the teaching of Jesus, just as we did in the Old Testament, that the salvation of God is still primarily future. The difference between Jesus and the prophets is that with him the age of salvation has dawned. But its full enjoyment still lies in the future, although it may be proleptically enjoyed in the present. It is the man who endures to the end who will be saved (Mk. 13.13 and parallels, also Matt. 10.22b). It is the man who loses his life for Jesus's sake (just as Jesus lost his for our sake) who will be saved (Mk. 8.35 and parallels). What form, then, will this final salvation take?

There are many metaphors used for it in the Gospels. It is likened for safety to a heavenly barn (Matt. 13.30). It is likened for glory to the sun shining (Matt. 13.43). It is likened for spirituality to the angels of God, who neither marry nor give in marriage (Mk. 12.25). It is likened for beauty to the garden of God (Lk. 23.43), for responsibility to thrones of judgement (Lk. 22.30), for joy to a wedding feast (e.g. Matt. 22.3ff.). This simile of the wedding feast is particularly instructive, for it speaks not only of the joy of the guests, of the grace through which they are invited and of the corporate nature of their enjoyment, but concentrates the attention of all upon the central figure. For the future, salvation involves two relationships, and indeed consists in them; fellowship with the Saviour, and fellowship with the saved. Perhaps the most wonderful indication of this future salvation given us in the Gospels is the least descriptive: "That where I am, there ye may be also" (Jn. 14.3).[1] Heaven and its salvation is essentially right relationship with the Lord himself or, as J. A. T. Robinson prefers to reinterpret it, "union in love with Love, the Ground of our Being".[2] The acme of salvation is what Jesus calls "entering into the joy of the Lord" (Matt. 25.21, 23). And that includes all that a man can hope for. It represents utter and ultimate satisfaction.

Salvation, then, according to the teaching of Jesus, concerns the whole man. It is concerned with his past, his present and his future. It is the work of rescue achieved by God through his Messiah. It belongs to the kingly rule of God brought into history by Jesus, the Son of Man. The conditions of its acceptance are repentance and faith; the very idea of merit is excluded by grace. But it demands a radical change of life in those who accept it. And this salvation is no narrow

[1] Similarly, Paul's delightful description of the state of Christians who have died is simply this: they are "with the Lord" (Phil. 1.23, 1 Thess. 4.14). His own expectation of death is "to depart and be with Christ, which is far better" (Phil. 1.23) while his most awful description of hell is "everlasting destruction from the presence of the Lord" (2 Thess. 1.9). Heaven and hell are basically a matter of relationship with God.

[2] *Honest to God* (1963), p. 80.

national ideal, but intended for all men, "that the *world*, through him, might be saved" (Jn. 3.17).

And that explains why, although Jesus came to fulfil the messianic hopes of Israel in the first instance (Jn. 4.22, 25, 26), he nevertheless gave hints, even within his lifetime, of his universal significance and appeal. With a great man's singleness of purpose he recognized the limitations of his earthly mission; "I am not sent but unto the lost sheep of the children of Israel" (Matt. 15.24). This was inevitable. The corn of wheat had to fall into the ground and die before there could be a harvest (Jn. 12.24, cf. v. 32). Before the cross and resurrection there were no saving acts to proclaim to the Gentiles, no gospel to preach outside Judaism. Nevertheless, even within his earthly life Jesus made exceptions to this general principle of the limitation of his mission to Israel. He could not remain inactive in the face of crying need. Hence the Samaritan (Lk. 17.16, Jn. 4.7), the Syrophoenician (Mk. 7.26) and even the Roman (Matt. 8.10) shared his blessing, and indeed evoked his praise.[1] He had a loving concern for all men. He offered forgiveness to all men.[2] In these two factors lies the secret of his universal appeal. A gospel which cares for all men, a gospel which is offered freely to the sinful, can know nothing of the limitations of age and class and race. Salvation indeed came from the Jews (Jn. 4.22). But both by his teaching and his practice, the Saviour, who came as the culmination of God's redemptive work in Israel, proved equally to be the Saviour of the world (Jn. 4.42).

[1] It is interesting to contrast the universalism and particularism of Jesus as recorded in Matthew's account (his mission was "to the Jew first, and also to the Greek", cf. Rom. 2.9, 10). Hence the restricted objective of the incarnate Jesus, 10.5, 15.24. But this must be balanced by the universalism of the risen Lord (28.19, 20). It can hardly be without significance in Matthew's pattern that, at the beginning of the Gospel, Gentiles seek Jesus while Jews do not (2.1-12), and at the end of the Gospel the Gentile mission progresses while few Jewish Christians stand firm (24.12, 14).

[2] Even to his Gentile murderers (Lk. 23.34).

CHAPTER 7

Salvation in the Evangelists

It is a fascinating but highly subjective enterprise to attempt to discover the doctrine of salvation held by the evangelists. Fascinating, because they are all early preachers, and if we could succeed in discerning their distinctive emphases it would shed light on the subject of our next chapter, the primitive *kerygma*. Subjective it must certainly be, however, if we are to try to decide what elements in the doctrine of salvation, as we meet it in the Gospels, we are to assign to the evangelists and what to Jesus. One way does, however, stand open to us. However little or much an evangelist diverges from the *ipsissima verba* of Jesus, it should be possible to see where his particular emphasis lies from the *selection* he makes of the teaching of Jesus bearing on the subject.

ST. MARK

When we examine the Marcan material, we notice at once that all but one of his references are parallel in both Matthew and Luke (5.34, 8.35, 10.26, 13.13, 15.31), in Matthew alone (5.28, 6.56, 13.20, 15.30 and the remarkable *lutron* in 10.45) or in Luke alone (3.4, 10.52). The single salvation reference peculiar to Mark is 5.23. Jairus beseeches Jesus to come and lay his hands on his daughter that she "may be saved and live". It is doubtful whether we should lay too great stress on this verse. For one thing the whole passage in Mark is much fuller than it is in Matthew, and considerably fuller than it is in Luke, so their omission of this phrase is not particularly surprising. For another, it is conceivable that $\sigma\omega\theta\hat{\eta}$ $\kappa\alpha\grave{\iota}$ $\zeta\eta\sigma\hat{\eta}$ are variants of the same Aramaic word, of which Matthew correctly gives only one. Furthermore, if it be thought strange that Luke of all people should omit a reference to salvation, it is noteworthy that he is the only evangelist to include it later in the same story, "only believe, and she shall be saved" (8.50).

If we are to seek particular significance in Mark's reference here, we may be right to look to Austin Farrer's interpretation of the incident. He sees Mark as a Gospel of prefigurement and fulfilment, and the

119

raising of Jairus's daughter as a hidden allusion to the resurrection.[1]
If so, then the σωθῇ will be a hint of that life after death which Jesus
pioneered and made possible for others. However, it is precarious to
base a theory on a single text, and that, perhaps, a mistranslation. We
shall get on to firmer ground by looking at the rest of the Marcan usage.

Of sōtēr and sōtēria he says nothing. There is his famous ransom-
saying which we have already examined, and fourteen places where
the verb "save" is used, apart from the statement in the later appendix
to the Gospel, "He that believes and is baptized shall be saved"
(16.16).[2] The majority of the instances appear to use sōzō ambivalently,
to apply to both spiritual and physical health (so 5.23, 28, 34, 6.56,
10.52). The raising of the dead, the cleansing of the menstruous woman,
the healing of the sick, the opening of the eyes of the blind are all
messianic activities; they are signs of the presence in the world of the
promised salvation. Furthermore, they make abundantly plain that the
concern of Jesus was with the whole man, and afford no justification
whatever for the disjunction between the physical and the spiritual,
the sacred and the secular, that has long typified the church doctrine of
salvation. It is interesting that in only one of these healings (5.43) is any
command to secrecy, so characteristic of Mark, enjoined. Perhaps it
was the use of the phrase talitha koumi which in this instance gave rise to
the injunction to silence. Jesus did not want to be identified with a
common thaumatourgos ("Wonder-worker") nor to set the precedent
of using terms like talitha koumi as though they possessed magical
properties.

What is, however, most interesting in all these deliberately ambiguous usages of sōzein is the emphasis that the evangelist puts upon
faith and on contact with Jesus. In each case it is contact with Jesus that
brings healing; this is not only an expression of the solidarity between
Jesus and the sufferer, but is also parabolic of the new "touch" by faith,
which brings salvation. Indeed, Mark mentions this contact with Jesus
in each of these healing miracles where he uses the word sōzein, and
in all but 6.56 (where it is strongly implied)[3] he connects this with

[1] A Study in Mark (1951), passim. He even goes so far as to suggest that Jairus
should be interpreted as "YAH awakens", and Jesus as "YAH is salvation". Hence
the use of the verb "be saved" in the context. It is nothing less than the Lord
Yahweh acting in Jesus to call the dead to life (op. cit., pp. 328f.).

[2] Doubtless the passage Mk. 16.9-20 is rightly regarded by all critics as a later
addition to the Gospel. Nevertheless the juxtaposition of belief and baptism is a
primitive trait, characteristic of the earliest preaching. It was soon replaced by a
probationary period of catechesis before baptism was administered.

[3] You do not bring your sick into the streets and beseech that they may "touch
if it were but the hem of his garment" unless you believe he can heal. Actually, the
phraseology is patterned on 5.28-34, which is treated as its paradigm, and which
places so great an emphasis on faith that it can readily be assumed here.

faith. There is no fortuitous link between faith and touch. To touch Jesus is to manifest faith in him (5.28 compared with 5.34). That is the whole point. Faith brings immediate contact with Jesus the Saviour; faith, therefore, saves. It takes little imagination to see how much this message would have meant to Mark's Roman readers who had not known the incarnate Jesus. It is faith that brings a man into living touch with Jesus, whether that man be his historical contemporary or a later disciple.[1] Perhaps that is why Mark has so much to say about people touching Jesus – a leper (1.41), the sick (3.10), children (10.13), the blind (8.22), the deaf and dumb (7.33) in addition to the ones which we have been considering, where the word "save" is specifically used.

Of Mark's other salvation references, three are concerned with the saving or destroying of life. In 3.4 Jesus asks, with heavy irony, whether it is permitted to save life (as he is planning to do to the man with the withered hand, and make him whole) or only to destroy life (as the religious leaders, so prim about their sabbath-keeping, were planning to do to him, 3.6). In 8.35 he propounds the paradox that man can only save his life by losing it; if he seeks to save it, he will assuredly lose it. This is the pattern of fulfilment through surrender, of life through death, set for the disciple by his Master (e.g. 10.45, cf. Jn. 12.24ff.).[2] Mark makes this point very clear in his other paradox, 15.30, 31. Jesus was faced with precisely the same dilemma as that with which he faces Everyman in 8.35. He *could* have saved himself and come down from the cross; of that the evangelist has no doubt. But he would not then have saved us. The ironical jest of the priests was, little though they realized it, the sober truth. He saved others; himself he could not save.

The other two references to salvation are in the "Little Apocalypse" (ch. 13), and refer specifically to the endurance of the Christians; they express the characteristic New Testament conviction that salvation belongs to the last day, and is only anticipated here and now by faith and perseverance. It is (13.13) the man who endures to the end who will be saved. Whether the tribulations he has to face are interpreted as those that accompany the fall of Jerusalem or the "birth-pangs" of the Messianic Age make little difference to the point the evangelist is making. Endurance is indispensable for salvation. This was a word of challenge and of comfort that was greatly needed by the martyr

[1] Peter, writing for the same Roman church, makes precisely the same point, I Pet. 1.7-9.

[2] The pattern *per ardua ad astra*, for the disciples as for himself, comes out most clearly in the teaching of Jesus to his disciples after Caesaraea Philippi: it culminates in the Transfiguration – an anticipation, surely, of heaven – which is linked by a unique time reference (9.2) to Jesus's teaching that both he and his followers must tread the way of the cross (8.31-38).

church of Rome in the sixties of the first century. It is a note that needs to be struck equally firmly in present-day preaching, where the comfort and realized eschatology of salvation is not infrequently prominently to the fore, and the hard unglamorous business of endurance is all too often soft-pedalled.[1]

No less significant is 13.20. Had God not "shortened the days", no one would be saved. The evangelist voices his conviction that God is sovereign in his world, that the perseverance no less than the salvation of his people is rooted and grounded in the sovereignty of God. While human free-will to persevere is essential, and is stressed in this context, even more important is the *magisterium* exercised by God over his world, a control which creates circumstances in which perseverance is possible.

ST. MATTHEW

There are no references to salvation common to Matthew and Luke alone, but in addition to the five Marcan references which are included in all the synoptics (Mk. 5.34, 8.35, 10.26, 13.13, 15.31), there are five where Matthew alone takes over the Marcan statements. Thus the woman with the issue of blood is saved (9.21, Mk. 5.28), so are the sick who touch Christ's garment (14.36, Mk. 6.56); the saying on perseverance (24.22), is taken from Mk. 13.20, so is the mocking invitation to Christ to save himself from the cross (27.40, Mk. 15.30) and the famous ransom saying (20.28, Mk. 10.45).

But the most interesting references are naturally those peculiar to Matthew. They seem to enshrine a threefold emphasis in his understanding of salvation.

In the first place, Matthew goes out of his way to emphasize the *human* side of salvation, the necessity to persevere with Christ. Not content with reproducing the saying, "He who endures to the end will be saved", in the apocalyptic discourse (24.13), he gives it again in the more general context of the Mission of the Twelve. In 10.22 it is made abundantly clear that hatred and opposition will be the lot of the Christian missionary, and that endurance to the uttermost is vital if salvation in its full sense is to be achieved. This was doubtless a message very necessary in the early days of the Christian endeavour for which Matthew's Gospel was written, where the discouragements afforded by the relative failure of the Jewish mission and the delay of the

[1] It was a commonplace with the rabbis that the Messianic Age would come to birth through "travail" or sufferings, just as a human baby does. The Old Testament suggested as much (Mic. 4.9f, Jer. 22.23, Hosea 13.13, Isa. 26.17, 66.8, etc). It is an important strand in later New Testament teaching that "we must through much tribulation enter into the kingdom of God", Acts. 14.22, I Thess. 3.4, Rev. 2.10, 7.14.

Second Coming must have tempted many to give up. As we shall see, the situation to which the Epistle to the Hebrews was addressed was very similar.

Secondly, Matthew lays great emphasis on the *physical* element in salvation, and here he stands squarely in the Hebrew tradition. In the story of the woman with the issue of blood he uses the word three times (9.21, 22); his final *kai esōthē*, stressing the completeness of the cure, is unparalleled in the other synoptists. Similarly, the use of the strengthened form *diesōthēsan* in the aorist tense instead of Mark's simple *esōzonto* in the imperfect, probably shows his interest in the completeness of the healing of the sick (14.36). Indeed, the importance he attaches to the healings as evidence of Christ's work of salvation is emphasized in 8.17, where he applies the quotation of Isa. 53.4 not to the atoning but to the healing work of the Servant of the Lord. With the origin of these "formula quotations" which figure so prominently in the first Gospel we are not here concerned, nor is it important to determine whether the application of Isa. 53.4 to the healings is a secondary use of a text originally applied to the cross of Jesus. The point is that Matthew uses it to demonstrate that in his work of healing and exorcism Jesus was fulfilling the portrait sketched long before of the ideal Servant of the Lord. Matthew remains a valuable warning against our readiness to over-spiritualize the salvation which Jesus brought. The words "took" and "bore" in this verse can mean either "remove", "deliver from", or "take upon himself", "bear the penalty of". It is clearly in the former sense that the words must be taken here, particularly in the context in which Matthew has placed the verse. Jesus did not transfer the diseases and demons of others to himself. But Lagrange is probably right in suggesting that the other, expiatory meaning is not far either from the mind of the evangelist or his hearers: "In taking away the pain the Servant also expiated the sin . . . it was this deliverance which Jesus began when he cast out demons and healed sick folk. It was understood that in so doing he assumed responsibility for the expiation of sin in the future; this the Christian readers knew very well" (*Évangile selon St. Matthieu* (1927), p. 169). It is also possible that Matthew's mind went back to the first of the Servant Songs, where, in Isa. 42.1, possession of the Spirit is to be the great mark of the Suffering Servant. Matthew saw the healings and exorcisms as manifestations of the Spirit's work (Matt. 12.28) and, like John (7.38f.), knew that they were inextricably bound to the suffering of the Servant; the two roles in Jesus could not be divorced. That is why he could use Isa. 53.4 of the healings – they were the firstfruits of that salvation which was to be consummated upon the cross.

The third group of verses on salvation peculiar to Matthew point to the *Christ-centredness* of the idea for him. Two of them are invitations to Christ to save; deliberately, it would seem, they are cast into the language of the cult. "Lord, save – we perish" is the plea of the disciples in the storm (8.25), and in a similar incident Peter, while walking on the water and beginning to sink, cries "Lord, save me" (14.30). In each case Jesus is invoked as "Lord"; in each case an explicit connection is noted between the faith of the disciples and the rescue of Jesus. True, both the disciples and Peter are rebuked for the smallness of their faith, but this merely serves to underline the fact that it is neither the quantity nor the quality of faith that is of primary significance, but its object. Faith, however superstitious or doubting, is never disappointed if it is placed in Jesus.

The Christocentric nature of salvation in this Gospel is underlined at its outset, in the famous promise of the angel to Mary, "Thou shalt call his name Jesus, for he shall save his people from their sins" (1.21). With this we may take a salvation reference peculiar to Matthew at the very end of his book (27.49), where the onlookers say, "Let us see whether Elijah will come to save him." Will Elijah come to save him? No, indeed. No one can save Jesus, for he is God's chosen Saviour for all men, and he cannot achieve this salvation short of the sacrifice of of himself. As with the other synoptic accounts of the crucifixion, Matthew uses the misunderstanding of the crowd to make his point about the nature of the Saviour and his salvation. Its essence lies in his self-oblation for others. Is he not Jesus, who shall save his people from their sins? This has been the keynote struck at the outset of the Gospel, and it is continued to the end. Jesus, of course, is the Greek translation of Joshua, and its meaning was so well known in Christian circles that Matthew does not even bother to translate it. Philo had said, "Jesus when translated means 'the salvation of the Lord'" (*de Mut. Nom.* 21), and the obvious point when this title was given to Jesus was that he would be a second Joshua, delivering people from their greatest enemies (their sins)[1] and bringing them into a better Promised Land.[2] But more profoundly, this would be the work of God. Not only is this clear from the name itself ("Yahweh saves", or "Yahweh is salvation"), but also from the fact that the promise, "He shall save his people from their sins" is an unmistakable allusion to Ps. 130.8, which says of God, "He himself (*autos* in the LXX is emphatically first word, as here) will

[1] See Acts 4.12, etc., where salvation is attributed to the *name* of Jesus.
[2] It is noteworthy that to Matthew, Jesus is also the new Moses (see W. D. Davies, *The Setting of the Sermon on the Mount* (1964), ch. 2). Like Moses, Jesus was snatched from death under a cruel tyrant. Like him, he was tempted in the wilderness. Like him he was prophet, miracle worker, lawgiver and supremely Saviour.

redeem Israel from all his sins." Jesus would do what the Old Testament had said God would do, and Matthew saw nothing surprising in this, in view of the supernatural birth which he is in process of describing. Quite literally, it would be God to the rescue of his people. In contrast to the nationalistic and materialistic hopes of salvation cherished, as we have seen, by many Jews of the time, Matthew's position is perfectly plain. He proclaims no human deliverer, but God himself come to save them – Emmanuel, God with us (1.23). And God's concern is not the restoration of the theocracy and deliverance from Rome, but the meeting of a deeper and universal need; in Christ he was about to fulfil the longing of the psalmist and provide men with a Saviour from *themselves*, a Saviour from sin. Thus for all the physical significance Matthew attributes to salvation, he sees Christ primarily as a Saviour from sin.

ST. LUKE

It is hard to overestimate the importance of salvation in the writings of Luke. It forms the subject of an important article by W. C. van Unnik, to which I am much indebted.[1] It is astonishing, however, that in view of the frequency with which Luke uses salvation terminology, more attention has not been paid to it. In the Gospel, in addition to the seven places where the verb *sōzein* is taken over from Mark, it occurs in no less than ten other places to which there are no parallels in the other Gospels. Furthermore, Luke uses *sōtēr* twice, *sōtērion* twice, *sōtēria* four times, *lutrousthai* once, *lutrōsis* twice, *apolutrōsis* once and *diasōzein* once; all of these occurrences are unparalleled in the other Gospels. When we turn to the Acts, there is an equally prominent stress on the language of salvation. *Sōzein* occurs thirteen times, *diasōzein* five, *sōtēria* six, *sōtēr* twice, *sōtērion* once and *lutrōtēs* once.

Since salvation is clearly a primary concern of St. Luke, it is worth enquiring, with van Unnik, whether this may not prove to be the key to that elusive problem, the purpose of Luke-Acts. We cannot help noticing how the early chapters of the Gospel make this a major theme. The "horn of salvation" had arisen in the ancient house of David (1.69), so that men may be saved (1.71), delivered (1.74), and receive the knowledge of salvation in the remission of sins (1.77). The angels proclaim to the shepherds the birth of a Saviour, Christ the Lord (2.11). And what is that if not Luke's understanding of Jesus the Messiah? He is both Saviour and exalted Lord. His saviourhood is recognized by Simeon (2.30). Indeed, Luke goes out of his way from the very outset of his Gospel to emphasize the universal nature of the

[1] "The Book of Acts, the Confirmation of the Gospel" in *Novum Testamentum* iv.i (1960).

salvation of God (1.47) brought by Christ (2.11).[1] Jesus is seen as the light to lighten the Gentiles as well as the glory of God's people, Israel (2.32). He is to give light to those sitting in darkness, as well as salvation to God's people (1.77-79). It is significant that in quoting Isa. 40.3f. Luke goes farther than either Matthew or Mark, so as to include the words, so important for his purpose, "And all the world shall see the salvation of God" (3.6). The two-volume work he wrote records just this, how all the world *did* come to see the salvation of God.

After this beginning, Luke goes on in the body of the Gospel to show what salvation means. The healing of a Gentile soldier's servant (7.3), the forgiveness of a fallen woman (7.50),[2] the restoration to wholeness of a demented man (8.36), the provision of new life for a dead girl (8.50) – are all described in the language of salvation by Luke, and are clearly intended to be paraenetic. He wants us to understand that this is what salvation is like – new life, wholeness, forgiveness, healing. It is the response of believing hearts to the *kerygma* that brings salvation (8.12), and this *kerygma* is nothing other than the proclamation of a person, Jesus. It is Jesus who comes to save men's lives, not to judge them (9.56 in some MSS.). He comes to save the lost (19.10). It is supremely by his death that he does this, as the repeated stress on salvation in the account of the crucifixion makes plain. Four times in 23.35, 37, 39 Luke stresses that the salvation of others was achieved at the cost of the self-sacrifice of the Saviour; he makes more of this point even than Mark does. He leaves us in no doubt at all that this salvation, achieved by Jesus at the cost of his own life, avails even for the most degraded of outcasts; the dying robber's prayer for salvation (23.39) was answered by the promise of the dying Saviour that he would be *with him* in Paradise. Salvation is thus inextricably linked by Luke with the person of Jesus. When Jesus comes to a man's home, salvation comes there (19.9). Salvation is not a matter for speculation (13.23), but for decision (13.24). It is secured by self-commitment to Jesus, that is to say, by faith (7.50, 8.12, 8.50, etc.).

The Book of Acts shows us the proclamation of this salvation through the ancient world. The early speeches in Acts, like the early speeches in the Gospel, are full of references to salvation. On the Day of Pentecost Peter quotes Joel to the effect that God's salvation,

[1] It is interesting that the word "Saviour", which Luke uses twice in his Gospel, should quite naturally be applied in one case to God and the other to Jesus.

[2] This verse makes it perfectly plain that the woman was saved because of her faith in Christ, not as a reward for her act of love, as a cursory reading of 7.47 might imply. This would, of course, make nonsense of the preceding parable of the debtors. The woman, like the debtor, loves much because she has been forgiven already – hence the use of the perfect, ἀφέωνται αὐτῆς αἱ ἁμαρτίαι.

promised in the Old Testament, is now available for all who will accept it, "Whosoever shall call on the name of the Lord shall be saved" (2.21). He means Jesus, of course, by "Lord", though he is well aware that the title referred to God in the Old Testament. The whole point of the early Christian preaching was that this Jesus, although repudiated by the Jewish leaders, was the divinely appointed Saviour for men (5.31, 13.23), and that his Lordship was vindicated by the resurrection, of the reality of which they were witnesses. In his name alone is salvation for a lost world (4.12), salvation designed as much for the Gentile as the Jew. Thus when preaching in the synagogue at Antioch Paul exhorts his Jewish hearers with the words, "To *us* is the word of this salvation sent" (13.26).[1] Yet, when they refuse to receive it, he can turn to the Gentiles confident that this is the fulfilment of the ancient Scriptures: "Lo, we turn to the Gentiles. For so hath the Lord commanded us, saying, I have set thee to be a light to the Gentiles, that thou shouldest be for salvation unto the ends of the earth" (13.47, 48). And that is Luke's repeated emphasis throughout the book. The gospel is the way of salvation (16.17). The challenge it makes is to "save yourselves" (2.40). The description of Christians is *hoi sōzomenoi* (2.47). Jews (ch. 2), Gentiles (ch. 13), godfearers like Cornelius (11.14), slaves (16.17), jailers (16.31) – all alike must be saved. The Council at Jerusalem was concerned with nothing less than this vital matter, the meaning and the way of salvation. "Except ye be circumcized . . . ye cannot be saved", said the Pharisee party. "Through the grace of the Lord Jesus we shall be saved, even as they," said Peter and Paul (15.1, 11). That was the issue at stake; that is why Luke spends so much time on it.[2]

[1] Not "to you" as in A. V. Nestle gives Acts 13.26 as a quotation from Ps. 107.20. If so, it is remarkable that Luke has inserted the words "of this salvation" into the text of the Psalm, just as he lengthened his quotation of Isa. 40.3 in Lk. 3.6 to include the salvation reference.

[2] The distinctive features that emerge in the treatment of salvation in Acts have been well treated by H. N. Ridderbos, *The Speeches of Peter in the Acts of the Apostles* (1962), pp. 28-31. He rightly stresses both its future and present aspects (2. 20, 21, 2.40, 3.19, 20, 10.42, compared with 4.9, 12, 4.30) and says, "Thus being saved relates to the whole of human existence, just as the fulfilment which has dawned in Christ has an all-embracing significance." He further shows how, for Luke, salvation is to be understood in the closest connection with the person of Christ. It is *in his name* (3.6, 4.10, 12, 30, 10.43) that men are saved; hence the vital importance he attributes to faith, commitment to that name. We have also noted the strong universalistic emphasis Luke lays on the scope of salvation. It is designed to avail for all men. But Luke is no "universalist". He is quite clear that those who reject salvation will be lost (e.g. 13.46, 17.31, 28.25-28). Like the rest of the New Testament writers Luke knows that "salvation is from the Jews", that it is all of a piece with the revelation of the Saviour God in the Old Testament. But he also sees that the Christian salvation fulfills not only the Old

Indeed, we may go farther. In ch. 4 Luke makes quite explicit what he implies in the Gospel, that he means us to see the healings of Jesus and the apostles as paradigms of salvation. In 4.9 Peter explains to the Sanhedrin how the impotent man has been healed (*sesōstai*). Immediately he goes on to stress the other meaning of this ambiguous word, and tells them that there is salvation in none other than Christ (4.12). "*Sōtēria* combines here the two meanings which we usually separate. This healing of the lame is the sign of the messianic era; this healing of the body visualizes the totality of Christ's saving power."[1]

The story of the shipwreck, whose length has been a source of amazement to scholars for generations, is probably to be seen in the same light. It is noteworthy that the language of salvation abounds (27.20, 31, 34, 43, 44; 28.1, 4). As we saw in ch. 1, and as reappears vividly in the description of heaven in Rev. 21.1 ("and there was no more sea"), the sea was to the ancient Hebrew the symbol of anti-God power, of chaos and danger, of the demonic. In the story of the shipwreck Luke would have us see the truth that not all the power of Antichrist can prevent the coming of salvation to the uttermost parts of the earth.[2] And so the book ends with Paul proclaiming without hindrance the salvation of God to both Jew and Gentile in the very centre of the ancient world. Although it is offered to Jew and Gentile alike, the response is once again most noticeable among the Gentiles, and the Gentile evangelist[3] ends his book with a quotation from Scripture warranting this sending of "the salvation of God to the Gentiles" (28.28) and assuring him that "they will hear it".

All this suggests that the purpose of Luke-Acts is apologetic in the broadest sense of the term. Not only does the author want to show the political harmlessness of the new faith, but he wants to show that although new it is not novel, but rather the outworking of the age-old plan of salvation to be found in the Jewish Scriptures. The two-volume work is, in fact, a piece of subtle teaching-evangelism; the speeches

Testament scriptures but the longings of the pagan heart for salvation (16.17, 30). Luke is not unaware of the corporate nature of salvation, as is clear from the household references he gives in the context of the saving faith of Cornelius and the jailer (11.14, 16.31 – on the οἶκος formula see E. Stauffer "Zur Kindertaufe in der Urkirche" in *Deutsches Pfarrerblatt*, 49 (1949), pp. 152-4). And Luke knows that salvation comes about when the self-surrender of Christ is met with the faith of the believer.

[1] Van Unnik, *op. cit.*, p. 51.

[2] In some ways it may be parallel to the extended treatment of the Passion at the end of the Gospel, where not all the anti-God forces arrayed against Jesus were able to prevent his bringing salvation to the world.

[3] Both at the turning point (13.47) and at the conclusion of his book (28.28), Luke cites the Gentile prophecy of Isa. 49.6: in both cases it is set in a context of Jewish rejection of salvation.

which constantly reiterate the saving events,[1] the thrice-repeated account of Paul's conversion, the repeated references to salvation and the change in those who accept it, the healings in the name of Jesus, the failure of any opposing forces of evil to quench this salvation of God – all these themes in Luke-Acts subserve the main central theme of teaching-evangelism, of "apology" in the distinctively Christian sense. In Lk. 21.11-13 Jesus foretells that Christians shall be brought before kings and governors for his name's sake, "and it shall turn to you for a testimony". For a commentary on that verse, we turn to Acts 26 where Paul stands before Agrippa "for his name's sake". He professes to be making his defence (26.2), but he turns it into a testimony; the speech is full of evangelistic overtones, and ends with an impassioned plea for faith. That, it seems to me, is what Luke himself is about. He is not merely writing apologetics for Christianity, not merely Church history. He is one of the great New Testament preachers, and he seeks to bring Theophilus and those like him to personal experience of Christian salvation, through faith in Jesus Christ.

Professor Moule has argued that Luke and John are both designed to be read by those outside, or on the fringe of the Christian communities, and he poses the question whether they are not the earliest written apologies.[2] Van Unnik takes much the same line when he urges that Luke-Acts was intended not only to proclaim but to confirm the gospel of salvation, "how it came to the world in Jesus Christ and how it built the solid bridge across to them who did not see Jesus incarnate. Acts as the confirmation of what God did in Christ as told in the first book."[3] Van Unnik places the main weight of his argument on the stress on witness, *marturia*, which is so prominent a feature of the book; the witness of men, the witness brought by God himself, the changed lives of those who receive the witness, all this is confirmation of the gospel in the sense of Heb. 2.3, 4 with which he links it. Professor C. K. Barrett[4] treads much the same ground when he emphasizes Luke's use of "The Word" or allied expression to show the the advance of the Church. He points out how no less than thirty-two times people are said to preach or hear or accept the Word, and concludes that Luke is anxious that the Church of his day should recall

[1] H. N. Ridderbos sees this clearly. He notices, with Dibelius, the significant *direct speech* of the Acts sermons, and observes, "They are directed not only to the original audience, but to all who read them. Just as the whole Book of Acts is a continued preaching of Christ, so it is also a concrete appeal to repentance and the forgiveness of sins" (*The Speeches of Peter in the Acts of the Apostles* (1962), p. 28).
[2] *New Testament Essays*, ed. A. J. B. Higgins (1959), p. 176.
[3] *Op. cit.*, p. 58.   [4] *Luke the Historian in Recent Study* (1961), pp. 68f.

and abide by the preaching of apostolic times. I myself wonder whether a different route might not lead us to much the same goal.[1]

It seems clear that van Unnik is right in seeing Acts as not only a proclamation but a confirmation of the gospel. It is designed to answer the question, always present in the minds of those who have not seen the incarnate Lord, "How can I be sure?" Indeed, this is what Luke explicitly sets out to answer in the Preface to his two-volume work, when he offers to show Theophilus the *asphaleia*, the certainty or assured reliability of the things believed in the Christian community (Lk. 1.4). How, then, can one be sure? The second-century apologists have three classic arguments for the divinely authenticated nature of Christianity. They refer to:

    a. Signs and wonders, which prove that Jesus was the Son of God, and vindicate the status of the apostles as well.

    b. Fulfilled prophecy, particularly concerning the death and resurrection of Jesus. This is particularly cogent to those who have no means of assuring themselves of the truth or otherwise of the reported miracles. Indeed, fulfilled prophecy has occupied a major plank in Christian evidences until very recent times.

    c. The success of the Christian mission proves its divine origin. The whole force of the argument from history is brought to bear – another feature of apologetic not unknown today.

Could it be that Luke was the first of the apologists? Do these classic arguments spring, in the last resort, from him? It can hardly be denied that Luke is distinctly fond of the miraculous. As a sheer matter of statistics, he speaks of signs and wonders, *terata kai sēmeia*, eight times in Acts as compared with seven in the whole of the rest of the New Testament. Is this accidental? Or does Luke not see the miracles of Jesus and the apostles as a confirmation of the truth of the gospel? Then again, his constant resort to quoting Old Testament prophecies comes immediately to mind, particularly concerning the resurrection. And finally, the whole account he records is one great success story. A handful of fisherfolk in a tiny province of the Roman Empire light a torch which, by the end of the book, has been blazed throughout the main areas of the empire, and is burning brightly at the metropolis itself.

Was Luke, thus, the first to see in the expansion of Christianity God's authentication of the gospel of salvation? Further, was he the first realized eschatologist? Not that Luke did not believe in the Parousia; he has as much to say about it as any other writer in the New

[1] J. C. O'Neill takes a broadly similar view in his *Theology of Acts* (1961), ch. 7.

Testament. But he knows that salvation is not only future but present; that the kingdom has come in the growth of the Church, although the restoration of all things lies still in God's future (Acts. 3.21). Was he among the first to grasp the truth that the coming of Jesus had split the "last day" into an "already" and a "not yet"? And did he write his Acts to show the *theological* significance of history since the cross and resurrection, that it is, in a word, the history of *salvation*?

ST. JOHN

John once speaks of "Saviour" (4.42, and again in 1 Jn. 4.14), once of "salvation" (4.22) and six times he uses the word "save" (3.17, 5.34, 10.9, 11.12, 12.27, 47). This is remarkably restrained usage for an evangelist who deliberately sets out to bring the uncommitted to faith in Jesus (20.31). Why should this be?

The answer may, I think, lie in the first of two remarkable emphases in the Johannine conception of salvation. To him, the *nature* of salvation is eternal life, and the *scope* of salvation is universal. John constantly equates salvation with eternal life; it is his favourite way of looking at it. This represents, of course, no innovation. The words "salvation" and "life" are identical in Aramaic, as we have seen. Furthermore, we have already met the identification, albeit implicitly, in Mk. 10, where "entering into the kingdom of God", "following Christ", "obtaining eternal life", and "being saved" are alternative modes of speech (10.17, 21, 24, 26). But for John the identification is quite specific, and indeed central in almost all his references. Thus in 3.16, 17 the phrase "have eternal life" is parallel to "be saved" and interprets it. In 5.34, coming to Jesus in response to John's testimony is called "being saved", while in 5.39, 40 it is called "having eternal life". In 10.9, 10 "being saved" and having "life abundant" are deliberately set in juxtaposition; and in 11.12 *sōthēsetai* is advisedly ambiguous and refers primarily to life. Finally, 12.47 speaks of the purpose of Jesus's coming as to save the world, while 12.50 speaks of it in terms of bringing eternal life. Since life is thus the major category in which John sees salvation, it is important to understand what he means by it.

In his treatment of the subject,[1] C. H. Dodd has shewn that three ideas underlie Jewish usage of this term; in all three cases there is reference to life beyond the grave. "Life" is contrasted with death; "life of the age", or everlasting life, is contrasted with temporary life; and "life of the age to come" is contrasted with the "life of this age". Dodd recognizes that it is from such a background that John develops

[1] *The Interpretation of the Fourth Gospel* (1953), pp. 144-50.

his doctrine of eternal life. It is something not merely quantitively but qualitatively different from the life we know before becoming Christians. It is defined primarily not by length but by relationship. "This is life eternal, that they may know thee, the only true God, and Jesus Christ whom thou hast sent" (17.3). Not only so, but it is experienced *now* (3.36, 5.24, 6.47, 54), although its fullness lies beyond the grave (5.21-29, 11.23-26). John sees that the life which the Jews expected in the age to come is present in Jesus, and can be enjoyed here and now by relationship with him who is the resurrection and the life (11.25). This is the utterly new thing in Christian salvation, something undreamed of in rabbinic Judaism, that men can enjoy living in God's eternal Today through knowing God and Jesus Christ whom he has sent to reveal him. That is not to say that John's conception of eternal life is one of timelessness. Far from it. We have still the characteristic Hebrew linear view of time in the Fourth Gospel, and are far removed from the cyclical conception of the Platonic world. There is a very specific note of *duration* about John's references to "life". The Christian will live for ever (6.51, 58), and will never die (11.26, 10.28); the "last day" lies in the future (6.39, 40), so does the judgement and resurrection (5.28f.), so does the parousia (21.22). Nevertheless, so strong is John's emphasis on realized eschatology, on present salvation, on the qualitative element in eternal life, that the judgement is seen as past for the Christian (3.18, 5.24), the resurrection life is enjoyed by relationship with Christ now (5.24, 11.25, 26), and the parousia of Christ is anticpated by the coming of the Spirit of Christ (14.16, 18). Salvation, the life of the age to come, is no timeless abstraction nor future hope, of God's own life, a category of existence so radically new that you have to be born again if you are to understand and enjoy it (3.3, 5). This is how John sees salvation. Though the terminology is different, his standpoint is characteristic of the early Church. The unitary conception of eschatology which they had accepted from their Jewish heritage was henceforth shattered into two by the coming of Jesus, than whom they could conceive nothing more ultimate; he had brought the life of the age to come to men of this Age. This was salvation.

John is just as certain of another aspect of eternal life, on which the early church was unanimous. Life was made available to men through the self-offering of Jesus. It came through death. This is made very evident in Jesus's soliloquy in 12.27-33. Jesus came, not to be saved himself but to save others; he would do so by his death on the cross. That is the context in which the famous saying about the corn of wheat occurs (12.24). The same thought is present in 3.16, 17 where the life of the doomed world is secured by the doom of the Son. It is in the background in the Lazarus story in ch. 11. Lazarus will indeed be "saved" (11.12) by the coming of Jesus to raise him from the tomb. But the real salvation of Lazarus and of all men will be achieved by the death on the cross in which that last visit to Jerusalem issued (the evangelist makes this plain in 11.8, 16, 53). The theme of life through death is even evident in the mention of salvation In 10.9, whether or not Dodd is right in detecting echoes of the Servant terminology from Isa. 49.9, 10 (op. cit., p. 246). For the good shepherd is the one who lays down his life to take it again, and who gives his life for the sheep (10.15, 17).

This life of God, released for men through the death of Jesus, is made available to them through the Spirit. The man who comes to Jesus drinks of the well of eternal life, like the wells of salvation of Isa. 12.3. This water John links with the Spirit who would come to apply the completed work of the Saviour to the believer after the passion and resurrection (7.37-39).

Such was one great way in which John looked at salvation. It meant life, the life of the age to come, made possible here and now by relationship with the crucified and risen Lord Jesus through the Spirit. His other great concern was to stress the universality of this salvation. It was meant for the whole world.

This is made particularly clear in the first instance in John where the language of salvation is used, 3.16, 17. "In the current Jewish eschatology, Messiah was to come as the Judge of mankind",[1] as we saw in ch. 3, and the Fourth Gospel does not deny this (5.27, 30, 9.39). Nevertheless, such was not the primary cause of his coming into the world. "God sent not his Son into the world to condemn the world . . . I judge no man . . . I came not to judge the world but to save the world" (3.17, 8.15, 12.47). Of course, judgement inevitably ensues when men face up to the light of God (3.18-20). The element of *krisis* cannot be evaded, but condemnation is incidental, not primary to his purpose. "Men by their response to the manifestation of the light declare themselves, and so pronounce their own judgement."[2] Nevertheless, the remarkable fact which John stresses here is well summed up by Bernard: "ἵνα σώσω not ἵνα κρίνω (as Jewish-Apocalyptic believed) expresses the final cause of the mission of the Son of Man",[3] and he compares Zech. 9.9, ὁ βασιλεύς σου ἐρχεταί σοι δίκαιος καὶ σώζων.[4]

The universality of this redemptive purpose is nowhere more strikingly portrayed than in ch. 4. There are two references to salvation

[1] Bernard in the *I.C.C.*, vol. i, p. 119.
[2] Dodd, *op. cit.*, p. 210.   [3] Bernard, *op. cit.*, p. 120.
[4] "Thy king cometh to thee, just and bringing salvation."

133

in this chapter. The first makes crystal clear that salvation[1] springs from the Jews. To be sure it is not their perquisite, but it originates with them; the Jews have down the centuries been the *locus* of God's saving acts. The second reference makes equally clear that if salvation is *from* the Jews it is meant *for* the whole world. The Samaritans recognize Jesus as the Saviour of the world (4.42). Can we suppose that the Samaritans would have spoken of Jesus in such terms? It is difficult to say. Bernard argues that there is only the most tenuous link between Messiah and Saviour in the Old Testament.[2] But this criticism is beside the point, since "The Messiah" in 4.42 is a later gloss. But it is by no means impossible that the Samaritans did see Jesus as *sōtēr*, since the title is applied freely to men sent by God[3] in the Pentateuch, which they accepted, and since they entertained far less nationalistic views of salvation than did the Jews.[4] "God's plan of salvation is not confined to a group of tribes in a small tract of territory. The whole world of mankind benefits from the salvation of the 'light of their life'." So wrote J. Macdonald (*op. cit.*, p. 352). However, it is possible that the use of the title here is a piece of indirect Christian opposition to its attribution to the emperor in the Graeco-Roman world,[5] although it must be confessed that there is no hint of any polemic aim in the context. Dodd's view is possible, if hardly convincing: "The evangelist may have been conscious of a certain dramatic propriety in putting [the title] in the mouth of Samaritans, who in this Gospel represent, in some sort, the Gentile world."[6] Of course, if, as Cullmann maintains,[7] the whole incident is rewritten in the light of the later Christian mission in Samaria which reaped where Jesus and his disciples had sown, then the title "Saviour" is quite comprehensible. He would then be right

[1] Westcott, in his *Commentary* on St. John, *in loc.*, comments, "*The* promised and expected salvation, ἡ σωτηρία, to be realized in the mission of the Messiah."

[2] *Op. cit.*, p. 161.

[3] "It became usual to regard 'the Saviour of our fathers' as the Saviour of the individual, though never in the full sense of a personal Saviour. This Christian-like stress only applies in Samaritan thought of very late times to Moses, also the Saviour of Israel. The Samaritans in the main preferred to apply the attributes of Saviour to God himself" (*The Theology of the Samaritans* by J. Macdonald (1964), p. 353).

[4] So Godet, *Commentary on St. John's Gospel* (1892), vol. ii, p. 131, and M. Dods, *The Expositor's Greek Testament*, vol. i, p. 732.

[5] See C. F. D. Moule, *J.T.S.* (N.S.), vol. x, p. 262. Certainly, as Deissmann has shown, the title "Saviour of the world" was freely bestowed on the emperors, particularly Hadrian (*Light from the Ancient East*, p. 369). If the title here is polemical, ὁ κύριός μου καὶ ὁ θεός μου (Jn. 20.28) must be even more so; it would represent a denial of Domitian's claim to be *dominus et deus noster*.

[6] *Op. cit.*, p. 239.

[7] "Samaria and the origins of the Christian Mission" in *The Early Church*, pp. 183ff.

in connecting this verse with the preaching of Christ as Saviour in Acts 5.31; it would be a title which was appropriate only after his death and resurrection – "*Sōtēr* very definitely presupposes his work of atonement."[1] However, Cullmann's view has not won wide acceptance, and it is impossible to be sure whether the use of this title here represents Samaritan or merely Johannine theology. That it *does* represent the latter is certain from 1 Jn. 4.14, the only other place in the New Testament where the full title "Saviour of the world" is applied to Jesus. It was John's conviction that the God of the Old Testament, who had shewn himself time and again to be the Saviour of *his people* (see especially Isa. 43.3, 11, 45.21, 49.26, 60.16, Jer. 14.8), had now intervened decisively in the person of Jesus to become the Saviour of the *whole world* (cf. 1 Jn. 2.2). Salvation comes *from* the Jews *for* the world, and John dedicated his life as well as his gospel to the spreading of the message of that universal salvation far and wide.

[1] Cullmann, *The Christology of the New Testament*, p. 243.

CHAPTER 8

Salvation in the Early Preaching

"The salvation brought in by Jesus is the theme of the entire apostolic age. Wherever we turn in the New Testament, whether it be the Acts, Hebrews, St. Paul or St. John, we are conscious of a note of confidence and triumph, as of men possessing a supreme good, in which they not only themselves rejoice, but which they are anxious to share with others. More significant than any change in doctrine is this consciousness of salvation as a glorious fact, dominating and transforming life." So wrote W. A. Brown over sixty years ago,[1] and it is a fair assessment. Salvation is a theme common, and indeed central to the whole of the New Testament. Or, to be more precise, it is everywhere taught that Jesus saves men; Christians are always seen as the objects of his saving activity. For the verb "to save", either in the active or passive, is a good deal more frequent in the New Testament than the noun "salvation"; and this leads some scholars[2] to conclude that the New Testament writers are not so much interested in a doctrine as in the experience of God's saving work brought about by Jesus.

However, in the Acts and Epistles this contrast does not hold good. The verb "save" is used over fifty times, "salvation" only slightly less, while the formal title "Saviour" is about half as common. Indeed, the distribution of the three terms throughout the New Testament is rather singular.

Thus Revelation, for instance, speaks of "salvation" but never of "save" or "Saviour". James, on the other hand, has five references to "save" but none to the other two. Hebrews has "salvation" seven times, but "save" only once and "Saviour" not at all; 2 Peter, by way of contrast, does not speak of "save" at all, only once of "salvation", but has "Saviour" five times!

It is easy to overestimate the significance of these divergencies, particularly when words of similar meaning like "redeem" and

---

[1] H.D.B. article "Salvation".

[2] E.g. P. Bonnard, s.v. "Salvation in the New Testament" in *Vocabulary of the Bible* (1958).

"deliver" are taken into account. This becomes very clear when we examine the usage of a single writer, Paul. Outside the Pastorals, he only twice speaks of the "Saviour", but uses "save" and "salvation" with equal freedom and frequency. Nevertheless, we find that whereas "save" comes eight times in 1 Corinthians, it comes only once in 2 Corinthians, while 2 Corinthians's thrice-repeated "salvation" does not appear at all in the first Epistle. And no sooner is one tempted to draw some inference from the absence of the entire *sōzō* root from Galatians and Colossians, than one recalls that Galatians speaks of redemption by Christ (3.13, 4.5), while Colossians tells of the deliverance that is ours, the redemption made available through his blood (1.13, 14). This ought to warn us against the assumption, commonly made, from the distribution of "Saviour" that the title is a late development. The rarity of the word in Paul's extant letters may well be fortuitous, if this evidence is anything to go by, for the idea is certainly everywhere present.

The language of salvation appears throughout the New Testament. It was common to the early Christian tradition. What did it mean to them?

THE SPEECHES OF PETER

Let us begin with the speeches attributed to Peter in the first part of Acts. The status of these speeches is, of course, much debated. Did Luke make them up? Did he, on the other hand, have transcripts of them? Both of these extreme views are very unlikely. But there is good reason to suppose that the speeches in Acts do give us a reliable summary of the primitive Jewish-Christian gospel.[1]

If it is argued that it is intrinsically unlikely that Luke had any evidence of what was said on each occasion, it might be well to remember that shorthand was much used in the ancient world, and that many Jews had their memories trained to an extent which we find almost incredible today with our reliance on the printed page.[2] But sometimes

[1] Among those who think highly of the reliability of Acts in general and the speeches in particular are C. S. C. Williams and F. F. Bruce in their recent commentaries, C. H. Dodd, *The Apostolic Preaching and its Development* (1935), and *According to the Scriptures* (1952), H. N. Ridderbos, *The Speeches of Peter in the Acts of the Apostles* (1962), B. Gärtner, *The Areopagus Speech and Natural Revelation* (1955), A. M. Hunter, *Paul and his Predecessors* (1961). E. Haenchen and M. Dibelius in their commentaries regard the speeches as Lucan compositions; so do D. E. Nineham (*Studies in the Gospels*, pp. 229ff.), and C. F. Evans (*J.T.S.* (1956), pp. 25ff.).
[2] See H. Riesenfeld, *The Gospel Tradition and its Beginnings* (1957), B. Gerhardsson, *Memory and Manuscript* (1961) and 'Tradition and Transmission in Early Christianity' in *Conjectanea Neotestamentica*, xx (1964).

the words of Thucydides about the purpose of his speeches are adduced to show that Luke, writing as a historian, would put into the mouths of his preachers what he thought appropriate. However, even Thucydides stood as close to what was said as he could; his speeches were not free composition; he "kept as closely as possible to the general gist of what was in fact said".[1] Furthermore, whereas in Thucydides and historians of his tradition, the speeches were the literary highlights, what Dionysius called "the summit of the author's literary perfection", in Luke they are stylistically poor. Indeed, it would seem that he has crucified his style in order to remain faithful to his sources. For it is indisputable that there is a strong Aramaic background to these early speeches in Acts. C. C. Torrey,[2] and to a lesser extent M. Black[3] have shewn that where the Greek is almost untranslatable, it turns easily into Aramaic (e.g. 3.16). The fact that Luke should have included in his book Aramaic translationese, and not always good translationese at that, to the prejudice of his own excellent Greek style, at least suggests the importance he attached to their reliability.

Furthermore, when we examine the doctrine of these speeches, it gives the appearance of being primitive and uncoordinated; certainly very different from that which prevailed in Luke's own day. Jesus is spoken of as the servant of God (3.13, 26, 4.27, 30), a title which did not retain currency in later Christology. He is called "a man approved by God" (2.22), a phrase which comes dangerously near adoptionism; and other titles are applied to him like "the prophet" (3.22, 7.37), "the righteous one" (3.14), "the prince" or "originator" of life (3.15, 5.31) which strike a primitive note and by no means savour of deliberate archaism. There is no thought-out doctrine of the atonement, of the church, of baptism even, to be found in the speeches, although the raw materials for later doctrinal formulations are there. Then again, the use of Old Testament citations in the speeches but not in the rest of the book is interesting. It suggests that this was not Luke's own method of preaching and teaching, but he knew that it was the apostolic one in the early days. The accuracy of his view has been demonstrated by Dodd's *According to the Scriptures* which shows how widespread in the early church was this appeal to certain passages of Scripture, which were seen as prophetic of the work of Christ and the Church.

Dodd has put us further in his debt by his earlier book *The Apostolic Preaching and its Developments*, in which he shows that there is a pattern

<hr>

[1] Thuc. *Hist.* 1.22.

[2] *Documents of the Primitive Church* (1941), and *Composition and Date of Acts* (1916).

[3] *An Aramaic Approach to the Gospels and Acts* (1946), though it is very sketchy on Acts.

of *kerygma*, the preached message, to be found in all these speeches; this pattern is almost exactly the same as that of Mark's Gospel as a whole, and many of the *pericopae* within it, and can be found with developments in Paul, Hebrews and John. He thus gives reason to suppose that we are on primitive ground in these speeches, and yet ground which is as independent of Paul in language as it is common with him in content.[1]

There are other straws in the wind. If the speeches were Lucan fabrications, there would have been still plenty of people alive to say as much, whether the Gospel and Acts saw the light in the 60's or the 80's. And the fact that Stephen's speech, for example, breaks off just before the distinctively Christian conclusions are drawn, suggests, at least to me, that we have here to do with authentic stuff. At all events, there is evidence enough to warrant our paying great attention to these speeches which purport to be so early. We shall try to see if they ring true, and if they contain what might reasonably have been preached in those early days. At the very least, they will show us what Luke, one of the "apostolic men", thought the primitive *kerygma* was. And no doubt he means us to see Peter's great sermon in Acts 2 as possessing a particular importance because it is to some extent determinative of what is to come after. So let us begin there.

At the very outset of the sermon, Peter is represented as quoting Joel 2.28-32 *in extenso*, concluding with "whoever shall call upon the name of the Lord shall be saved" (Acts 2.21). Joel, of course, was speaking of God's cataclysmic break into history of which the plague of locusts was a foretaste. He was looking to the last days, messianic days we might call them, in which the Spirit would be generally available; critical days in which God's judgement as well as his mercy would be revealed, days marked with cosmic signs, days that would drive many to repent and call on the name of the Lord. Those days would be days of salvation, for those who fulfilled the conditions.

On the day of Pentecost, Peter tells the crowds that these days have come. The essentially apocalyptic picture of Joel has been brought about by the human deliverer of prophetic expectation, the man of David's house (2.25, 30). This man bore the ancient name of "God the Saviour", Jesus. His mission was from God. It was proved to be so from the signs and wonders that God did by him in their midst, and these they could not deny. Having drawn their attention to the fulfilment of Scripture, the person of Jesus and the signs attesting that

---

[1] Needless to say, Dodd's thesis has been attacked, e.g. by D. E. Nineham, *Studies in the Gospels* (1955), pp. 223ff., and C. F. Evans (*J.T.S.*, 1956, pp. 25ff.) but their objections do nothing to disturb Dodd's main position (see his *Historical Tradition in the Fourth Gospel* (1963), p. 234).

person, Peter goes straight on to speak, not of his teaching, nor any other notable feature of his life, but of his shameful death upon a cross – the very last thing one would expect him to talk about. He had jibbed at the cross when first he had some inkling of Jesus's person and probable death (Mk. 8.29-33). It was the prospect of the cross that caused his denial of Jesus, and crushed all his hopes.

Yet now he glories in the cross. Not only does he dare to blame the religious leaders for their wickedness in putting Jesus there (2.23, 36, and this is a constant pattern, cf. 3.13-15, 4.10, 11, 5.30, etc.), but he claims that the fate of Jesus was no disaster. It had to happen. So far from putting out of court his claim to be the Messiah, it was all part of the eternal plan of God (2.23 cf. 3.18, 4.28).[1] God had proved it by raising him from the dead. Fantastic though this might seem to them, the resurrection is fact. It is attested not only by eyewitnesses (2.32, cf. 3.15, 4.20, 33, 5.32, etc., cf. 1 Cor. 15.6), but by their own Old Testament Scriptures as well. This is particularly plain in Ps. 110.1 and Ps. 16.6-11,[2] where David confesses that his descendant, who will sit upon his throne (2.30, cf. 2 Sam. 7.12, 13), is not only greater than himself (his "Lord") but will, instead of "seeing corruption", find life and joy in unclouded communion with God (2.28).

This, then, according to Peter, is what has happened. Jesus who died in shame has been raised in glory; he is even now with the Father in heaven; and his gift to his followers is the Holy Spirit who has already begun to transform them, by giving them a quickened understanding of Scripture, a tremendous courage, an infectious enthusiasm, and by turning them into men with a message. These historic events constitute Jesus as Messiah, and indeed Lord (2.36). This latter word, so frequently used of God in the Old Testament, was common in the Hellenistic world, and was applied to all sorts of cultic deities. Writers like Bousset[3] and Bultmann[4] think that it was taken over by Christianity from this background, and that therefore it is quite out of place in Palestinian Christianity, let alone on the lips of Peter at Pentecost. However they overlook or minimize two important points. The first is that the

[1] The necessity for the sufferings of the Messiah was a cardinal point in Christian apologetic. In 3.18 it is stated; in 26.23 (Greek) it is argued. In 1 Peter 1.11 it reappears, as it does in Lk. 24.26, 27, 46. The Old Testament does not specifically teach a suffering Messiah – but then it never speaks of a Messiah as such at all! It assuredly does look for a Suffering Servant, and the early Christians followed Jesus himself in interpreting his Messiahship in terms of the Servant prophecies.

[2] Ps. 16 is used not only here but in 13.35 and may have had wide currency in the early Church. But Ps. 110.1 was fundamental to the preaching of the Gospel, and is cited independently in Mark, Acts, Paul, Hebrews and 1 Peter. See Dodd, *According to the Scriptures*, p. 35.

[3] *Kyrios Christos* (1913).   [4] *Theology of the New Testament*, i., pp. 52f., 121ff.

worship of Jesus as Lord was firmly grounded in the Aramaic-speaking Church before ever it embarked on a programme of expansion, and we have the formula *marana-tha*[1] to prove it (1 Cor. 16.23). Paul is clearly quoting a very old prayer (or credal statement) here; it had a liturgical usage, as we see from *Didache* 10.6, and liturgy is notoriously conservative. This phrase anchors the worship of Jesus as "Lord" in the earliest Christian community, and there is no reason why Peter should not have used it here, particularly in view of the Joel prophecy. Peter sees that to call on the name of the Lord is to call on Jesus,[2] through whom this salvation is available. But perhaps an even more decisive reason why we must look for the origin of the worship of Jesus as Lord in the earliest Christian community is the fact that he is himself reported to have used that very passage of Scripture to which Peter here refers, in discussion with the scribes (Mk. 12.35ff. and parallels quoting Ps. 110.1).

[1] "O our Lord, come!" It is probably to be divided thus, and seen as a prayer, rather than *Maran-atha* ("Our Lord has come") and seen as a primitive creed. However much or little content they put into the word "Lord", which can, of course, mean anything from "sir" to "almighty God", it is remarkable because it is used as an *invocation*. One does not invoke a mere rabbi!

[2] What precisely is meant by "those that call upon the name of the Lord"? In a paper delivered to the Society for the Study of Theology in April, 1963, W. C. van Unnik argued that the phrase was a primitive self-designation of the early Church. It is found not only here but in 9.14, 21, 22.16, Rom. 10.13, 14, 1 Cor. 1.2, 2 Tim. 2.22, and, in a somewhat different form, in Acts 15.17 and James 2.7, Dr. van Unnik rejected as inadequate the normal explanations of the phrase as "those who pray to the Lord", "those who belong to the Lord" "those who worship the Lord", and "those who confess the Lord". He examined the Old Testament background of the term, and concluded that it denoted prayer from a man in distress directed towards God as his Saviour, a man who knew God, and trusted him to save him. And in Christian use it means having a living trust in Jesus as Saviour, through whom we will be saved. He argued that the background of distress was everywhere present in the New Testament, and that the characteristic of the Christian is to cry constantly to the Lord (Jesus) for help in the midst of a life which must inevitably be characterized by *thlipsis*, "affliction". This approach was most illuminating, but could it be that the phrase was brought into Christian usage more directly through Joel 2.32, where the distress, the calling on the name of the Lord, and the salvation are all specifically linked together? Dodd has shewn reason to suppose that this verse became a current *testimonium* in the early Church (*op. cit.*, pp. 47f.), as indeed its use in Rom. 10.13 among other proof texts from the Old Testament indicates. As Dr. van Unnik pointed out when dealing with the passage in Romans, Paul leaves the word he has been using, *homologeisthai* for *epikaleisthai* here in order to bring in the quotation from Joel. Salvation is not achieved even by confessing the name of the Lord, but by the Lord himself saving men. The whole context shows that salvation depends not on men but on God alone, and this consideration reinforces his conviction as to the proper meaning of *epikaleisthai ton theon*, to cast oneself on the saving mercy of God out of a background of danger, affliction and need.

The use of this psalm is as ancient as anything we can discover in the early Church, and its wording may well have determined Peter's language at this point. In the psalm David speaks of his descendant as Lord; and Peter is adding nothing new to it when he says, "God has made this same Jesus both Lord and Messiah" (Acts 2.36) – apart from applying it to Jesus. Thus it is not surprising to find that the earliest creed of all is the confession that "Jesus is Lord". It is obviously a traditional formula in 1 Cor. 12.3, and may well be as ancient in Phil. 2.11, another passage which seems to be pre-Pauline.[1]

This conviction of the present Lordship of Jesus shewed Peter what his Master had seen so clearly, that the eschatological event was split in two. He is already Lord – but the day of judgement is still to come (2.35). And in one of his other speeches in Acts Peter has a good deal more to say about this future element in salvation (3.19-26).

In view of these historic but eschatological events, it was clear that men must make up their minds, and decide whether they would commit themselves to the crucified Jesus, the risen Lord, or not. It would involve repentance (2.38) and of course belief (2.41, 44); it would also mean baptism in the name (that is to say, the character, the possession) of Jesus, if men were to receive the forgiveness and the Holy Spirit promised by the prophets. Just as the continuity of this new preaching with the Old Testament has been preserved, so here we see a strong link with the teaching of the Baptist. Like him, the early Christians required baptism of *Israelites*, thereby demanding a complete repudiation of any reliance on religious privilege or heritage, a recognition of the righteousness of God's judgement, and a trust in him to save. Peter's advance on John the Baptist, indeed, the fulfilment of what John had looked for, was to show the availability of the Spirit which he promised Jesus would give.[2]

The long-promised forgiveness and new power were meant for all, so Peter said (Acts 2.39), as he continued to quote Joel (2.28, 32). All could be saved if they would make a decisive break with the "untoward generation" of those who had rebelled against God's purpose.

[1] See R. P. Martin's *An Early Christian Confession* (1960), for a good summary of current discussion on Phil. 2.6-11, also Hunter *op. cit.*, pp. 122f. Jeremias, Cullmann and Bultmann all agree that this is a pre-Pauline hymn of great antiquity.

[2] As we have seen, the Messiah was closely associated with the Spirit in the Old Testament (e.g. Isa. 11.1f., 42.1, and particularly 61.1 – where the word "anoint", used of the Spirit, is of the same root as Messiah). This link is preserved in the play (in the Greek) on the word "Christ" and "anoint" with the Spirit in Acts 4.26f. For intertestamental hopes that the Messiah would not only be filled with the Spirit but offer him to others, see C. K. Barrett, *The Holy Spirit and the Gospel Tradition* (1947) pp. 42-45, where the evidence is readily grouped together; see also *supra*, pp. 93f. for the Qumran material.

These words echo Deut. 32.5, but Peter gives them a remarkable, indeed revolutionary, change of application (as does Paul in Phil. 2.15 – doubtless this became a piece of anti-Jewish apologetic). In Deuteronomy the words applied to renegade Israelites; here Peter applies them to all Israel (2.40)! Just as the prophets had sometimes seen Israel as a whole to be apostate (e.g. Hos. 1.6, 9), just as Jesus has said much the same of the generation of Israelites who rejected their Saviour (Lk. 9.41, 11.29, 17.25), so Peter proclaims that Israel as a whole has ceased to be Israel. It has crucified Israel's hoped-for Messiah, and repudiated the promised salvation. That is why, in order to be saved, Peter's hearers had to make a clean break with this attitude of the majority of their countrymen.

Their decision was, of course, individual; but salvation meant integration into a community of those "who were being saved" (2.47), a community which, in repentance, faith and baptism had committed themselves without reserve to Jesus as Messiah, a community bound together in a common belief, a common worship and a common fellowship (2.42-47). Their salvation was a present experience between the past and the future terms in salvation. So here in this first speech in Acts we have the essence of the primitive *kerygma*. The same pattern reappears, with minor variations, in the other speeches (3.12-26, 4.8-12, 5.29-32, 10.34-43, 13.16-41, etc.) and, as Dodd has shewn, throughout the New Testament there *was* a common basis to the early preaching. And "salvation" was one of the most comprehensive words they used to describe its contents. It became, probably very early, a technical term to sum up all the blessings brought about by the gospel. Thus we find the New Testament writers speaking of "the gospel of your salvation" (Eph. 1.13), "the gospel . . . by which ye are saved" (1 Cor. 15.1, 2), "the words of this salvation" (Acts 13.26), "our common salvation" (Jude 3), and "the grace of God that bringeth salvation" (Tit. 2.11). In contrast to all the previous deliverances which God had wrought, in Jesus he had introduced *the ultimate* in salvation; just as, in contrast with all the previous fragmentary revelations of himself which God had given, the person of Jesus enshrined the ultimate in revelation (Heb. 1.1, 2). Jesus, they were convinced, had brought in a salvation as historic and as total as that of the Exodus, and much more far-reaching; for it was an "everlasting salvation" (Heb. 5.9), the salvation of the age to come.

The uniqueness of Jesus's salvation is nowhere more clearly emphasized than in Acts 4.12. It is, as the context shows, a salvation which concerns the whole man (*sōzein* is ambivalent in 4.9, 12, as it is so often in the Gospels). It is made possible through Jesus of Nazareth, crucified, risen and active in his disciples. He was "the stone set at nought by you builders", says Peter courageously (as he uses the text from Ps. 118.22 which his Master had used before him, Mk. 12.10), and through God's action he "is become the head of the corner". This verse became an important one among the early Christians. It comes from a psalm sung at all the festivals, and Jewish Christians would never be able to forget its words, and the striking light they shed on the fate of Jesus. There are, in fact, many verbal links between this psalm and the whole incident of the healing of the lame man to which this speech is the sequel. "The gate of the Lord" which "the righteous enter" (Ps. 118.20) corresponds with "the gate of the temple" (Acts 3.2) which the restored cripple (now made "righteous"?) "enters" (3.8). "This is the Lord's doing, and it is marvellous in our eyes" of the psalmist (118.23) is matched by Peter's insistence that the healing is God's doing (Acts 3.12, 16), and by the repeated statements that the crowd "marvelled" (3.10, 11, 12). "I will praise thee, for thou hast heard me and art become my salvation" (Ps. 118.21) is illustrated by the man who has been "saved" (Acts 4.9, 12) "praising God" (Acts 3.8, 9). In short, the idea of God's salvation is quite a feature of Ps. 118 (21, 25), as it is of this man's cure (Acts 4.9, 12). Just as the salvation teaching of ch. 2 is based on Joel, so here in chs. 3 and 4 we have another important Old Testament quarry for the references to salvation, not only in the words from Ps. 118 that are specifically cited, but in their whole context.[1] "Thou art become my salvation," cries the psalmist. "Neither is there salvation in any other," proclaims the apostle. In so doing he has quite deliberately applied to Jesus the words spoken of God in the Old Testament, as he did in ch. 8. He is clear that in Jesus God is uniquely at work. He accepts the scandal of the cross, and once again glories in it, claiming that God has reversed it by the resurrection. The divine *peripeteia* of cross and resurrection is seen both as the vindication of Jesus and the condemnation of the Jews.

But Peter goes farther than in his first speech, or so it would seem. He stresses that salvation is something given, and that it is something available and necessary for all mankind. There is no salvation to be found in any additional saviour (*allo*); nor is there any alternative way (*heteron*) of salvation (4.12). It is to be found in him (remarkable phrase, suggestive of the characteristic New Testament "in Christ"), and in him alone. Already we meet the scandal of particularity which made the gospel so hard for the Greek to accept, accustomed as he was to find his wisdom in universals; already, too, the proclamation of a

[1] This, for what it is worth, provides some slight support for the argument of Dodd's *According to the Scriptures* that the early Church did not ransack the Old Testament for isolated proof texts, but more often than not had in mind whole passages, to which the words actually quoted were intended to act as a pointer.

crucified Messiah as the way of salvation, a proposition which seemed to the Jew to be a contradiction in terms (cf. 1 Cor. 1.23).

This concentration of salvation in the person of Jesus prepares us to some extent for ch. 5 where he is given the title "Saviour" by Peter (5.31). This recurs in 13.23 but not elsewhere in Acts. It is applied to Jesus once in Luke (2.11), once each in the Gospel and Epistle of John, and infrequently until the Pastorals and 2 Peter. The reason for this is difficult to determine. Cullmann thinks that the common use of the title was late because it "presupposes the Christology of the exalted Kyrios";[1] and it is possible, I think, that the use of the term in Hellenistic religions and the Imperial Cult gave pause to the Christians in applying it to Jesus. Under Nero and Domitian it probably had a polemical meaning, denying that the emperor is *Sōtēr*.

However, it may well have been used in Jewish-Christian circles quite early. For one thing Jesus means "God the Saviour", and Matthew was certainly not the first person to realize that (1.21). The link between Jesus's name and his work of dealing with sin must have been apparent from the earliest days of the Church. For another, the early Christians were certain that in Jesus God was uniquely at work saving men; and Saviour was a common title for God in the Old Testament. But quite apart from this, men in whom God was at work were often called saviours in the Old Testament, as we saw in ch. 1. Perhaps this helps to account for the usage in the Pastorals, where both God and Jesus are called Saviour (e.g. Tit. 2.13[2]). And thirdly, when "save" and "salvation" are so often applied to Jesus, it is not difficult to see how the title of "Saviour" became attached to him also.[3]

It is important, therefore, to notice in what connection he is called Saviour here. It is as one who was *hanged upon a tree* by men, and raised by God to give repentance and remission of sins. Never is *xulon* used of the cross in non-biblical Greek. The allusion is to Deut. 21.22f., "He that is hanged upon a tree is accursed of God." This frank recognition of the meaning of the cross is found also in 10.39, 13.29, Gal. 3.13, 1 Pet. 2.24, and possibly underlies the "tree of life" in Rev. 22.2, 14, 19. It meant that to Jewish eyes Christ hung in the place of cursing. Hence the scandal of a crucified Messiah; not only did he fail to rid them of their enemies, but his end shewed that he rested under the curse of God. Hence, perhaps, the cries of execration, "Anathema Jesus!" of which we read in 1 Cor. 12.3. Neither Peter, here and in 10.39, nor Paul in 13.29 give a rationale of the cross, as they were both

[1] *Op. cit.*, p. 243.
[2] See also the title used first of God and then of Jesus in Tit. 3.4, 6; Lk. 1.47, 2.11.
[3] See F. F. Bruce in *The Saviour God* (1963), pp. 51ff.

to do later.[1] They had not yet, perhaps, grasped the significance of all
that Jesus accomplished in that place of curse. But from the earliest
days they express the conviction that the one hanging upon that
accursed tree was acting as Saviour, and a Saviour from sins at that.[2]
They see that the curse was reversed by the act of God which raised
him from the dead, and vindicated him completely. That is why he is
able now to lead men to repentance and offer them forgiveness.[3] We
have here an interpretation of the cross, which it is entirely credible
that the early Christians could have used. It is not worked out into a
coherent theology; but they know the cross dealt somehow with
sins, and that the resurrection proves that the curse has been exhausted.
Jesus died in the place of cursing. That is agreed by Christians and non-
Christians alike. Jesus was raised and exalted by God. That is agreed
by Christians and cannot be gainsaid by the others. Jesus is therefore
Saviour. Cullmann comments, "We are clearly in the realm of Jewish
Christian thought here; Christ is *Sōtēr* because he has saved from sins."[4]
   In these speeches of Peter, then, the work of salvation has always been
specifically related to an Old Testament passage (Joel 2, Ps. 118, Deut. 21)
which has been reinterpreted in the light of the staggering events of the
life, death, resurrection and ascension of Jesus of Nazareth. It is not a
salvation of the soul alone,[5] but a total salvation, an historic deliverance.
It brings the age to come into the present, together with forgiveness
of sins and the gift of the Spirit. It opens up vistas of sharing God's life
after death (3.15, 5.31,[6] and most clearly in 3.19-21) though these are not
explored; the early Christians were too full of the present gift to wonder
overmuch about what lies ahead. This is a picture which is eminently
credible; the doctrine of salvation is entirely Jewish as opposed to
Greek, though naturally the eschatology has been altered by the teaching

[1] In 1 Pet. 2.24 Peter sees Jesus going up to that place of cursing, bowed down
with the load of *our* sins which he took to the tree, in fulfilment of Isaiah ch. 53.
Perhaps some inkling of that was with him from very soon after the resurrection,
for in Acts he calls Jesus "Servant" in 3.13, 26, cf. 4.25, 27, 30. In Gal. 3.10, 13,
Paul recognizes that Jesus, in dying on the tree, indeed bore the curse; but the
curse he bore was *ours*, deserved by our breaking of God's law. And in Revelation
the tree of curse and death becomes for believers the tree of blessing and life,
the counterpart of the tree of life in the primeval garden of God (Gen. 3.22).

[2] Note the juxtaposition of 5.30, 31, 2.36-38, 3.18, 19.

[3] 2.38, 5.31, 10.43.   [4] *Op. cit.*, p. 243.

[5] Indeed the soul is never mentioned.

[6] ἀρχηγός means not only prince or leader, but founder, originator. He is the
leader, the pioneer in the life of the age to come; he is also its initiator so that his
followers may enter. See Bruce's comment on Acts 3.15 τὸν ἀρχηγὸν τῆς ζωῆς
'The Author of life': in Aram. this could be the same as τὸν ἀρχηγὸν τῆς σωτηρίας
in Heb. 2.10, as Aram. ḥayyē is the equivalent of both ζωή and σωτηρία" (*The
Acts of the Apostles* (1950), p. 109).

of Jesus on the subject, and supremely by his death and resurrection. Peter's other speeches have little to add. In 11.14 the word *sōthēnai* is a synonym for entering the realm of the Holy Spirit through the preaching of the Word, faith and baptism. Then there is an interesting contrast, in 15.1, 11 between Jewish Christians who had, and those who had not, emerged from the legalism and the anthropocentric hopes of salvation current in debased quarters of late Judaism. The latter still saw salvation as the fruit of human ritual and ethic. Peter, however, had come to see that salvation is by grace, not by works; achieved by Christ, not by human attainments; and designed for all men, not merely for Jews. Incidentally, this verse shows Peter actually using the word "be saved" of the *future* state of the Christian to which he had referred in different terminology in 3.19ff.

There are two remaining passages which deal with salvation and they are quite important. Both are connected with Paul; the first comes in a sermon, the second is addressed to an individual.

The sermon of Acts 13 was, we are told, preached in Pisidian Antioch, where there were vast numbers of Diaspora Jews, who doubtless spoke Greek. Indeed, the juxtaposition of the two words "a Saviour, Jesus" (13.23) could only be made in Greek; in Aramaic it would be tautologous, *Yeshu'a Yeshu'a*. This Saviour is seen as the longed-for King of David's line. Paul's language reflects 1 Sam. 13.14, Ps. 89.20, and the actual promise is found in various places in the Old Testament (e.g. 2 Sam. 7.12, 22.51, Ps. 132.16, 17). Both these last two references state that in fulfilling this prophecy God will bring in salvation, and this may account for the use of the title "Saviour" here. Clearly one of the uppermost themes in the context is that of the kingly rule exercised by great David's greater son. And this takes us back to yet another strand in the Old Testament conception of salvation.

In 13.26 it is made clear that this salvation is meant, in the first instance, for Jews and "God-fearers", as Gentile adherents of the synagogue were called. It is the culmination of God's saving activity displayed in the whole history of Israel. The content of the *kerygma* is much the same as in Peter's speeches.[1] Once again we find the use of

[1] It is frequently a matter for complaint among those who doubt the historicity of these speeches that the Pauline speeches are too Petrine, and Peter's speeches too Pauline. Why should not the essence of the primitive *kerygma* have been common ground for both? Indeed, it is impossible to explain the growth of the early Church if they spoke with a divided voice. The attitude betrayed by such criticism is, as J. Munck has shown, an unrecognized but real vestige of the discredited Tübingen hypothesis (*Paul and the Salvation of Mankind* (1959), especially ch. 3).

Psalm 16. In addition, Paul uses Ps. 2.7 to prove the Messiahship of Jesus. It is just possible that this text was applied to the Messiah in pre-Christian times,[1] and if so might have been common ground between Paul and his Jewish hearers. In any case, it rapidly became an important text for the early Christians (Heb. 1.5, 5.5, 7.28) and is embedded deep in the story of the Baptism of Jesus (Mk. 1.11 and parallels; 2 Pet. 1.17).

Paul makes two other significant Old Testament allusions, which shed light upon what he means by the salvation terminology of 13.23, 26, 47 and, incidentally, relate to what he wrote in his epistles. In the first place, he proclaims forgiveness of sins through Jesus (13.38), and tells them that the justification which was impossible by the law of Moses is possible in Christ.[2] He then quotes Hab. 1.5 to warn them that they must come to terms with God's offer of salvation (13.40, 41). In Habakkuk this was a warning of the approaching terrors of the Chaldaean invasion. Here it becomes a warning of God's rejection of rebellious Israel as manifested in those who reject the gospel. Paul, in fact, is working with exactly the same ideas as Peter in Acts 2.40, and Jesus before him. The sequel is described in 13.47, the turning point of Acts. Having consistently preached to the Jews first, and been largely rejected, Paul sees the Gentile mission as the logical outcome. "Behold, we turn to the Gentiles."

How was Paul to justify this momentous step? He turned to the Songs of the Servant, which had so influenced the teaching and death of Jesus. All that Paul did was to carry out the implications of what was clearly there in the sacred Scriptures of the Old Testament. He saw that the Servant had a mission not only to fallen Israel but also to the Gentiles. "I have set thee a light to the Gentiles, to be my salvation unto the end of the earth" (Isa. 49.6). Simeon had foreseen that Jesus would fulfil this role (Lk. 2.32). But he could not be the light for all men until he had died for all men. It was left to that "body" of Jesus consisting of the Christian Church (Acts 9.4)[3] to fulfil the destined role of the Servant of the Lord.[4] It is on this authority that Paul and his friends turn to the Gentiles to preach the gospel to them; "for thus the

[1] See Strack-Billerbeck, *Kommentar zum neuen Testament aus Talmud und Midrasch* (1922), vol. 3, pp. 15-22.

[2] It is interesting that the only speech in Acts where this word "justify" is used should be Paul's speech here. Justification is said to be *in Christ*, another Pauline touch. It is interesting to note that Paul again quotes Hab. 2.4 for his doctrine of justification in Rom. 1.17, etc.

[3] Paul thought he was persecuting the Church, but he found, on the Damascus road, that he was persecuting Jesus. Was it here that he saw for the first time the solidarity between Christ and his people that later became so important a part of his theology in metaphors like the body?

[4] See A. T. Hanson's *The Church of the Servant* (1962), esp. ch. 3, where this is worked out in detail.

Lord commanded us" (13.47). This same prophecy of Isaiah, and the other Servant Songs, meant a good deal to St. Paul, and he makes a number of allusions to them in his letters. Indeed this very passage of Isa. 49 is in his mind in 2 Cor. 6.2 when he quotes verse 8, "For he saith, I have heard thee in a time accepted, and in the day of salvation have I succoured thee." And Paul comments with exultation, "Behold now is the accepted time; behold now is the day of salvation." The Church carries on the work of its ascended Lord. It is the Church of the Servant.

Ch. 16 brings us to pagan soil, the Roman colony of Philippi. We see here the Gentile mission in operation. Paul preached to such effect that Lydia, an Asian businesswoman, believed and was baptized. A slave girl whom Luke calls a "pythoness", that is to say a woman inspired by the god Apollo, followed the missionaries around, and advertised them as the "servants of the most high God" who proclaimed "the way of salvation" (16.16f.). Gone are the days when it was thought impossible for a pagan medium to speak in such terms.[1] The longing for salvation was prevalent throughout the ancient world (as we saw in ch. 4) and "the most high God"[2] was a title for the supreme deity among the Jews and pagans alike.[3] Apollo was primarily a saviour in the sense of healer;[4] he was the god of prophecy and divination;[5] and in Rome from the time of Augustus[6] he was virtually equated with Jupiter Optimus Maximus – the most high god! And it was the slave of this healer god, this inspired god, this most high god, who recognized in a superior power a greater inspiration and a better saviour. She was not disappointed, but came to taste the salvation she had recognized.

The jailer uses the same word, "What must I do to be saved?" (16.30). Perhaps he used it in a neutral sense, meaning, "What must I do to be safe?" i.e. from the results of the earthquake, the escape and the inevitable enquiry that would follow. Probably, however, his request

[1] See W. M. Ramsay, *Bearing of Recent Discovery on the Trustworthiness of the New Testament* (1915), pp. 136ff. and 173-98, and his *Teaching of Paul in Terms of the Present Day* (1913), pp. 95ff.

[2] Professor C. F. D. Moule has kindly drawn my attention to an article on 'The Guild of Zeus Hypsistos' in *Harvard Theological Review* (1936), pp. 39ff.

[3] See Westcott's note on Heb. 7.1 and Pearson on *The Creed* (1859), p. 136, for a conspectus of the evidence, also *T.W.N.T.*, vii, p. 1006 (Götter als σωτῆρες). As we have seen, "Saviour" was a common Old Testament name for God. It was meaningful both for Jew and pagan.

[4] He was addressed as Apollo Paean, Apollo Medice, by the Romans (Macrobius, *Sat.* 1.17.15).

[5] The Delphic Oracle was his shrine; that is why he was called the Pythian god, after the snake (python) of Delphi. Hence, too, the name pythoness for his female prophetesses.

[6] Augustus venerated him highly, and built him a temple on the Palatine, because his famous victory of Actium occurred near the temple of Apollo.

went deeper. Is it too much to suppose that he shared the hunger of antiquity for salvation, and that he had heard the persistent way in which the pythoness claimed that these men held the answer to that hunger? At all events, he asked them, perhaps hardly knowing what he asked. Paul, needless to say, turns this unexpected opportunity to good use. He tells the man of the salvation Jesus came to bring, "Believe on the Lord Jesus Christ and thou shalt be saved, and thy house" (16.31). He meets this inchoate hunger for salvation with the message for which it was a *praeparatio evangelica*. The jailer must believe in the Lordship and the Messiahship of Jesus. He must be baptized. And so he gathers his household to share in the good tidings which he is beginning to grasp; Paul and Silas preach "the word of the Lord" to them, and the whole household (i.e. including slaves) is baptized. Faith and baptism link them with the Saviour. It is important to notice the communal or societary aspect of salvation here. We are only told that the jailer believed (16.34 – singular in the Greek); nevertheless, both he and his household were baptized. The family solidarity in baptism[1] goes back to the predominant Old Testament concept of salvation; thus Noah and his house are saved (Gen. 7.1), as are Abraham and his seed (Gen. 17.4, 5). The head of the household acts on behalf of his house both for good and evil in the Old Testament, and that presumably is the reason for the repeated reference to the baptism of whole households in the New Testament when, as here, it is only specifically stated that the head of the house believes.[2] Here, then, in this jail at Philippi we find salvation achieved by Christ, received in faith, sealed in baptism. It was a present possession, and it was marked by some of the characteristics of life in the new age, such as exultation, fellowship, good deeds and love – all proof that the Holy Spirit had become present, though in this instance he is not mentioned.

Such was the earliest preaching of salvation, according to the speeches in Acts. Its main points were common to the whole of the New Testament. It was a historic salvation achieved by Jesus of Nazareth, acting as God's representative. It was connected with his death upon the cross, as their use of several Old Testament texts and the whole concept of the Servant makes plain, though the link between the death of Christ and the forgiveness of sins is never made quite explicit in these speeches.[3] Salvation was from sin's guilt and power, into the

[1] On this whole point see P. Ch. Marcel, *The Biblical Doctrine of Infant Baptism* (E.T. 1953), pp. 63–95; J. Jeremeias, *Infant Baptism in the First Four Centuries* (E.T. 1960), especially pp. 19ff.

[2] Acts 11.14, 16.15, 33, 18.8, 1 Cor. 1.16.

[3] The nearest to a *doctrine* of the atonement is 20.28, where the Church is seen as brought into God's ownership at the cost of his own blood, or better, at the cost of the blood (i.e. the death) of his Own One (i.e. Jesus).

life of the age to come which was made present through the Holy Spirit, and was now, as the prophets had promised, available to all who would repent, believe and be baptized. Salvation involved a new relationship not only with God and Jesus, but with other believers, and manifested itself in the new quality of life. All this, they were convinced, was in accordance with the Scriptures of the Old Testament, which they unhesitatingly used in order to make good their claim before their Jewish hearers. The whole of mankind, Jew and Gentile, came within the scope of this salvation of God; it concerned the whole man, too. Springing entirely from God's initiative and love for sinful men, it could only be received in simple faith, not earned by any merit.[1] It was entered individually as each man was baptized into the name of Jesus, from henceforth dedicated to him as Lord of his life. But it brought the believer into a community, the kingdom of God, and thus involved him in a new relationship with brother Christians, and a new attitude of responsibility towards those who did not yet share this good news of salvation. It spoke, too, albeit sketchily, of a future with God, in an endless life which Jesus had pioneered by his resurrection.

There is no carefully thought out soteriology in the Acts of the Apostles. That is to be expected. These men knew from their experience that Jesus was the bringer of that ultimate salvation of which all the Old Testament prophets had spoken. "This is that which was spoken by the prophet," said Peter, and it was the conviction they all shared. *This is that!* The days of salvation had dawned. The Last Day, the day of the age to come, had become a present reality to them through the achievements of the Messiah and the gift of the Spirit. Experience preceded theology, and these men rejoiced in salvation as a glorious reality. Reflection on the significance of these great events would come later. It would not add anything to what they experienced and what they preached, though it would interpret it. But they were so conscious of their risen and ascended Lord, and his ability to save men by curing their ills, forgiving their sins and giving them the Holy Spirit, the mark of the new age, that they "went everywhere preaching the word" (Acts 8.4) and before long "turned the world upside down" (Acts 17.6) with their gospel of a God who has saved men from their sins, can save them from themselves, and will save them eternally.

[1] As if to emphasize that the movement from "lost" to "saved" is accomplished by God's grace alone, not by any human process of "spiritualization", the verb is most frequently employed in the passive. Salvation, like baptism its sacrament, is done *for* us; we are recipients, not contributors.

CHAPTER 9

Salvation in the Thought of Paul

St. Paul has a great deal more to say about salvation than any other New Testament writer: about as much, in fact, as all the rest of them put together. This is only partly because there is more of Paul than of anyone else in the Canon. It is no less due to the fact that salvation is at the very heart of St. Paul's theology.

It has been customary, since the Reformation at all events, for Protestants to see "justification by faith" as the key which unlocks the thought of the great apostle; important though it is, however, particularly in Romans and Galatians when he is defending the gospels against legalism, justification is not wide enough to express Paul's Christianity. It concerns only the past, and there is more to the Christian life than that. Seeing this, Deissmann began what has proved an influential trend by regarding the phrase "in Christ" as the key thought of St. Paul. Union with Christ, both individually and corporately, is indeed of vital importance to Paul, but it is no more comprehensive a description than justification. It concerns only the present,[1] and there is more to the Christian life than that.

Salvation has, perhaps, a better claim than either to come near to the heart of Christianity according to Paul. For to him salvation covers past, present and future. It is the total work of God in Christ for man. God has come to man's rescue. As a result of what he has done, man has been saved from the need to remain alienated from God; man can be saved from the spiritual foes of fear, defeat and doubt which dog his path; and man will, one day, be saved from the very presence of corruption of any kind, enjoying the glorious liberty of children of God, in his presence where nothing that defiles can enter in (Rom. 8.21, Rev. 21.27). Whether or not it is apocryphal, the story told of Bishop Westcott and the Salvation Army girl is instructive. They happened to be travelling in the same railway compartment, and the Salvation Army girl, seeing that her companion was a bishop, had the

[1] The New Testament knows well that there was a time when the Christian was not yet in Christ. It speaks, too, of the future bliss of the believer in different terms. The Christian dead are "with Christ" (Phil. 1.23, 1 Thess. 4.14, 17).

gravest doubts whether he could possibly be a Christian. So she plucked up her courage and asked him if he were saved. Westcott was reading his Greek Testament, and replied, "Do you mean *sōtheis*, *sōzomenos*, or *sōthēsomenos*?" What the Salvation Army girl made of that is not recorded, but the bishop's reply succinctly summarizes the way in which Paul uses the term. Salvation is indeed in three tenses. It is the work of God "who has delivered . . . who does deliver . . . and in whom we trust that he will yet deliver" (2 Cor. 1.10). It will be convenient to follow this chronological distinction as we attempt to examine Paul's development of the doctrine of salvation.

A. SALVATION AS A PAST EVENT

In contrast to a good deal of pietistic and evangelical usage, St. Paul does not often speak of salvation as a thing of the past. He would not, I think, have been too happy to say, "I was saved on such and such a day", because he was intensely aware that salvation, in its fullness, was something that belonged to God's future. Accordingly, most of his references speak of this future aspect of salvation. Nevertheless, for him as for all the New Testament writers, the unitary eschatological event of Jewish expectation has been shattered by the coming of Jesus. The age to come is no longer entirely future. It has invaded this age in the person of Jesus, and this bridgehead is, so to speak, kept open and indeed enlarged by the presence in the Church of the Holy Spirit. He it is who is described by Paul as the *aparchē*, the firstfruits of the age to come (Rom. 8.23). He whose coming was promised in the last days (Joel 2.28) has come, since Pentecost, into the hearts and lives of believers; so much so that, "If any man have not the Spirit of Christ, he is none of his" (Rom. 8.9).

The early Christians, in short, were confident that 'the last days' had broken in upon them (Acts 2.17, Heb. 1.2, 1 Jn. 2.18), and that they tasted even now the powers of the age to come (Heb. 6.5). Of that justification, that acquittal before the ultimate Judge, which properly belonged to the last day, the Christians were assured *now* (Rom. 5.1, 8.1); of that final salvation, involving deliverance, safety and victory which also belonged to the age to come, they were no less confident. The man in Christ is justified, and he is saved. Paul dares to say that in several places. Could realized eschatology go further?

There are, in fact, four places where Paul speaks of salvation in the past tense, once in Romans (8.24), twice in Ephesians (2.5, 8), and twice in the Pastorals[1] (2 Tim. 1.9, Tit. 3.5). To these we must add Tit. 2.11,

[1] I shall without discussion take the Pastoral Epistles along with the other Paulines partly because, together with Spicq (*Les Epîtres Pastorales* (1947)),

153

where the rare adjective *sōtērios* is applied to the incarnation; 1 Tim. 2.6 where Christ's death is interpreted in terms of the ransom metaphor derived ultimately, I believe, from Isa. 53, via Mk. 10.45; a few occasions where the language of redemption (bringing to mind the *go'el* and *padah* of the Old Testament) is used of a past deliverance (Rom. 3.24, Eph. 1.7, Col. 1.14, Tit. 2.14); and a couple where the simple verb *rhuomai* is relevant (Col. 1.13, 1 Thess. 1.10).

Now the remarkable thing about these verses is that they maintain the tension between the past and the future of which we have just spoken. Christ "gave himself as a counter-ransom for all", yes, but "to be witnessed to at his proper time" (? the parousia, 1 Tim. 2.6). "The grace of God that brings salvation *has* appeared" – certainly; but it is intimately connected with the blessed hope of the Saviour's future appearance in glory (Tit. 2.11, 13). In Tit. 3.5 we read that "by his mercy he saved us ... that we should be heirs according to the hope of eternal life" (3.7). In Eph. 2 the eschatological emphasis is strong in the immediate context of 2.5, 8; so it is in the context of Eph. 1.7 and Col. 1.12, 13. In fact the significance of each of these references to a past salvation could not be better summed up than in Rom. 8.24, "we were saved", indeed, but only "in hope". There is in Paul a deep understanding of what Bultmann calls "the Christian's betweenness".[1] We enjoy here and now an authentic first instalment of salvation; but the best is yet to be.

Nevertheless, when the existence of this eschatological tension between the "already" and the "not yet" has been emphasized, the fact remains that Paul does say that the Christian has been saved. What does he mean by this? What are the enemies from which we have been delivered?

(i) *What have we been saved from?*

Simply to ask this question is to see how far we have moved from the Old Testament use of the term. There salvation from sin was the exception; in Paul it is the rule. True, he does, on occasion, talk of salvation from perils like lawsuits (2 Tim. 4.18), illness (2 Cor. 1.6-10) enemies (Rom. 15.31) and, for the woman, deliverance through the dangers of childbearing (if that is what 1 Tim. 2.15 means), but these

Jeremias (*Die Pastoralbriefe* (1953)), Guthrie (*New Testament Introduction: the Pauline Epistles* (1961)) and, most recently, J. N. D. Kelly (*The Pastoral Epistles* (1963)), I think it most probable that these letters were written by Paul; and partly because in any case the doctrine of salvation is precisely the same in the Pastorals as in the Paulines (see C. K. Barrett, *The Pastoral Epistles* (1963), pp. 21ff. He does not regard these letters as coming from St. Paul, but can find no significant difference in the doctrine of salvation).

[1] *The Theology of the New Testament* (1955), vol. ii, p. 185.

are peripheral usages for him, whilst in the Old Testament they were central. Salvation to Paul is nothing less than deliverance for man from all his spiritual foes, from all that keeps him in alienation from God and in thraldom to evil powers. We shall gain a good idea of what he means if we look at the four main contexts where he claims that we have been saved.

(a) Salvation from the old aeon

Rom. 8.24 comes in a chapter which is the culmination of the doctrinal part of Romans. Few have put the situation more clearly than Nygren,[1] who understands Paul to be saying in chs. 5-8 of Romans that we have been delivered in Christ from the four great foes that held the human race in bondage. The Christian is saved from wrath (ch. 5), from sin (ch. 6) from law (ch. 7) and from death (ch. 8).

It is probably a mistake to try to separate too distinctly these destroying powers which rule in the old aeon. They belong together, and together they make life so hopeless for man left to his own devices. But they deserve at any rate a cursory glance, if we are to understand the human plight as Paul saw it.

(i) The basic trouble is sin. Ever since the first man disobeyed God and went his own rebellious way, sin has entered God's world and spoiled man's life (Rom. 5.12ff.). Sins, to Paul, are by no means unconnected failures of various sorts. They are the fruit of a principle of evil which is endemic in our nature. As he puts it in one graphic metaphor, sin is a master, a slave owner (Rom. 6.16); we are sold under sin (7.14) and therefore act as slaves of sin (6.17) and do sin's wishes (6.19). Eventually, if we do not come into living contact with the Deliverer, we shall draw sin's wage, which is death (6.23). If we ask what Paul means by sin, the combined nuances of three of the words he uses for it will give us a good idea.

Sin is *parabasis*, for one thing. It is the deliberate breaking of divine law (Rom. 2.23, 25, 27, etc.). It is what Adam did when he deliberately disobeyed God's plain command (5.14). It is what the man with standards does every time he breaks them (2.23). Sin is also, and most frequently in Paul, described as *hamartia*, "missing the mark" – the metaphor was originally drawn from archery. All have sinned, i.e. come short of the mark for human conduct, the glory of God (3.23). What that "glory" or glorious standard of God is can be seen from the life of Jesus (2 Cor. 4.6). All, whatever their respective merits, fall far short of *that* quality of life. A third devastating description of sin can be seen in the word *anomia*, "lawlessness". "We have turned every one to his own way" was how the prophet

[1] *Commentary on Romans* (1952).

described this attitude we adopt of keeping God out of our lives (Isa. 53.6). Like the men in the parable, we say of God, "We will not have this man to reign over us" (Lk. 19.14). Transgression of God's laws, falling short of God's standards, rebellion against God's loving rule; this to Paul is what is meant by sin, and it holds sway over Jew and Gentile alike (Rom. chs. 1-3), so that "all the world is guilty before God" (3.19).

(ii) Sin finds a surprising ally in the Law. This is conceived of in a number of slightly different ways in Paul's letters, but God's standard, as set out in the Decalogue, the Five Books of Moses, or the whole Old Testament covers most of these. The Law thus conceived is "holy and just and good" (Rom. 7.12). It is God-given and enshrines his principles for human life, but as a means of communion with God it is wholly defective. While it is true that if any man could keep the Law he would be fit for life with God (Rom. 10.5), the fact is that nobody keeps it (Rom. 3.19, 22f.). So far then from being an agent of life, the Law becomes an agent of death (Rom. 7.9, 10). It is not, of course, the Law that "kills". If there were no such thing as sin, the Law would not be a power of destruction. It would merely delimit the path of duty in which we were in any case walking. But because sin has taken hold of us, the Law finds itself in a paradoxical situation. God-given though it is, it exposes sin (Rom. 7.7, 13), it inflames sin and brings it out of seclusion into open disobedience (Rom. 7.7, 8). Paul knew from bitter experience that an explicit "Thou shalt not" produces the reaction "I most certainly will". Moreover, the Law was powerless either to pardon the sinner or to give him the power to start a new life (Rom. 3.20, 1 Cor. 15.56). For all these reasons the Law which was meant to be a friend became an enemy to man, particularly to religious man. The Jew thought that his possession of the Law gave him some sort of a claim on God; in fact it merely increased his guilt (Rom. 2.17-29). Nor was all this a failure of God's plan. He never intended the Law to be a means of salvation. He *meant* it to expose sin and to lead men to trust the divine mercy (Rom. 5.20f.). In the long view, it was intended to lead men to Christ (Gal. 3.24). But because the Jews chose to treat the Law as a ground for claiming merit (thus effectively depersonalizing the relationship with God) it became not a stepping-stone but a stumbling-block. The rabbis called the Law "the strength of Yahweh"; Paul, with deeper insight, recognized it as "the strength of sin" (1 Cor. 15.56).

(iii) Naturally, this rebellion of self-centred man, fortified as it was by a legalistic self-righteousness, provoked the wrath of God, which to Paul is the third of the forces of destruction operative in human society. This is a concept which is given little prominence in current Christian thought, but it figures prominently enough in the New

Testament, and particularly in Paul. "The wrath of God is his personal (though never malicious, or in a bad sense, emotional) reaction against sin."[1] "The relation of man to God being one of hostility," wrote T. W. Manson, referring to Rom. 5.10, "the corresponding relation of God to man is also described in one word – wrath. This is not an affective condition in God, corresponding to what we should call 'anger' or 'rage'. It is rather to be defined as the will of God as opposed to evil."[2] And it is a very serious thing. It is already at work in the world (Rom. 1.18), judicially giving over sinners to the sin they have chosen (see the threefold "God gave them up" in Rom. 1.24, 26, 28); for there is as indissoluble a connection between transgression, law and wrath as there is between faith, the promise and grace (4.14f.). Moreover, wrath has a future consummation (2.5). Indeed, like salvation and justification, it is primarily a word which refers to the age to come but like them is proleptically experienced in the present.

(iv) Death is the last of the four powers which hold men in subjection. It is, of course, a natural phenomenon, but was seen by the Jews to be sacramental as well. It speaks of separation from God. This is most clearly brought out in the Genesis story to which Paul so often refers. God had told Adam that disobedience would mean death (2.17). The tempter had told Eve, "Ye shall not surely die" (3.4). But die they did. They died physically later on; whether or not physical death would have come to man, had there been no Fall, we have no means of knowing. But death in its totality is certainly seen in the Bible as penal, the result of sin. For by death the biblical writers do not merely mean physical dissolution. Adam and Eve died spiritually as soon as they had tasted the forbidden fruit. They immediately sought separation from God (Gen. 3.8), and their choice was confirmed by God as their penalty: they were excluded from his presence (3.24). They were dead while they lived. That is what the New Testament writers mean when they speak of living men as being "dead in trespasses and sins" (Eph. 2.1), and when they speak of the "wage" paid by sin as "death" (Rom. 6.23). Man is spiritually dead already; this state, if it is not altered, will be finalized by his physical death (e.g. Jn. 8.21, 24). That is why Paul can say, "Sin came into the world by one man, and death came in by sin; and so death spread to all men, inasmuch as all men sinned . . . From Adam to Moses death reigned even over those whose sins were not like Adam's transgression" (Rom. 5.12, 14). Death is thus the penal consequence of sin; and it is the logical consequence as well. There is nothing arbitrary about it. If man chooses to turn his back on the life of God (and life, we recall, means salvation), then death alone remains. And man has made that choice. Our first forefather

[1] C. K. Barrett, Romans (1957), p. 33.   [2] On Paul and John (1963), pp. 41f.

157

committed the race when he turned aside from God.[1] Since then the human race has been infected with this poison of rebellion against God,[2] this *sin* which unfailingly produces *sins* in every man, and brings him inescapably under the domination of death. The sin of Adam is the sin of Everyman; the penalty of Adam is the penalty of Everyman.

Such is the human situation, as Paul sketches it in Romans. We have looked at it in some detail not only because it supplies a necessary background to the assertion in Rom. 8.24, but also because it is the backcloth against which we must understand much of what Paul has to say about salvation.

(b) Salvation from the old state

In Eph. 2 Paul gives a somewhat similar analysis. The main emphasis lies on the fact that men through sin are dead, devoid of God's life, cut off from him (2.1, 3, 5). But we meet the other evil powers as well, sin (2.1-5) and wrath (2.3), and, by implication, Law as well, for there is a repeated denial that we can achieve or deserve our salvation (2.5, 8, 9). Thus far we are on familiar ground. But in verses 1-3 Paul gives a further description of the characteristics of non-Christian man. He uses a word "walk", common among the Jews to describe their laws of conduct (*halakah*), in order to draw attention to the "laws of conduct" according to which these converts used to behave. They lived according to a threefold principle.

First, they fashioned their behaviour according to the pattern of the age[3] – what Paul elsewhere calls "this present evil age" (Gal. 1.4). They were dominated by the worldly standards which actuated all their neighbours, the standards to which the Christian is not to be conformed, but from which he is to be transformed by the indwelling Spirit of God (Rom. 12.2). It is the mark of Demas's defection from Christian living that he is recorded as having loved this present age (2 Tim. 4.10).

[1] The literature on Rom. 5 is immense. H. Wheeler Robinson, *The Christian Doctrine of Man* (1926), pp. 112f., and F. R. Tennant *The Fall and Original Sin* (1903) pp. 253f., deny that there is a causal connection between Adam's sin and that of his posterity, and together with T. W. Manson, *op. cit.*, p. 44, find the clue to Paul's thought in the conception of Adam as corporate personality. Mankind is certainly an organic unity to Paul, organized under one head; he does not have our atomistic view of man. But he does see humanity's fate as resting on the action of its head, be that head Adam or Christ (Rom. 5.18, 19, 1 Cor. 15.45, 47).

[2] See W. D. Davies, *Paul and Rabbinic Judaism* (1948), on the *yetser-hara'*, the "evil inclination" which the rabbis recognized as born in all men.

[3] κατὰ τὸν αἰῶνα τοῦ κόσμου τούτου. This is a unique combination of two phrases, both common in Paul, ὁ αἰὼν οὗτος and ὁ κόσμος οὗτος; the phrase strictly is a pleonasm, as both are translations of the Hebrew phrase which denotes "this age" in contrast to "the messianic age", "the age to come".

Secondly, their behaviour showed that they were dominated by the evil one. He is described as the spiritual being who is at work in the "sons of disobedience" (a Hebraism for the disobedient), the one who is "ruler of the power of the air". Paul is using the Jewish language of the day, which saw the air[1] as the realm of evil spirits. It is his habit to use the current terminology in order to express Christian truth; he is impatient with the details (see Eph. 6.12, Col. 1.16, Rom. 8.38f.). His point here is the same as his Master's (Matt. 4.1-11, 13.39, Lk. 8.12, Jn. 8.44, 13.2, 14.30, 12.31), that there is an organized, spiritual force of evil opposing the work of God. Perhaps he puts it with greatest clarity in 2 Cor. 4.3, 4, where three things are noted about this evil being. He is called "the god of this age"; that is to say he has a widespread dominion, indeed a universal one, over those who have not been reached by the saving power of God (see Acts 26.18, Col. 1.13, and Lk. 4.5-7, where Jesus does not dispute Satan's claim). His great objective is not necessarily to make men wicked, but to keep them from being reached by "the rays of the enlightenment of the gospel of Christ's glory", to keep them, that is to say, within his realm. And the weapon he uses most particularly in order to achieve his purpose is spiritual blindness; "he blinds the minds of those who do not believe." He blinds them to their need of Christ, and to what Christ can do for them as Saviour. Such is "the prince of the power of the air" of whose influence Paul speaks so feelingly in Eph. 2.2.[2]

The third characteristic of non-Christian man noted in this passage is that his way of life is determined by the desires of his "flesh" and of his "mind". He is basically self-centred. Paul's use of the word "flesh" (sarx) is important. The word is used in the first place, as we might expect, to denote man's bodily existence; it is even so used of Jesus (Rom. 1.3, Eph. 2.15). By a natural extension the word comes to mean anything outward (e.g. Rom. 2.28), and is thus applied to man himself to emphasize his creatureliness (Gal. 1.16). Sarx, in fact, speaks of the material, the transitory; as distinct from God who is power and life, sarx stands for the impotence (2 Cor. 10.3, Gal. 4.13) and the mortality (Gal. 6.8) of the creature. Hence the third sense of sarx in Paul. Man as "flesh" is part of the world that is estranged from God. He is subject to the rulers, the god, the spirit of this age (Eph. 6.12, 2 Cor. 4.4, 1 Cor. 2.12). Though the flesh is not, pace Bultmann, to be equated with sin, it provides a bridgehead for sin (Rom. 7.8) and thus becomes not merely a sphere but a force of evil (8.12, 13, 14). The sarx cannot

[1] See Philo, de gigant. 2, ψυχαὶ δέ εἰσι (sc. οἱ δαίμονες) κατὰ τὸν ἀέρα πετόμεναι, and de somn. 1.22, ὁ ἀὴρ . . . ἐστι ψυχῶν ἀσωμάτων οἶκος.

[2] The Theology of the New Testament, ii, pp. 201ff. On sarx see also J. A. T. Robinson, The Body (1952), and the Kittel T.W.N.T. article 'Sarx' by E. Schweizer.

please God (Rom. 8.7); in it nothing good dwells (Rom. 7.18);[1] it is, in a word, the lower nature with which we serve the law of sin (Rom. 7.25), and with which even the Christian resists the godly promptings of the Holy Spirit within him (Gal. 5.17). Thus the same word is used to denote both our human creatureliness and our human sinfulness. *Sarx* as the former is neutral and to be accepted (2 Cor. 10.3). *Sarx* as the latter is evil and to be eradicated (Gal. 5.24). Barclay's summary is a fair generalization, "The flesh stands for human nature weakened, vitiated, tainted by sin. The flesh is man as he is apart from Jesus Christ and his Spirit."[2]

The world, the devil, the flesh; these three conspire to dominate the life of non-Christian man. It is from them that the Christian has been saved (Eph. 2.4-8).

(c) Salvation from the old fears

This is the main emphasis of the third passage which deals with salvation as a past event, 2 Tim. 1.9. In saving us, God has replaced the old spirit of *deilia*, "cowardice and dread in face of the unknown" (particularly death, 1.7) by the Holy Spirit, who brings love, and power, and self-control. There was much dread, *Angst*, in the ancient world of the first century, as we have seen in ch. 4. There was a hankering for salvation from war, famine, death and disease, yes, and from personal failure as well. This is what gave the Mystery Cults such popularity. They offered some sort of assurance, however illusory, to those who were racked by *deilia*. It is interesting that the language in 1.9, 10 has a distinctly Hellenistic flavour. In reminding Timothy of the glorious gospel of the *Saviour* Jesus, whose royal *advent* has seen the end of death's tyranny, and brought *life* and *immortality* to *light*, Paul perhaps unconsciously expresses himself in terms used by the pagan world to enunciate their hopes and fears. The fears are, perhaps, best described in the immortal lines of the *Odyssey*, where Achilles refuses to be comforted about death; "For I would rather act as serf upon the earth, yes, even with a poverty-stricken owner, than reign as king over all the dead below" (*Od.* 11.487f.). Indeed, the whole object of the Epicureans was to rid men of two fears, the fear of death and the fear of the gods, which were seen as the two great obstacles to human *ataraxia*, "tranquillity".[3] Epicurus's confident conclusion that

---

[1] This is precisely where σάρξ differs from σῶμα, the other word sometimes translated "flesh". The σῶμα can be the vehicle of the Holy Spirit. The σῶμα will be raised to immortality. The σῶμα is for the Lord (1 Cor. 6.13, 19).

[2] W. Barclay, *Flesh and Spirit* (1962), p. 22.

[3] Freedom from "the most cruel of tyrants, eternal terror and fear by night and day" was the aim of the Epicureans (Cicero, *Tusc. Disput.*, 1.21, 48) and of the entire *de Rerum Natura* of Lucretius.

the gods need not be feared because they do not enter into life at all, and that death need not be feared because it is extinction, nothingness, did not still the hearts of men; and the Christian gospel that God himself offered to man both immortality in the future and his Spirit of love, power and self-control here and now, must have spoken very clearly to their longings.

(d) Salvation from the old habits

This is the main theme of Tit. 2.11-3.6. 2.11 tells us that God's grace which brings salvation has appeared; 3.5 tells us that God our Saviour in his love and kindness has saved us. In each case the habits contracted in the old life are in the forefront of the author's mind. The qualities outlined in 2.1-10 have only to be negatived to see what the old habits were. Or, as he puts it positively in 3.3, "We ourselves were once foolish, disobedient, led astray, in bondage to desires and pleasures of every kind, living our lives in envy and malice, hateful creatures, and hating one another." These are some of the ways in which the sin principle mars the life of man; these are what Paul calls in Gal. 5.19 "the works of the flesh".

Such is the condition of the man outside Christ, according to Paul. He is still in the old aeon, dominated by sin, law, wrath and death. He is at the mercy of the flesh, the world and the devil. He is subject to the fears and frustrations of which the contemporary world, both Jew and pagan, was all too well aware, and his life was spoiled by bad habits which he was powerless to alter. These are the things from which man needs to be saved. These are his deepest needs. And it is just these needs, Paul tells us, that God himself has come to deal with.

(ii) How have we been saved?

Paul's answer is no different from that of the rest of the New Testament *kerygma*; indeed he uses salvation language when he recalls, in 1 Cor. 15.1-3, that extremely primitive creed which was handed on to him after his conversion. Paul is at one with the rest of the early Christians in his understanding of the salvation wrought by God for man.

(a) He is clear, in the first place, that *we have been saved by God*.

It is all "of God that Christ Jesus is made unto us . . . redemption, that, according as it is written, He that glorieth, let him glory in the Lord" (1 Cor. 1.30f.). Thus in the Pastoral Epistles[1] Paul often speaks of "God our Saviour" (1 Tim. 1.1, 2.3, 4.10, Tit. 1.3, 2.10, 3.4). It is his will that all men should be saved (1 Tim. 2.4).

[1] On the increased use of the substantive "Saviour" in the Pastorals and 2 Peter, see pp. 145, 197. Whether or not these letters are, as they claim, apostolic,

(*b*) He is no less clear that *we have been saved by Christ.*

Jesus is called Saviour by Paul in Acts 13.23, Eph. 5.23 (?), Phil. 3.20, at least three times in the Pastorals (Tit. 1.4, 3.6, 2 Tim. 1.10), and probably also in Tit. 2.13, though such is the identity between the Father and the Son that this title could be construed with either. The point is clear. There is no difference between the attitude of the Father and the Son in redemption, and any theory of the atonement that drives any wedge between them cannot claim to be true to the New Testament. If 1 Tim. 2.4 reminds us that God wills salvation for his world, 1 Tim. 1.15 makes clear that it was to save sinners that Christ came into the world. In Jesus Christ we meet God at work for our rescue.

(*c*) This is another way of saying that *we have been saved by grace.*

That we are in fact saved by God's gracious intervention and not by anything that we ourselves do is stressed in three of the four contexts where salvation is spoken of as past (Eph. 2.5, 8, 9, Tit. 3.5-7, 2 Tim. 1.9), while the other, Rom. 8.24, comes after the most devastating attack ever made on the efficacy of "works" to achieve salvation.

Why was St. Paul so sure that works have nothing to do with it? For at least three good reasons. In the first place, the whole attempt to establish a claim on God by doing certain things is impersonal; merit is not the appropriate basis for a lasting relationship between persons (Rom. 10.1-3). Secondly, the clocking up of merit merely panders to the arrogance endemic in man; we are not saved by "works" lest any man should boast. If heaven were full of brazen, self-made men, it would become hell. Thirdly, the method of "works" is impossible. Those who rely on it inevitably come under the curse of God which rests on any offence against his holy law (Gal. 3.10). Paul, like James, knew that if a man were to keep the whole law, and offend in only one point, he would be guilty of breaking the whole (Jas. 2.10, Rom. 7.7-11). He saw that the way of legalism, the way of self-establishment before God, must lead to ruin; it was the primal sin of pride, nothing less, and it broke the basic principle of loving dependence proper to a creature before his Creator. It is the clarity with which he recognizes the hopelessness of relying on "works" of any kind that

or as many think pseudepigraphic, they were presumably written in the second half of the first century when *Sōtēr* was being applied freely to Emperors like Nero and Domitian, not to mention other θεοὶ σωτῆρες. Christian polemic, therefore, may account for the increased use of the title, but the title itself is very old. F. F. Bruce has shewn how it occurs in many strata of the Old Testament. (*Our God and Saviour; A Recurring Biblical Pattern* in the Collection of Essays presented to E. O. James, 1963). See also ch. 1, *supra.*

gives Paul such exultation in the gospel of the free grace of God, God who justifies the ungodly (Rom. 4.5).

Justification is linked with salvation, not only in the Psalms and Deutero-Isaiah, but also in several places in Paul. In Tit. 3.5-7, Rom. 5.8-10, 10.10 and 1.16f. the connection is explicit. Paul saw salvation, in so far as it was a past event, at least partly in terms of justification. The meaning of this term has been hotly debated since the Reformation. At that time the Reformers saw it as God's declaration of acquittal on penitent, trusting sinners, while Roman orthodoxy[1] (though both beforehand and later[2] recognizing the basic truth of the reformed interpretation) saw it as God's making a man righteous ethically by inner renewal. There is a general agreement today that it is not possible to make this meaning fit the majority of Pauline references.[3] His synonyms for "justify" are "reckon righteous" "remit sins" and "not reckon sin" (Rom. 4.3-8). But many critics are unwilling to give full force to the evident forensic background of the term, lest justification be thought of in sub-personal categories, or be conceived of (as admittedly it has not infrequently been represented) as a legal fiction by which God declared us righteous (when clearly we are nothing of the kind) by virtue of a transfer of Christ's merits to our account in the ledger of heaven. Thus, for instance, T. W. Manson regards justification as the language not of the court but of the throne room – a regal rather than a judicial act, whereby God regards us as righteous. "He does not declare that the unrighteous is righteous, but treats him as if he were . . . God does not acquit the guilty, he issues an amnesty or a free pardon."[4]

Others find the background of this term in those few passages in the Psalms and Deutero-Isaiah (e.g. Ps. 98.2, Isa. 45.8, 46.13, 56.1) where God's righteousness appears as the equivalent of his salvation; accordingly they interpret Paul's doctrine of justification as God's

[1] As formulated at the Council of Trent (sessio vi).

[2] See H. Küng, Rechtfertigung (1957) and "Justification and Sanctification according to the New Testament" in Christianity Divided (1961).

[3] Nowhere in Greek literature does δικαιόω mean "to make righteous". In common with other verbs in – όω denoting moral qualities, the causative element (often to be found in – όω verbs) is absent. Thus ἀξιόω means "to account worthy" not "to make worthy"; δικαιόω means "to account righteous" not "to make righteous".

[4] Op. cit., pp. 56f. His argument is developed in a curiously inconsistent way. He recognizes that "God must be δίκαιος as well as δικαιῶν", but instead of adopting Paul's answer as to how this may be, suggests that man's repentance, made possible by Christ, is satisfaction for sin (pp. 58f.). He ends up, however, by asserting roundly that "salvation is absolutely and entirely the gift of God . . . All that man can do . . . is to take what God gives. This is what Paul means by faith" (p. 63).

vindication of his people. This is fairly unconvincing. Not only does Paul never refer to any of these verses which are supposed to be the background of his teaching, while he does refer to others, like Ps. 32.1 where the judicial putting away of sin is prominent; but the main thrust of Romans is to show that God acquits even the Gentiles who had no claim on him (9.24ff., 10.19ff.), whereas the whole point of the identification of justification and salvation in Deutero-Isaiah is that God is faithful to his covenant promises to his people, Israel.

How then, according to Paul, does a just and holy God find it possible to justify the ungodly? The answer is found in the cross of Christ, to which we now turn.

(d) We have been saved by the life, death and resurrection of Jesus Christ.

But supremely by his death. Without the perfect life that preceded it, his death would have been of no avail; the New Testament is clear about that. Without the resurrection that followed it, we could have had no assurance that his death had availed and no experience in our lives of the risen Lord. That, too, is clear. But undeniably the New Testament teaches that salvation is primarily due to what Christ achieved for us upon the cross. That cross is interpreted by various metaphors in Paul's writings.

(i) He uses, in the first place, the language of the law court, *"justification"*. We have been justified by his blood (Rom. 5.9), that is to say by his death.[1] In Gal. 3.8-14 Paul is speaking of how a man can be justified with God, how he can properly be accepted by a holy and loving God. He shows his readers that this cannot take place through law-keeping, "for it is written, 'Cursed is every one that continueth not in *all* things written in the book of the law to do them' ", and in any case, "that no man is justified by the law in the sight of God is evident, for 'The just shall live by faith'. And the law is not of faith." But he goes on to show how that Christ "has redeemed us from the curse" which lay upon us as lawbreakers, "when he became a curse for us; for it is written 'Cursed is every one that hangeth on a tree', that the blessing of Abraham [i.e. justification, see verse 6] might come on the Gentiles through Jesus Christ." Christ on the cross took the place of the law-breakers, the place of cursing, that the law-breakers

[1] On the meaning of the word "blood" in Scripture, see A. M. Stibbs, *The Meaning of the Word 'Blood' in Scripture* (1947), J. A. Motyer in the symposium *Eucharistic Sacrifice* (1962), pp. 36ff., L. Morris, *The Apostolic Preaching of the Cross* (1955), pp. 108-24. As Armitage Robinson rightly notes, in opposition to Westcott, "To the Jewish mind, 'blood' . . . was especially the life poured out in death; and yet more particularly, in its religious aspect, it was the symbol of sacrificial death" (*Ephesians*, p. 29). "Blood" in Scripture is *not* primarily life, *nor* life released for future usefulness, but life laid down in death.

might be accepted through him. Once again we find this primitive use of *xulon*[1] which runs through the early proclamation of the cross,[1] and on this occasion we are explicitly taken to its source in Deut. 21.23. God, in Christ, himself entered into the "entail" of man's wrongdoing. He himself endured the being-in-the-wrong-with-God which was sin's heritage.

Paul asserts much the same in Rom. 3.24ff., where he can say in the same breath that we are justified *gratuito* and *propter Christum*, "freely" and "through the redemption that is in Christ Jesus". So closely does he identify the action of the Father and the Son in redemption that he sees no discrepancy between these two assertions. Would that it had been the same through the history of theories of the atonement! In this most concentrated piece of writing, Paul explains how God could have been righteous in not taking notice (in judgement) of transgressions throughout previous history, which he characterizes as "the time when God forbore". His answer is that in the cross of Christ God has now shown himself to be both "just and the justifier of him that believes in Jesus". The sacrificial death of Jesus on that cross demonstrates not only God's righteousness and his mercy, but his righteousness *in* his mercy. And if we enquire farther into what took place on Calvary to make possible this astonishing reversal in the fortunes of sinful men, the answer is given by Paul in 2 Cor. 5.21. He has just reasserted the unity of the Father and the Son in the work of reconciliation (5.19) so he will not be misunderstood when he says that God made Christ to *be sin* for us, Christ who knew no sin. Christ was, as it were, identified with the sin of man, in order that, united with him by faith, we might be identified with the very righteousness of God. Christ became what we were, that we might become what he is; he shared our estate that we might share his. That is the ground of justification. Christ, who was one with us, and, unlike us, lived a life of perfect obedience even unto death (Phil. 2.8), was representatively "made sin" in our stead and for our benefit. No wonder Paul can cry out in triumph "Christ is made unto us . . . righteousness" (1 Cor. 1.30).[2] No wonder he can exult in the work of the last Adam, through whose "one act of righteousness" the free gift came "unto all men to justification of life" (Rom. 5.18). It is because God himself has assumed responsibility for the outcome of man's misdoing that he can proclaim acquittal to the believer in Jesus. And belief is important; it constitutes

[1] See pp. 145f.
[2] In Rom. 4.25 Paul says Christ was delivered up because of our offences, and was raised again because of our justification. He means that the resurrection is the guarantee of our acceptance with God. It is the risen Christ, victorious over sin and death, who "is made unto us righteousness".

a union with the Just One, Jesus, without which we could never be "accounted" righteous. It is only as we are "in him" that we are "made the righteousness of God" (2 Cor. 5.21, Gal. 2.17). Without the twofold solidarity of God with us in Christ, and of us with Christ in God, the New Testament doctrine of justification, so far from establishing God's righteousness, would be immoral. As it is, there is no question of "legal fiction", for believers *are* in Christ, and share his status of righteousness. As J. I. Packer rightly says, "God accounts them righteous not because he accounts them to have kept his law personally (that would be a false judgement), but because he accounts them to be 'in' the one who kept God's law representatively (which is a true judgement). So, when God justifies sinners on the ground of Christ's obedience and death, he acts justly . . . for by setting forth Christ as a propitiation for sins, in whom human sin was actually judged and punished as it deserved, he revealed the just ground on which he was able to pardon and accept believing sinners in Old Testament times (as in fact he did: Ps. 130.3f.), no less than in the Christian era."[1]

Exception can, therefore, only be taken to Paul's doctrine of justification when it is misunderstood, either as God punishing an innocent Christ for guilty men, or as a cold legal transaction whereby his merits are imputed to us. Certainly when Paul's teaching of the solidarity of God with Christ and of us with Christ is neglected the first error can easily be made, and when his teaching about justification only as we are in Christ (or as we "believe onto him", as he more frequently expresses it) is forgotten, the second error follows. Even when full weight is given to what he says about the place of faith in justification, it is often misunderstood as though faith were a giant "work"[2] which God decides to accept as a soft option instead of law-keeping; rather than the adoring self-devotion of the sinner to his Lord who devoted himself for us. How faith like that can be misconstrued as something sub-personal defeats me! Justification, so far from being a legalistic category, brings us to the heart of personal relations with a God who is willing to have dealings with sinners, to forgive them, to take upon himself the consequences of their sins, and to confer on them a new status of justified, of "accepted in the Beloved". This, of course, does not at once make a man just in the ethical sense; this comes with time, as the Spirit of God makes him empirically what he is theologically. "The knight has been dubbed knight, but he is still in his condition a commoner," writes Brunner. "His nobility has not yet

[1] Article "Justification" in *New Bible Dictionary* (1962), p. 685.
[2] This was Bonhoeffer's complaint about pre-war Lutheranism; see his *The Cost of Discipleship* (1937).

permeated his whole nature."[1] But it will, as we shall see when examining Paul's conception of salvation as a present experience. Meanwhile there are other aspects of the cross which must be reviewed.

(ii) A second metaphor which Paul applies to the cross as a means of salvation comes from the language of *redemption*. In Rom. 3.24, 1 Cor. 1.30, Eph. 1.7, Col. 1.14 Christ's death is interpreted as *apolutrōsis*, "redemption". Closely connected with this word is the noun *antilutron* in 1 Tim. 2.6. Christ, the one mediator between God and man, gave himself as a "counter-ransom-price" on behalf of all.[2] In Tit. 2.14 the verb *lutroō* is used, with the same meaning. Christ gave himself for us in order to redeem us from all iniquity. The same use in 1 Pet. 1.18f. specifies that the ransom-price was nothing less than "the precious blood of Christ"; here, more succinctly, it is simply said that he gave himself. This language all seems to stem from the famous "ransom-saying" of Jesus in Mk. 10.45, and farther back to Isa. 53 and the redemption language of the Old Testament (*go'el*, *padah* and *kōpher*), where it was supremely used of the Exodus, the mighty act whereby God set his people free from the hostile forces that had been oppressing them. And, of course, the redemption that Christ wrought is often in the New Testament seen as the new Exodus (e.g. Lk. 9.31, Greek). But the word had another significance to the Gentile, which made it doubly useful in the missionary vocabulary of Paul. *Apolutrōsis* meant deliverance to him, too, and again the idea of the costliness of deliverance was present. For it was the word used to describe the manumission of a slave upon the payment of a price. Deissmann shed a great deal of light on Paul's usage from contemporary inscriptions.[3] One of the most common forms of manumission was the fictitious purchase of the slave by some god, e.g. "Apollo the Pythian bought from Sosibius of Amphissa, for freedom, a female slave . . . with a price of three minae and a half of silver." St. Paul would, therefore, be alluding to a very well-known custom when he used such language as, "Ye were bought with a price" (1 Cor. 6.20, 7.23),[4] "For freedom did Christ set us free" (Gal. 5.1), and "Ye were bought with a price; become not

[1] *Man in Revolt* (1942), p. 491.
[2] This passage is particularly illuminating. The μεσίτης was sometimes appointed in Greek law to mediate between two estranged parties, and to bring them together whatever the cost to himself (Diod. 19.71, 4.54, Polyb. 28, 17, 8). This Christ has done at the cost of his life in the stead of ours. Josephus uses a similar phrase when (*Ant.* 14.7) he records that Eleazar the priest gave Crassus, when he invaded Jerusalem, a gold beam from the Temple to save the rest from spoliation τὴν δόκον λύτρου ἀντὶ πάντων ἔδωκεν.
[3] *Light from the Ancient East* (1910), pp. 327f.
[4] Paul saw all men as slaves of sin and the consequent death which was its wage; in addition the Jew was the slave of the law (Gal. 4.1-7, 5.1) while the pagan was slave of his gods (Gal. 4.8, 9).

slaves of men" (1 Cor. 7.23). "Christians cannot become slaves of men," writes Deissmann, "because they have become 'slaves of Christ' by purchase, and have entered into 'the slavery of God' or 'of righteousness' (Rom. 6.22, 6.18). But, as in every other case of purchase by a god, the slave of Christ is at the same time free; he is the Lord's freedman (1 Cor. 7.22)."[1] He further points out that "the union of the idea of manumission with the idea of sacrifice was made easier for the ancient Christians by the fact that sacral manumission, e.g. at Cos, was not complete without sacrifice", while there was an "affinity between the idea of redemption (manumission) and the idea of forgiveness (remission) of our trespasses, which was established for the ancients by the legal procedure they were accustomed to. In cases of non-payment of a money debt, the system . . . allowed slavery for debt."

Of course, the emphasis we have given to the full background of this word does not mean we must ask literalistic questions never raised in Scripture, such as, "To whom was the ransom paid?" No metaphors are perfect, and none must be over-pressed. But it is difficult to deny that when this ransom language is applied to God's work for man through the cross of Christ, the themes of freedom by the payment of a costly price, of our belonging henceforth to him, of the cancellation of our "debts" to God, of our release from an unwilling slavery to hostile powers which held us in captivity, are all present. We can be no less certain about the Hebrew overtones of the *go'el* (Christ acting the part of our kinsman), of the *kōpher* (where a life is given in exchange for a life) and the *padah* (the gracious counterpart to the release from Egypt's slavery and death). This is all part of the salvation which Jesus Christ achieved for man through his death and resurrection. It enables us to say as confidently as the Israelites when they had crossed the Red Sea that there is a sense in which we *have* been saved by God's intervention on our behalf.

(iii) There remains one other metaphor which Paul uses to describe our salvation by the cross of Christ, that of *reconciliation*. It is possibly significant that, like the Old Testament writers, Paul never brings the language of salvation into direct contact with the realm of the sacrificial system, although he did see Christ's death as the culmination of that system, and the reality which gave meaning to it (1 Cor. 5.7, Rom. 3.24). But in Rom. 5.10 he says, "If, when we were enemies we were reconciled to God by the death of his Son, much more, being reconciled, we shall be saved by his life." It is by the cross that we have been reconciled. Our attitude was one of enmity to God, the latent rebellion of which we have spoken earlier. This could not but evoke the

---

[1] *Op. cit.*, p. 329.

wrath of God.[1] But from this we have been saved by the reconciling work of Christ upon the cross. This is not a common Pauline metaphor, being confined to Rom. 5.10, 11 and 2 Cor. 5.18, 19.[2] But it is a useful one, for it indicates the restoration of personal relations between God and man. It is important to notice that the initiative in this restoration of fellowship, as always in salvation, comes from God. Paul never speaks of God as being reconciled to us, but always *vice versa*. For "all things come from God who has reconciled us to himself by Jesus Christ" (2 Cor. 5.18). It is also important to notice that the Greek word *katallagē* does not precisely correspond to the English "reconciliation". We speak of reconciliation as achieved only when both parties are in fellowship once again, but God's *katallagē* is something which Paul can speak of as complete and finished, which is offered to men. The Christian message is that "God has reconciled us" (2 Cor. 5.18) – and yet men must still "be reconciled to God" (5.20). The word would better be translated as "remove the obstacles to fellowship". There existed a dual barrier to fellowship between God and rebellious man; man's *echthra* and God's *orgē*. The latter barrier to fellowship was broken down at the cross,[3] and in that sense God has reconciled us (so far as he is concerned). The former barrier to fellowship is broken down only when man the rebel becomes man the penitent and commits himself in faith to the Saviour who died to achieve our reconciliation. Only then is "reconciliation", as we would call it, complete.

Justification, redemption, reconciliation – salvation seen as a past event includes all three. But how are we to make this rescuing action of God our own?

(e) We have been saved through faith

Faith is the hand, the empty hand, by which we receive the divine gift of justification, redemption and reconciliation. It is not the ground on which God accepts us; for then it would become a meritorious "work", something of which we could boast before God. That is very far from being Paul's view of the situation. He is careful to say that we are accepted "by faith" (*pistei*), "arising out of faith" (*ek pisteōs*),

[1] Indeed, many commentators think that the "enemies" of Rom. 5.10 and 11.28 may be descriptive not only of our hostility to God but of his to our sin. At any rate the latter point is emphatically made in the concept of the wrath of God.

[2] The intensive *apokatallassō* is also used of the atonement in Eph. 2.11f. and Col. 1.19f.

[3] It is noteworthy that in both passages where *katallassō* is used (Rom. 5 and 2 Cor. 5) and in the two where *apokatallassō* occurs, the means whereby this is achieved is invariably stated; it is through what Jesus did on the cross that the barrier to fellowship with God has been removed.

"through faith" as through a door (*dia pisteōs*), but never "because of faith" (*dia pistin*). Faith is man's personal response to God's personal initiative. It is the total response of man to the total self-giving of God – "thus by grace you have been saved, through faith" (Eph. 2.8). Faith is opposed to the principle of works, of earning the favour of God (Gal. 2.16); it is wholehearted reliance on what Christ has done. Or, if we prefer to think of it in this way, faith is counting on the promises of God, as Abraham did (Gal. 3.6, 7, Rom. 4.3-5). Faith is born when men hear these gracious promises, this glorious gospel of God (Rom. 10.8, 9, 17). That is why the Scriptures (2 Tim. 3.15), that is why the preaching of the gospel, or of the cross, is described as a means of salvation (Rom. 1.16, 1 Cor. 1.18). For it is the proclamation of what God has done to save man which demands his response. That response is faith, and that faith is seen in Paul both as an initial act (Rom. 10.9) and as a constant attitude (Gal. 2.20). Trust is at the beginning and at the end of the Christian way; "we walk by faith not sight" (2 Cor. 5.7) and faith will never be superseded until we see him whom now we trust (1 Cor. 13.8-13). Such faith in the Lord means obedience to him, as we shall see (cf. "the obedience of faith", Rom. 1.5), and issues in love (Gal. 5.6) and good works (Eph. 2.10).

What happens when we thus trustingly put our hand in the hand of God, and entrust ourselves to his saving mercy? The Holy Spirit of God comes into residence in the life of the believer, and he is then baptized. The two results are brought together in Tit. 3.5, 6. "He saved us through the water of rebirth and of renewal by the Holy Spirit." Despite a certain ambiguity in the Greek expression it is clear that two things are in Paul's mind, the rite of baptism[1] and the gift of the Spirit to the believer. These two are juxtaposed equally naturally in Gal. 3.26, 27 where entry into Christ is said to be by faith and by baptism, and is identified, earlier in the chapter, with receiving the Spirit by faith (3.1-3). The New Testament saw no tension between salvation by faith and salvation by baptism; they are properly regarded as belonging together, and this was all the easier in a missionary situation where infant baptism was probably the exception. Tension would only arise with an automatic doctrine of regeneration through baptism irrespective of faith. This would have come under the same strictures

[1] On the complex New Testament teaching on baptism, see W. F. Flemington, *The New Testament Doctrine of Baptism* (1953), O. Cullmann, *Baptism in the New Testament* (E.T. 1950), J. Jeremias, *Infant Baptism in the First Four Centuries* (E.T. 1960), and *The Origins of Infant Baptism* (E.T. 1963), together with K. Aland's reply, *Did the Early Church Baptize Infants?* (E.T. 1963). Marcel, *The Biblical Doctrine of Infant Baptism* (E.T. 1953) is strong on the covenant element in baptism and its relation to faith, while D. E. H. Whiteley (*The Theology of St. Paul* (1964)) has a useful survey of baptism in the thought of Paul.

as Paul passed on circumcision; it would have assumed the proportions of a work, if not, indeed, of magic. Paul's own teaching on baptism is very different. It carries with it the implications of dying with Christ and rising to newness of life with him (Rom. 6.1-16), precisely as faith – union with Christ does. And it is the Holy Spirit, given access to the life of the believer when he turns in faith to God for salvation, who actualizes in him the death to sin and the life to righteousness of which his baptism speaks.

Faith, then, is sealed by the "outward and visible sign" of baptism, and the "inward and spiritual grace" of the Holy Spirit received into the life. This marks the beginning of a new life, life in Christ. It is interesting to see how Paul here describes it. Nowhere else does he use the language of rebirth or regeneration adopted by John, James and Peter (Jn. 3.5, Jas. 1.18, 1 Pet. 1.23); he avoided it perhaps because such language was commonly applied to the initiate in the Mystery Religions. The nearest he gets to it is to call the man in Christ a "new creation" (2 Cor. 5.17); and here in Tit. 3.5 he uses a word which comes only once more in the New Testament, where it refers to the new world of the last days (Matt. 19.28). This wider usage suggests, perhaps, that the new birth is no merely individual thing. Rather, in line with the corporate salvation teaching of the Old Testament, it means that the individual is brought within the work of gracious rescue and restoration which God is doing in the last days. This is emphasized by the phrase used of the Holy Spirit in Tit. 3.6; he is *"poured out"* upon us in full measure "through Jesus Christ our Saviour". In these words we are taken back to the Day of Pentecost and Acts 2.17, where the pouring out of the Spirit is seen as the fulfilment of Joel 2.28, and the inauguration of the last days, the days of salvation. Because those days have begun, the apostle can say that we *have* (albeit in hope) been saved.

B. SALVATION AS A PRESENT EXPERIENCE

When we come to see how Paul uses salvation language of our present Christian experience, we discover that he does so in three contexts. Salvation as a present reality means protection in Christ, power through the Spirit, and preaching to the lost. It can be argued that he ought to have used the term more widely,[1] and referred it to church life, the Eucharist and so forth. The fact remains that he has not, and we shall restrict ourselves here to considering the actual Pauline usage.

[1] It is interesting to note how modern treatments of Paul's doctrine of salvation, e.g. T. W. Manson, *On Paul and John*, A. M. Hunter, *Interpreting Paul's Gospel*, and C. Ryder Smith, *The Bible Doctrine of Salvation*, all desert Paul's actual linguistic usage at this point, and expatiate on allied themes.

(i) Salvation means protection

How can Paul, with all his harsh experience of life (e.g. 1 Cor. 4.9-13, 2 Cor. 11.23-28) possibly speak of the Christian as secure? Simply and solely because the Christian is "in Christ", his only and sufficient security. On several occasions when speaking of salvation, Paul stresses that it is "in Christ" (2 Tim. 2.10, 3.15, 1.9, cf. Eph. 1.4). Jesus Christ, God's final Saviour, offers more than any of God's other agents down the history of salvation; he can and does incorporate the believer in himself. Our salvation in Christ was given us, in the purposes of God, before the world began. There are, to Paul, two corporate or inclusive personalities in the history of salvation; Adam through whom paradise was lost, and Christ, through whom paradise was regained. Their respective acts commit those who are in solidarity with them. All men are "in Adam" by nature; believers are "in Christ" by grace. Solidarity with Adam involves all his members in sin and death; solidarity with Christ, on the other hand, involves all his members in life. This is the theme of Rom. 5 and 1 Cor. 15. The Christian is intimately implicated in all his Lord has done; he is safe with him. Thus some of Paul's favourite metaphors for Christian living are corporate ones, which stress the organic union between Christ and his people. In so doing he was true to the emphasis of Jesus. The very idea of Christ or Messiah involved the corollary of a Messianic people; you cannot have Messiah without his *qahal* or *ekklēsia* (Matt. 16.18). He called himself the Good Shepherd, and you cannot have a shepherd without a flock (Lk. 12.32). Indeed, Jesus' favourite self-designation, Son of Man, is essentially a corporate word, denoting "the people of the saints of the Most High" (Dan. 7.13, 27). It is not otherwise with the figure of the Suffering Servant[1] which in Deutero-Isaiah oscillates between the personal and the collective. Again, nothing in Christianity is more primitive than the sacraments, and baptism is seen as baptism into Christ and the Eucharist as joint participation in his Body and Blood. Nothing could express more graphically the integration of Christians with their risen Lord. Paul stresses this organic union in several ways; not only by the famous metaphor of the Body in which we are all members (1 Cor. 12.12-27; Rom. 12.4, 5; Col. 2.17-19; Eph. 1.23, 4.4-16). He also sees us as branches in the olive (Rom. 11.16-21) and stones in the building (1 Cor. 3.16, 17, Eph. 2.20-22); united with each other we are united with the risen Lord. The New Testament knows nothing of solitary Christianity. "On the contrary, New Testament Christianity is nothing if not social; the Semitic traditions on which it arose are themselves strong in a corporate sense; and, still more, it was quickly found to be

[1] For the development of the theme of the Servant in the New Testament see my *Called to Serve* (1964), chs. 1 and 2.

172

impossible to describe Christ himself otherwise than as an inclusive, a corporate personality. To become a Christian was, therefore, *ipso facto* to become an organ or limb of that Body, and the Christian Church is essentially the household of God (see Gal. 6.10, Eph. 2.19, 1 Tim. 3.15, Heb. 3.5f., 10.21). Indeed, for all its corporeity in the Old Testament, Israel was never so fully organic a concept as God's Israel, the Church."[1]

- Because the Christian was thus united with his risen Master, he was safe. The world might do its worst to him, but could not touch his inmost being; "for you are dead, and your life is hid with Christ in God" (Col. 3.3). The early Christians were utterly convinced that Jesus was even now at the place of power in the universe (1 Cor. 15.24f., Phil. 2.9-11). He was the *Lord* Jesus Christ.[2] He had overcome the world (Jn. 16.33). They knew, therefore, that nothing could separate the man in Christ from his Lord; neither life nor death, angels nor powers, things present nor things to come could separate him from the love of God in Christ Jesus his Lord (Rom. 8.38f.). All these forces had been disarmed by the death and resurrection of Christ. Jesus had borne all the attacks of evil in every conceivable form, and had risen triumphant. And what was true of the head was true of his members. The Christian was immortal and invulnerable till his work was done. And when it was done, even if it led to martyrdom, why, that meant sharing more intimately than ever in fellowship with Christ. Such was their faith that they dated the deaths of the martyrs *regnante Jesu Christo* "in the reign of Jesus Christ"! Here was no shallow optimism, that "God's in his heaven! All's right with the world". Far from it. It was sober Christian logic, based on the fact of the resurrection. Evil could not finally triumph over the members any more than it had over the head. It may be very uncomfortable for us, of course, but "if we suffer with him we shall also reign with him" (2 Tim. 2.12). And so, throughout his missionary work and trials, Paul has implicit confidence in the protection of God. Does he come near to death at Ephesus? It is God who delivers and protects him (2 Cor. 1.9, 10). Does he fear the plots of evil men as he writes to the Thessalonians? He knows God will preserve him (2 Thess. 3.2). And in looking back over his experiences at the end of his life he acknowledges that it is God who has preserved him through the persecutions, afflictions and sufferings he has endured (2 Tim. 3.10f.). Even in the trial before Nero, the first part of which had just been concluded when he wrote, he has been conscious of the preservation of the Lord, through which he was "delivered out of the mouth of the lion". Human friends had let him down, but he is quietly

[1] C. F. D. Moule, *The Birth of the New Testament* (1962), p. 135.
[2] See O. Cullmann's essay "The Reign of Christ" in his book *The Early Church* (1956).

173

confident of divine protection until he enters the heavenly kingdom, when he will no longer need it (2 Tim. 4.17, 18).

In fact, throughout his writings there is the joyful assurance that "*now* is the day of salvation" (2 Cor. 6.2). Just as the husband saves or protects the wife, so Christ saves his people (Eph. 5.23). In him, the Christian is invulnerable. The demonic powers cannot touch him (Rom. 8.38f.) – they were disarmed by Christ's victory on the cross, when he "stripped off the cosmic powers like a garment; he made a public spectacle of them, and led them as captives in his triumphal procession" (Col. 2.15).[1] Danger and opposition cannot thwart him; even a rigorous imprisonment can turn out to the furthering of his salvation (Phil. 1.19). For God will not scrap what is precious to him; he will not discard what he has saved. He who has begun a good work in the Christian will continue it until the day of the Lord Jesus (Phil. 1.6).

(ii) Salvation offers power

The old life was bedevilled with powerlessness, the inability to do right. That is the whole burden of Romans 7, and the poignant cry rings out in 7.24, "Who shall deliver me from the body of this death?" He means, of course, the *massa perditionis* – the whole weight of sin, frustration and death which belongs to him as to every other son of Adam. Thank God there *is* deliverance – "through Jesus Christ our Lord". For "the gospel is the *power* of God unto salvation to every one that believeth" (Rom. 1.16). What does Paul mean by this?

The clue is given us by that similar passage in 1 Cor. 1.18. Paul does not say that the proclamation of the cross meant salvation to him once, as though it were a thing of the past. He does not say that it *was* the power of God to us who *have* been saved. No. He says it *is* the power of God to us who *are* in process of being saved. What he here alludes to rather enigmatically (as he does in a precisely similar use of the present tense in 1 Cor. 15.2, when he speaks of the cross and resurrection as a present means of our being saved) he expands more fully elsewhere (e.g. Gal. 2.20, Rom. 6.6f., 2 Cor. 4.10, Phil. 3.10 and Col. 3.1-5). The cross and resurrection are not only a unique event in past history, concerning Christ alone. They concerned us then; we were implicated in his representative death and resurrection. They concern us now; we must reproduce his death and resurrection.

Our old sinful nature was taken to the cross with Christ (Rom. 6.6). The old "I" of self-will was crucified with Christ (Gal. 2.20). It is now a defeated foe. When Christ rose to newness of life, he took with him the

---

[1] On Christ's victory over evil powers, see, e.g. H. Schlier, *Principalities and Powers* (1961) and C. D. Morrison, *The Powers that Be* (1960).

total new humanity into which we are incorporated by faith and baptism; "we have been buried with him, through baptism, into that death of his, so that just as Christ was raised up from the dead by the glorious power of the Father, so we too should walk in newness of life" (Rom. 6.4). The cross and resurrection are thus not only something that happened once for us, but something that must be repeated constantly in us. The principle of life through death is the one by which the Christian lives. The cross and resurrection are intended to have a counterpart in our own daily lives. Perhaps Rom. 6 puts this doctrine of identification with our Lord most clearly. If I *know* that he has taken my sinful human nature to death with him (6.6), I must *reckon* myself dead indeed unto sin (6.11), I must count on the truth of this fact, and while not living any longer under inevitable defeat at the hands of my sinful impulses, must treat them as dangerous, albeit caged animals, with which I dare not trifle. Instead, I must completely *yield* my members, the different aspects of my personality, to God for him to use; this is the least I can do in gratitude to my Saviour (6.13). In other words I must consciously and constantly put off "the old man" and put on "the new man" which, in Christ, is recreated in the Creator's image (Col. 3.10). I must become, what, in Christ, I already am. That means that I must carry about in my body the dying of the Lord Jesus, in order that his risen life may be manifested in my mortal body (2 Cor. 4.10). I must be made conformable to his death, if I am to know the power of his resurrection (Phil. 3.10). This is the secret of victorious living which made the cross and resurrection a daily source of power to the apostle. This enabled him to progress in Christ's triumphal procession, not, like Roman captives in an imperial triumph, a sullen prisoner of war; the paradox of Christian victory was just this. Once he had allowed himself to be utterly conquered by Christ, he *shared in* Christ's triumph (2 Cor. 2.14). He found unleashed within his life the very power of God which raised Christ from the dead. This was good news indeed, and he prayed that the Holy Spirit would make known to his Asian friends "the surpassing greatness of his power towards us believers, according to the working of the power of his might which he wrought in Christ when he raised him from the dead . . ." (Eph. 1.19). Paul piles word upon word to depict the mighty power of the resurrection which can raise the Christian, who was dead in sin, to a new quality of life altogether. This is what salvation as a present reality meant to him.

Another way of looking at this whole experience of victorious living, which should be the normal Christian life, is in terms of the Holy Spirit. The Holy Spirit is the Spirit of Jesus (Rom. 8.9), given us in order to actualize within our lives something of the character of Jesus. "The diffused and little defined and fitfully manifested Spiritual presence of God (viz. as we meet it in the Old Testament) becomes sharply contracted to a 'bottle-neck' so as to be defined and localized in Jesus of Nazareth; God who formerly spoke at various times and in many different fragments has now spoken to us in one who is a Son. But the pattern, thus contracted to a single individual, widens again, through his death and resurrection, to an indefinite scope, though never again to an undefined quality. However widely diffused, however much more than individual, it bears henceforth the stamp of the very character of Christ." Such is Professor C. F. D. Moule's helpful comment on the nature of God's gift to men.[1] Accordingly, when we heard the gospel of our salvation and believed, we were sealed with that Holy Spirit who had been promised long ago (Eph. 1.13). "Seal" is a property word. It speaks of ownership. He is given to us in order to possess us, and mark us out as God's people by transformed lives. He is given, moreover, here and now as an "earnest" or "first instalment" of our future inheritance, until the day when God comes to collect his purchased possessions (Eph. 1.14). Paul changes here to a commercial metaphor, one that should be very readily intelligible in these days of "down payments". The Holy Spirit is that part of the age to come which is already present, the foretaste and the guarantee of heaven. The transforming, sanctifying work of the Spirit in the Christian is the consequence of his calling by God, and the prerequisite of his final salvation. We must, as those who have been saved and will be saved, evidence the fact by working *out* in our lives that salvation which God by his Spirit is working *in* us (Phil. 2.12, 13). The Bible nowhere encourages us to think that any man can have tasted the past deliverance of God who does not manifest in his life any of the signs of the Spirit's present work and power. If he cannot show a blameless, shining life as a son of God in a dark world, if he is never holding forth the word of life to those who perish for lack of it, then Paul fears his labour has been bestowed in vain upon such a man (Phil. 2.13-16). God our Saviour would have us adorn his doctrine in all things—and that includes our talk, our behaviour, our relations with children and marriage-partners, our drink and our honesty, our self-control and sincerity. The Christian is to be nothing less than a pattern of good works, a variegated yet harmonious whole which points unmistakably to "God our Saviour" (Tit. 2.1-10). This is, perhaps, what is meant in Tit. 3.5 when the Holy Spirit is said not only to regenerate the objects of salvation but to renew them. His work is to make us Christlike, to "conform us to the image of God's Son" (Rom. 8.29). The

[1] In an unpublished lecture, *The Holy Spirit in the Church*, p. 7, given to the Society for the Study of Theology, 1963.

Lord the Spirit indwells us in order to create in our lives the fruit of Christ's life (Gal. 5.22f.), and to change us, as we live with Christ, from one degree of glory to another (2 Cor. 3.18).

Of course, this process of sanctification requires cooperation on our part. It necessitates renewed repentance, constant faith and instant prayer. All three are attributed to the salvation that the Spirit works out in us (2 Cor. 7.10, 2 Tim. 3.15, 2 Thess. 3.1, 2). Unrepented sin grieves the Spirit (Eph. 4.30); lack of faith quenches his working (1 Thess. 5.19); and through prayerlessness we cut ourselves (and others, cf. the link in Phil. 1.19) off from his divine resources.

In a word, salvation in the present tense means *living with Christ* (1 Thess. 5.10). It was to this end that he died for us, to this end that he brought salvation within our grasp. Christ is not satisfied, and his death is to some extent frustrated of its purpose, unless we live in his company throughout our lives and in the hour of our death ("whether we wake or sleep"). In the intimacy of this fellowship, the Church is meant to know the protection and the power of her Saviour God.

(iii) *Salvation leads to preaching*

The third way in which Paul uses the language of salvation as a present reality concerns the proclamation of this power and protection, which are inherent in God's salvation, to others. St. Paul sees the world as falling clearly into two categories, no more; those who are being saved, and those who are being lost (2 Cor. 2.15, 1 Cor. 1.18, 2 Cor. 4.4-6, Col. 1.13, etc.). The Christian has responsibilities to both.

God intends those who are already the objects of his saving power to be helped along the way of salvation by the life and words of Christian brethren. Thus Timothy, by taking heed to himself (in meditation, dedication and stirring up the gift within him) and to the doctrine (teaching, exhortation and public reading of the Scriptures) will further his own salvation and that of his presumably Christian hearers (1 Tim. 4.14-16). When God saves a man like Paul, it is in order to make him a pattern to those who should hereafter believe (1 Tim. 1.15, 16). By this it is clear that he means an example not only to the outsider but to the fellow Christian (Phil. 4.9, 1 Thess. 2.10). All Christians have this responsibility to their fellows, a responsibility which the Thessalonians discharged so well (1 Thess. 1.7).

Not only a Christian's example, but his prayers (2 Thess. 3.1, 2, Phil. 1.19) can further the salvation of his brethren in Christ. So, too, can his suffering, if patiently borne. Paul sees his "afflictions" in this light as contributing to the salvation of his friends to whom he writes (2 Cor. 1.6). Presumably the encouragement of his example would deepen their dependence on their Saviour. Similarly, in 2 Tim. 2.10,

Paul sees his sufferings as contributing to the salvation of others. It is possible that by "the elect" in this verse, Paul means those whom God has chosen but who have not yet responded to his call; it is more probable, however, that he sees his sufferings as encouraging other Christians to follow suit, and as demonstrating the sustaining power of the Lord to keep him. No doubt here, as in Col. 1.24, Paul is influenced by the idea, common in rabbinic circles, that the messianic age could only be ushered in through suffering[1] (see Matt. 24.6ff., Mk. 13.7ff., Lk. 21.23f., 2 Thess. 2.1-12). How right he was. The way of salvation is the way of suffering for the followers as for the Master (2 Tim. 3.12, Jn. 15.20). And with characteristic self-forgetfulness, Paul is willing to shoulder more than his share of sufferings if it will relieve the lot of his brethren, and hasten the coming of his Lord.

But if the Christian who enjoys the power and protection of Christ is in duty bound to give himself in service to, and, if necessary, in suffering for those who are in Christ with him, he is under an even more pressing obligation to those who are perishing. So long as there are men without Christ and without hope in the world (Eph. 2.12), men living in the old aeon under the old foes, they have a claim on the Christian Church. It must never become a ghetto. It is there to serve the world. In 2 Cor. 2.15, Paul leads on immediately from the exultation of being in Christ's triumphal procession to the sombre thought of those who are lost. He knows he must be a "savour of Christ" among them, and must give an honest and balanced presentation of the good news, while he trusts God to speak to their hearts. "Who is sufficient for these things?" he asks ; . . . and answers, "Our sufficiency is of God" (2 Cor. 3.5). To save others became Paul's master passion. It sent him all over the Middle East, wearing himself out in the service of the gospel. It was his deepest concern and most earnest prayer that all Israel should be saved (Rom. 10.1). A remnant had indeed been saved, as Isaiah had foretold (Rom. 9.27), but the majority of Israel had rejected their Saviour. Why? He concludes that God has allowed it, in order that the Gentiles might be grafted into the olive, and find salvation (11.11). Surely God will, in due time, provoke his old people by the sight of the Gentiles streaming into salvation (11.14). That is one result which Paul hopes his Gentile mission will have; when the "fullness of the Gentiles has come in, then all Israel shall be saved" (11.25f.).[2]

[1] "An evident token of salvation" is "to stand together for the faith of the gospel", and to take the ensuing suffering and opposition as a privilege, a gift of God, who not only allows us "to believe on him, but also to suffer for his sake" (Phil. 1.28f.).

[2] For an acute interpretation of Paul's hopes for the salvation of Israel, see F. J. Leenhardt's *Commentary on Romans* (1961), *in loc.* See also J. Munck, *Paul and the Salvation of Mankind* (E.T. 1959), though he spoils his case by exaggeration.

Throughout all his missionary work, Paul has this great concern to save the lost, just as his Master had. That is why he accommodates himself, as far as conscience allowed,[1] to the scruples of Jews when he was with Jews, and of Gentiles when he was with them – "so that by all means I may save some" (1 Cor. 9.22, 10.33). The Christian partner in a mixed marriage has the same responsibility to seek to save his partner (1 Cor. 7.16). Not, of course, that the Christian can save anyone by himself. But by bearing testimony to the gospel of God's saving work, he can (Rom. 1.16). In the New Testament the work of saving is predicated of human agents just as readily as it was in the Old. It is the task of every Christian to pass on what he himself enjoys. For this is the will of God (1 Tim. 2.3), who is in design the Saviour of all men, but in practice the Saviour of those who believe.[2] "And how shall they believe in him of whom they have not heard? And how shall they hear without a preacher?" (Rom. 10.14). God's answer to this problem is the principle of incarnation; he entrusts his message to redeemed men and women whom he trusts to pass it on. "He manifests his word through the *kerygma*, which is committed to me," says Paul (Tit. 1.3). That responsibility and privilege drives him on to preach even when men "receive not the love of the truth that they may be saved" (2 Thess. 2.10), or when others "forbid us to preach to the Gentiles that they may be saved" (1 Thess. 2.16). For in the *kerygma* lies the power of God to save men (Rom. 1.16). Every Christian is called upon to proclaim it. Indeed, he cannot be called a Christian until he does. For "with the heart man believes unto righteousness; and with the mouth confession is made unto salvation" (Rom. 10.10). You cannot be saved, the previous verse reminds us, unless you confess with your mouth as well as believe in your heart. For it is a scriptural principle that, "Whosoever believeth on him shall not be ashamed" (10.11). Only in this way can salvation spread; only thus can God's will for the extension of his saving work in this age be accomplished.

C. SALVATION AS A FUTURE HOPE

This is a major theme in the teaching of Paul. "Our salvation is nearer than when we believed", " we have been saved in hope . . . of the resurrection of the body", "We look for that blessed hope, the glorious appearing of the great God and our Saviour Jesus Christ." These are some of the ways in which Paul expresses his Christian hope

[1] And it allowed a lot. See H. Chadwick, "All things to all men" in *New Testament Studies* (1955), pp. 261ff.
[2] This seems to be the meaning of the verse. Alternatively it may mean that God is the preserver of all men, and especially (i.e. in the distinctively Christian sense) of believers. See the further consideration of it in chs. 10, 11.

that "he who has begun a good work in you will perform it until the day of the Lord Jesus" (Phil. 1.6) Salvation is through and through eschatological for Paul, just as it was in the developed prophecy and apocalyptic of the Old Testament. The "day of the Lord" would not be merely a point in history but beyond history, not merely its conclusion but its goal.

But there is the characteristic Christian difference in eschatological perspective to be found in Paul. The last days have begun in Jesus Christ. Johannes Weiss put the paradox very clearly when he said, "Although Christ is already present, his coming is still expected; although Christians are already redeemed, still must they wait for the full redemption; sonship is theirs now, and yet they have still to obtain it; they are already glorified, and yet hope for glory; they possess life, but life they must receive."[1] In a word, the last days have been inaugurated, but they have not yet been consummated. To borrow a metaphor from Dr. Robinson, the decisive move in the game of chess has been played (although the opponent may not realize its significance), and the outcome is assured, although the game has yet to be concluded.[2] Oscar Cullmann's wartime analogy of "D"-Day and "V"-Day has become even more celebrated, and it is difficult to better it. The Allied invasion of Normandy is rightly seen as the decisive battle in the war; it is comparable to God's invasion of hostile human soil in the incarnation, cross and resurrection of Christ. "V"-Day lies ahead – how far ahead none can say before it happens. The one thing that is certain is that when it does dawn it will be seen to be nothing but the unfolding of the event of "D"-Day. So it will be with the last day. It will be seen to consummate what has already been inaugurated in Christ. At present the Christian lives "between the times" – beyond "D"-Day and this side of "V"-Day. Like the Allied troops in Europe after the invasion, he faces foes who are in principle defeated but who refuse to acknowledge it – and at times counter-attack most effectively. But, despite it all, the issue is assured and in due course the outcome will be revealed. As Althaus graphically put it, "The parousia removes the hiddenness of the reality of Easter for history."[3] We cannot afford to neglect this element in salvation without denying the significance of history, of a God who acts within time to save men. There must be a goal in view; without it the decisive battle would have been won but the cease-fire never applied; the teeth of death and sin would have been drawn but their final doom left in abeyance. God has acted decisively in Christ. Paul knows that. Indeed, as Albert Schweitzer said, "While

[1] See *Das Urchristentum* (1917), p. 421.
[2] J. A. T. Robinson, *In the End, God* (1950), pp. 54f.
[3] See *Die letzten Dinge* (1922), p. 244.

other believers held that the finger of the world-clock was touching on the beginning of the coming hour and were waiting for the stroke which should announce this, Paul told them that it had already passed beyond the point, and that they had failed to hear the striking of the hour, which, in fact, struck at the Resurrection of Jesus."[1] For that very reason Paul never underestimates the significance of future salvation. He would agree with Cullmann's conclusion: "The final act of the drama of the history of salvation cannot be neglected without disparaging the previous acts. If the death and resurrection of Christ are not to be consummated in the future, they cease to be the central event in the past, and the present is no longer located in the space between the starting-point and the consummation of Christology."[2]

With these last words Cullmann has come to the very heart of Paul's eschatology. It is in fact a department of Christology. The changed view Paul had of the life to come after he became a Christian was entirely due to Jesus Christ, his person and his work.[3] It is "through him" that we shall be saved (Rom. 5.9), and Paul's three main convictions about the life to come are, accordingly, integrated with him. He is clear that the Christian will share Christ's presence, his life and his likeness.

(i) We shall share his presence

This is one of Paul's most characteristic convictions about heaven. We shall be *with the Lord*. In the early letters like 1 Thessalonians, his assurance about the present state of the dead Christians is this; they are with the Lord. Furthermore, this is the supreme description of the bliss of the saved after the parousia – "the dead in Christ shall be raised first, then we which are alive and remain shall be caught up together with them in the clouds, to meet the Lord in the air; and so shall we ever be with the Lord" (4.16, 17). When he wrote the Corinthian letters, in the middle part of his ministry, Paul is still clear on this basic theme. "He which raised up the Lord Jesus shall raise us up also by Jesus, and shall present us with you" (2 Cor. 4.14) – and even before that final resurrection, when the soul after death is disembodied and lacks its full bliss,[4] the overriding compensation is this, that we are present with the Lord (2 Cor. 5.8). As Rom. 6.8 expresses it, "Now if we be dead with Christ, we believe that we shall also live with him." And

[1] *The Mysticism of Paul the Apostle* (E.T. 1931), p. 99.
[2] *The Early Church* (1956), p. 160.
[3] It will not be possible here to touch on the whole vast field of Pauline eschatology (see G. Vos, *The Pauline Eschatology* (1952)). Instead we shall restrict ourselves to what falls within his salvation language.
[4] See p. 182, n. 1.

in his later letters the picture has not changed. When, in a context where he is considering his salvation, Paul weighs up the pros and cons of life and death, he acknowledges that his continued life would be more useful for his Philippian friends than his death, but confesses to them his "desire to depart and to be with Christ, which is far better" (Phil. 1.23). Christ was now already his "life"; how could it be other than "gain" to depart into his closer presence (Phil. 1.21) where faith would be exchanged for sight (2 Cor. 5.7)? Nothing could break the union between the Christian and his risen Lord; thus, "when Christ, who is our life, shall appear, then shall ye also appear with him in glory" (Col. 3.4).

It is interesting to see how this deep conviction that the hereafter was qualitatively defined, and was essentially a state of relationship with the Lord and with others who were in him, is stressed by Paul throughout his writings, irrespective of the thought forms in which his language about the future life happened at any time to be couched. Clearly the background to the Thessalonian passage is very Jewish; equally clearly the thought forms in 2 Tim. 1.10, Tit. 1.2, 3 and perhaps in 2 Cor. 5,[1] are designed to appeal to a Hellenistic readership. But irrespective of the "furniture" of the hereafter (which, after all, can never be other than symbolic, for it remains in principle empirically unverifiable now just because it *is* the future), the conviction that the life to come is life with Christ is unshakable. That is the heart of salvation as a present experience, life with Christ; it will not be otherwise in the future. For the life to come has already dawned, and the part which still is future is all of a piece with what we already enjoy.

John Baillie, in his book *And the Life Everlasting* (p. 199), has a charming story which, as he says, is an artless tale, but embodies the authentic Christian temper. An old man lay dying, and asked his Christian doctor "if he had any conviction as to what awaited him in the life beyond. The doctor fumbled for an answer. But ere he could speak, there was heard a scratching at the door; and his answer was given him. 'Do you hear that?', he asked his patient. 'That is my dog. I left him downstairs, but he grew impatient and has come up and hears my voice. He has no notion what is inside that door, but he knows that I am here. Now is it not the same with you? You do not know what lies beyond the Door, but you know your Master is there.'"

<hr/>

[1] The view of Bultmann *op. cit.*, vol. 2, pp. 201ff., W. L. Knox, *St. Paul and the Church of the Gentiles* (1939), pp. 128ff., that Paul has here "sold the pass" to Hellenistic thought about the survival of the soul as opposed to the resurrection of the body, will not stand close investigation. See J. Lowe, *J.T.S.* (1941), pp. 129ff., W. D. Davies, *Paul and Rabbinic Judaism* (1948), pp. 310ff., Cullmann, *Immortality of the Soul* (1958), pp. 52f., R. Berry, *S.J.T.*, March 1961.

(ii) *We shall share his life*

The Christian does already share Christ's life (Rom. 6.10, 11, Gal. 2.20), and after death he will continue to share it. We live "in hope of eternal life" promised by God our Saviour – and he cannot lie (Tit. 1.1-3). It is interesting that Paul seems to reserve the phrase "everlasting life" for the sequel to physical death; such is the certain meaning of Rom. 2.7, Gal. 6.8, Tit. 1.2, 3.7, and probably holds good of Rom. 5.21, 1 Tim. 6.12 (in the light of 6.19) and Rom. 6.22, 23, though the last mentioned may well be thought of as a present state reaching out into the future, as "death" in the parallel clause does. In any case Paul freely applies "life" both to the now and to the hereafter. Already we share "life in God" (Col. 3.3, cf. Eph. 4.18), "life in Christ" (2 Tim. 1.1, 2.11) and "life in the Spirit" (Rom. 8.6, 10). This life is no bare attribute; it is qualitatively defined by the Holy Trinity. So it will be in the life to come. Eternal life to Paul is only secondarily life that will go on for ever; it is primarily a new quality, a new dimension of living. As Baillie acutely points out, when commenting on pagan views of immortality, "Nobody ever wanted an endless quantity of life until discovery had been made of a new and quite particular and exceptional quality of life."[1] It is this quality of life which is the Christian's present enjoyment and his future hope together. If he does not know it now, he will not know it then. If we are strangers to the life of God here, we shall be strangers to it there. Indeed, life with God hereafter would not be heaven but hell if we have not learnt to "crucify the flesh" and "live in the Spirit" (Gal. 5.24f.) it would be what Althaus calls "inescapable godlessness in inescapable relationship to God"[2] (cf. 2 Thess. 1.9). "Life with God for ever" means salvation from death and the associated "wrath" which we saw to be one of man's greatest enemies under the old aeon. Paul is at pains to stress this ultimate eschatological deliverance from death and wrath (1 Thess. 5.9, 10 – contrast 1 Thess. 2.16, 2 Tim. 1.10, Rom. 5.9). For the Christian is, in his present life, only delivered "in hope". Thus Paul can say we have been delivered from the wrath to come (1 Thess. 1.10), or that our deliverance is past and at the same time future (see the contrasted uses of "redemption" in Eph. 1.7, 14). These foes of man have received their death blow, but are not yet dead; their sentence is signed but not yet executed. The tension of our living now both in this age (where we are still subject to these evil powers) and in the age to come (where we are finally freed from them) is well brought out in the use of the Greek word *katargein*. The "principalities and powers" have been decisively defeated, and are already on the way to destruction (1 Cor. 2.6), but they will not be annihilated until the End (1

[1] *Op. cit.*, p. 205. [2] *Op. cit.*, p. 183.

Cor. 15.24). Death has already been *conquered* by Christ when he "brought life and immortality to light" (2 Tim. 1.10), and yet Paul uses the same word when he says that the last enemy that shall be *destroyed* is death (1 Cor. 15.26). It has been conquered but will not be abolished until the last day. That which is already final awaits its completion. Such is the future hope of sharing the life of Christ who "being raised from the dead, dieth no more; death hath no more dominion over him" (Rom. 6.9) which is the "helmet of salvation", the hope of *living* together with him (1 Thess. 5.9f.). Saved by his life now, we shall be saved by it then (Rom. 5.9), for we shall share it in its fullness, when the last enemy has not only been conquered but destroyed.

It need not be supposed that life after the removal of all foes will be a dull and static affair. Life is never static, nor is love dull. If there is to be life, there must be growth; if the life to come is one of perfect understanding, it will be one of perfect love both to the Saviour and to the saved (1 Cor. 13.8, 12). Instead of development *towards* goodness, there will be development *in* goodness. Professor A. E. Taylor has expressed this well. "The moral life would not disappear even from a world in which there were no wrongs to be righted. Even a society in which no member had anything more to correct in himself, and where 'Thou shalt love thy neighbour as thyself' were the universally accepted rule of social duty, would still have something to do; it would have the whole work of embodying the love of each for all in the detail of life."[1] This emphasis is important, for the ultimate salvation is essentially corporate. Indeed, almost all the metaphors used in Scripture to describe it are corporate ones – the kingdom of God, the Messianic Banquet, the elect, the Body of Christ, the New Man (or Humanity), the Israel of God, the fellowship of the Spirit, and so on. That is why love will be the all-important quality of the saved, the very life of heaven; it is "we with them" who will ever be with the Lord (1 Thess. 4.17). And so, to quote Professor Taylor again, "If we are to think morally of heaven, we should, I suggest, think of it as a land where charity *grows*, where each citizen learns to glow more and more with an understanding love, not only of the common King, but of his fellow-citizens." He continues, after remarking that we can begin to learn this lesson now, "But even where there is no ill-will or indifference to interfere with love, it is still possible for love to grow as understanding grows."[2]

[1] *The Faith of a Moralist* (1930), vol. 1, p. 400.
[2] *Op. cit.*, vol. 1, p. 421.

(iii) *We shall share his likeness*

Once again, the life to come is represented to us as continuous with this life. Death has been robbed of its significance, and the two poles in the Christian's existence are his conversion and the Coming of Christ. He does even now share Christ's likeness – increasingly as the Spirit is allowed mastery in his life. We are transformed into Christ's likeness, "from one degree of glory to another, even by the Lord the Spirit" (2 Cor. 3.18). But that likeness is still blurred in every Christian, however sanctified. It is, as John put it, not until Christ appears that "we shall be like him; for we shall see him as he is" (1 Jn. 3.2). St. Paul's perspective is precisely the same. He knows that it has been God's purpose from all eternity that mankind should be "conformed to the image of his Son, that he might be the firstborn among many brethren". And this is the result of what he calls predestination, calling, justification and glorification (Rom. 8.29, 30). Not until the process is complete shall we effectively and fully share his glory.

This important Pauline word "glory" is frequently connected with salvation. Indeed, salvation in its future consummation (after "belief of the truth" and "sanctification of the Spirit") means "obtaining the glory of our Lord Jesus Christ" (2 Thess. 2.13f.). Salvation is "in Christ with eternal glory" (2 Tim. 2.10) and it is reserved until the "appearing of the glory of the great God and our Saviour Jesus Christ" (Tit. 2.13). The word "glory" (*doxa*) in the Bible is primarily associated with God or Christ. It has nothing to do with the meaning current in Greek philosophy of "opinion" or in Greek politics of "honour", but means the manifestation of God's character and presence, pictured, to help our understanding, in terms of light or radiance. Thus when Jesus was born, the angels rightly sang, "To God in the highest, glory" (Lk. 2.14), for the divine radiance had become incarnate, and men saw in terms of a human life "the glory as of an only Son from the Father" (Jn. 1.14). Jesus had come to restore what was man's original destiny, to be the image and the glory of God (1 Cor. 11.7). Progressively as we are transformed into Christ's image (which is "the image of the invisible God" – Col. 3.10) we come to share his visible manifestation of character, his glory. This will be perfected at his return.[1] Even now "Christ in you" is "the hope of glory" (Col. 1.27). *Then* those saved by Christ will obtain glory (2 Tim. 1.10), and will perfectly reflect in a redeemed human nature the character God intended them to have; they will be like Christ. Perhaps the most famous passage which links salvation with the return of Christ and the obtaining of his glory is

[1] On the recovery through Christ of man's original status as creature made in God's image, see A. M. Ramsey, *The Glory of God and the Transfiguration of Christ* (1949).

Phil. 3.20f. Paul is writing to a city proud of being a Roman colony. He reminds his readers that we Christians constitute a colony of heaven, and from this relationship we can expect vindication at the hand of our Saviour when he comes, just as the Roman colonists could from their Saviour, the Emperor.[1] But Christ's salvation is incomparably superior to Caesar's; for he will change the body of our low estate, our corporate existence in all its frailty and sin, and make it like the body of his glory. This verse raises acutely a theme which runs right through the Apostle's teaching on the future aspect of salvation, the resurrection of the body at the parousia.

The Resurrection of the Body

Christian eschatology stands in striking contrast to Greek. By the first century A.D. most people in the Hellenistic world who had anything constructive to say about the after-life were influenced to a greater or lesser extent by Plato. The soul is by its nature immortal and at death is delivered from the hindrances imposed by the body.[2] "The body is our tomb," said Plato,[3] and such was the common conviction of those who cherished the hope of immortality. Bodily resurrection would seem repugnant and incredible to the Greek mind. It would be the perpetuation of something sordid and material – for the body and the created world were widely considered the work of some Demiurge, some inferior power. And a dualistic world-view has no place for the resurrection of the body.

The Christian conviction was quite different. It rested not on intellectual speculation, but upon a fact they could not deny, the resurrection of Jesus. That resurrection had only given demonstration to the Hebrew conviction about the after-life as it appears in the Old Testament, a conviction which is unashamedly physical, or rather, total. The Hebrew could not possibly write the body off; he could not sit loose to history – for in history God's saving acts had been revealed to him. How could he disparage the body or the created world when he knew that both sprang from a good God who "saw every thing that he had made, and, behold, it was very good" (Gen. 1.31)? Robert Davidson summarizes the position well when he writes, "Nature and man in the Old Testament form one indivisible whole, both utterly dependent upon and pliable in the hands of God, and linked in destiny to each other. For good and for ill, nature reflects the condition of man. Thus . . . Adam's disobedience reacts upon the whole world in which he lives." Of course, as he goes on to point out, "The converse

---

[1] He was increasingly, as we have seen, called *Sōtēr* in the first century, particularly in the Eastern Mediterranean.

[2] Plato, *Phaedo* 64C.   [3] Plato, *Gorgias* 493A.

also holds good. When the Old Testament looks for a renewed people of God enjoying a rich fulness of life, then it cannot but speak of this fulness of life in terms of a recreated universe from which all pain, disharmony and ruthlessness have been banished."[1] The New Testament doctrine of bodily resurrection is indeed the fulfilment of the hopes of Isa. 11.6-9, Ezek. 47.10-12, Joel 3.18, 20, etc. It is the logical outcome of realistic ethical monotheism. If you have come to believe in one good God as the author of the world and all that is in it, what other conclusion of the whole matter could there be? The Pauline stress on the resurrection of the body is simply another way of saying that the Christian doctrine of redemption is the complete counterpart of the Jewish doctrine of creation. Redeemed men will inhabit a redeemed universe where God will be all in all.

But if Paul follows the Old Testament in insisting on redemption of the whole man by grace as opposed to the Greek idea of the natural immortality of man's soul, that does not mean that he joined hands with the crass Jewish materialists of the day whom we know to have held the most crude and literal views about the resurrection body. Thus, for example, the Apocalypse of Baruch reads, "The earth shall then assuredly restore the dead (which it now receives, in order to preserve them). It shall make no change in their form, but as it has received them, so shall it restore them" (2 Baruch 50.2). Indeed, it seems probable that in his doctrine of the "spiritual body" in 1 Cor. 15 Paul is fighting on two fronts; against those with a Greek background who believed in a disembodied immortality, on the one hand, and against the Jewish materialists on the other, who believed that the very same bodily particles which had been buried would rise again in the last day. We shall indeed rise, Paul counters, but with a spiritual body. By "spiritual" Paul appears to mean one perfectly adapted for heavenly conditions, a body that will no longer hinder, but rather express the new life in Christ, a body that has become the perfect and transparent instrument of the Holy Spirit. By "body" he means the whole man, his entire personality, set within the *material* context of the created world and the *social* context of his fellows. The Christian doctrine of the resurrection of the body means that our ultimate destiny is thus neither reabsorption into the Infinite, nor the resuscitation of our present existence, nor a solitary and selfish enjoyment of God *solus cum solo*, but a social matter. Final bliss, the ultimate consummation, is not meant for us individually but corporately; it will not be enjoyed by *any* until it can be enjoyed by *all*, "that they without us should not be made perfect" (Heb. 11.40). The present state of the Christian dead before the parousia is something of which Paul says little; doubtless,

[1] *The Old Testament* (1964), pp. 222f.

until towards the end of his life he hoped that he would be alive at that great day and "be changed" without having to undergo death (1 Cor. 15.51). In 2 Cor. 5. we see the same thought;[1] he hopes to be "clothed upon" (*ependusasthai*) and have immortality superinvested upon his mortality, rather than face disembodied existence from which, as a good Hebrew, he shrank (5.3). If, however, he does have to endure this "nakedness", he has an abundant compensation; he is *accepted* with the Lord, *present* with the Lord (5.8, 9). To depart does mean "to be with Christ which is far better" (Phil. 1.23), although the resurrection body itself belongs to the last day. The dead in Christ are still *in* Christ, they are *with* Christ, they live on the farther side of Easter and death has been both overcome and passed, they have the earnest of the Holy Spirit (2 Cor. 5.5), but they await, as we do, the goal of all history, when man's social as well as individual aspirations will be fully satisfied. That is what is meant by the resurrection of the body. And that is why the parousia is of such cardinal importance. God's plan is for a new world of renewed men, not just for individuals, God's plan involves relationship among all the saved, not merely personal enjoyment of the Saviour. The parousia will usher in the consummation of the new age; it will mean the resurrection of the body for those who are dead in Christ, and the transformation of the body for those who are alive. Death will be swallowed up in victory (1 Cor. 15.54), and the saved will be at length like their Lord, with a body like his, which adequately expresses their transformed character.

If, like the incredulous Greek, we ask, "How are the dead raised up, and with what body do they come?" (1 Cor. 15.35), St. Paul can no more draw the curtain than we can. But he does give two most illuminating insights into the nature of the resurrection body. He gives us the famous parable of the seed, an illustration which had parallels in Judaism.[2] When we sow grain in the ground, it dies and decomposes. Only the germ lives on, and from it the new body is formed. It is the old principle which Paul knew to be central to the Christian religion, of life through death. So it will be with the resurrection body; a continuity of life through death, while this physical frame returns to the dust as surely as the husk of the grain of corn. But the analogy does not stop there. We do not expect an identical grain to emerge from the cornfield, but something far more wonderful, a plant, a blade, an ear of corn. Had we never seen the latter, we could never

[1] See p. 182, n. 1. It seems to me thoroughly unconvincing to suppose with E. E. Ellis (*New Testament Studies*, April 1960) that we have here nothing to do with the intermediate state. Paul *is* talking about the intermediate state (the "naked" here are equivalent to the "sleeping" of 1 Thess. 4.14 and 1 Cor. 15.51), and his eschatology is consistent throughout the period covered by his letters.

[2] *Sanhedrin*, 90 b.

have guessed what it would be like, simply from looking at that bare grain in our hands the autumn before. But once we have seen it, we can recognize that there is not only a continuity of life with that grain, but a real likeness, albeit greatly enhanced and beautified. "God has given it a body as it pleased him . . . So also is the resurrection of the dead . . . it is sown in corruption, it is raised in glory" (1 Cor. 15.38, 42f). We cannot conceive what a "spiritual body" will be like, but we may be sure that, once we possess it, we shall recognize that there has been both continuity of life and a real though transfigured likeness to the body we knew. Can we get any farther than that?

We can do so only by comparison with the risen body of Christ, and this is Paul's last word on the subject. Our resurrection body will be like the risen body of the Lord. There are two corporate solidarities in the world, two bodies, he says – Adam and Christ. All men are related to Adam, and all therefore bear his likeness; similarly all who are related to Christ will bear his likeness – for likeness depends on relationship. As the old solidarity in Adam characterizes our physical life, it is bound to end in death like his (15.22, 48). Similarly our new solidarity in Christ marks our spiritual life and will likewise issue in life like his. Christ is the firstfruits of the great harvest. Where there is a firstfruits, there will be a main crop. In short, "as we have borne the image of the earthy, so we shall bear the image of the heavenly (man)" (15.49), though this will not be until the Saviour appears, and gives us, as a final act of grace, a sharing in his own exalted body; the whole of redeemed mankind will at last reflect the Redeemer – Christ will be fully formed in us (Gal. 4.19). "The Body of Christ is the only corporeity which is 'eternal in the heavens'. Not until a man has put on *that* will he know salvation; and not till *all* have found themselves in it, and everything is finally summed up in Christ, will this salvation be complete for *any*."[1]

[1] J. A. T. Robinson, *op. cit.*, p. 98.

CHAPTER 10

Salvation in the Rest of the New Testament

THE PETRINE EPISTLES

Let us begin our survey of the non-Pauline teaching on salvation with the Petrine letters. I do not propose to argue the apostolic origin of 1 Peter, which is widely accepted in this country.[1] As might be expected, if the author is indeed the preacher of Acts. 1-12, there is a good deal of teaching on salvation in this Epistle. The verb comes in 3.21, 4.18 and the noun in 1.5, 9, 10, and probably 2.2. "Saviour" does not appear, but we meet with "redemption" in 1.18.

The tension between realized and unrealized eschatology is everywhere apparent. It is nowhere more clearly set out than in 1.18ff., an important passage to which we shall pay some attention.

Peter's readers are to recognize, in the first place, the *fact* of their redemption. He speaks of it as something already accomplished. The word *lutroō* is not common in the New Testament, and Hort believed, plausibly, that each instance echoes the words of Jesus in Mk. 10.45.[2] It is a word that would mean to the Gentile reader manumission from slavery, and to the Jew deliverance of a more general kind, with the great rescue from Egypt never far from his mind. Both, incidentally, were sealed in sacrifice. Peter's words here take us back explicitly to that prototype of all God's deliverances, as far as the Jew was concerned, redemption from Egypt. The Israelites who sheltered under the blood of the paschal lamb (Ex. 12.5) were delivered from that land of bondage and death, and were brought into the freedom of Canaan. It was, of course, in this sense and in this context that Moses was called a *lutrōtēs*, a deliverer, in Act 7.35. And now Jesus has achieved a new Exodus. All men, not just Israelites, have been ransomed from a bondage and a death far worse than Egypt's, by the costly ransom-price of the death of the Messiah; they are brought, furthermore, into an inheritance far better than that of Canaan, for it is "incorruptible, undefiled,

---

[1] This has been effectively argued in recent times by E. G. Selwyn, A. F. Walls, and C. E. B. Cranfield in their commentaries. See, however, F. W. Beare's commentary (1958) for the opposite view.

[2] See F. J. A. Hort's commentary (1898) *in loc.*, especially pp. 78ff.

and that fadeth not away, reserved in heaven" for them (1.4).

The *nature* of this deliverance is interesting. Peter says nothing about sin. What he does mention is the emptiness of their own previous way of life, and that of their fathers before them. To the Jew this would speak of the burdensome traditions imposed upon the faithful by the religious leaders (Lk. 11.46 and Matt. 23 *in toto*); indeed, Peter himself refers to these traditions as the yoke of bondage "which neither our fathers nor we were able to bear" (Acts 15.10). To the Gentile, this would speak of the old heathen life, characterized by ignorance of God, absence of objective moral standards, lack of purpose, and what Hort calls "the yoke not merely of personal inclination and indulgence but that which was built up and sanctioned by the accumulated instincts and habits of past centuries of ancestors".[1] It was from all this slavery to futility and custom that the suffering Messiah offered redemption.

The *purpose* of this deliverance is also clearly stated. It is to enable men to become what God requires in those who are related to himself. Indeed, in the paragraph beginning 1.13, Peter gives three compelling reasons for living a holy life. It is essential because relationship with God is impossible without it (1.14-16), because we must all render account to the God who is Judge (17), and because of the tremendous moral claims of the death of Christ who died to redeem us (18-21). That is why Christians must be holy. The nature of this holiness, what Selwyn calls the "neo-Levitical holiness" of a ransomed people dedicated to their God, is too wide to examine here. It affects the whole way of life (1.15), and gives rise to obedience and love (1.22), glad submission (2.18, 3.1, 5.5) and suffering (4.12, 13). It involves worship (2.5), and means a life of courtesy and compassion (3.8), a tongue that is both purified from unkind and immoral talk (3.9) and also ready to give a reason for the hope within (3.15).

But most significant of all in this verse 1.18, is the emphasis on the *cost* of our redemption. To quote Hort once more, "The idea of the whole passage is a simple one, deliverance through payment of a costly ransom by another" (p. 79). Nevertheless, the Old Testament allusions are complex. The primary reference is, of course, to the Exodus, where deliverance of the people from death at the hands of the destroying angel took place through the death of a lamb. This was closely associated, in the minds of later generations, with the Exodus from Egypt itself, which properly followed it.[2] Thus the Midrash on Ex. 12.22

---

[1] *Op. cit.*, p. 76.

[2] Bigg seems to have grasped the broad scope of the verse when he writes, "The blood of the Paschal Lamb . . . was, as a shadow, both an Atonement and a Ransom; it covered the houses of the Israelites from the destroying Angel, it redeemed the firstborn, and it was a condition of the deliverance of the whole people from the house of bondage," C. Bigg in the *I.C.C.* (1901), p. 120.

says "The Israelites were delivered from Egypt with the blood of the paschal lamb."[1] The actual language of 1.18, however, is borrowed from Isa. 52.3, a passage which, as we have already seen, teaches that God's deliverance is not achieved by money, but none the less costs him dear. And further, Peter seems to be thinking in 1.20, 21 of Isa. 53.12, 13 as he certainly is in 2.24 and 3.18 where, as in Acts, we find him interpreting the cross in terms both of the Suffering Servant and the Curse. So great was the cost to God, that it meant the death of the Messiah for us; a death wherein he suffered for sins, the just for the unjust, in order to bring us to God. Once again we meet his assertion that the Christ had to suffer (cf. Acts 2.23, 3.18); his death was part of the eternal purpose of God, and has now been revealed in time. Because of this redeeming death, and the glorious resurrection which crowns it (1.3), we can be assured of a salvation which is in every respect complete.

But the strength of Peter's faith in a finished work of Christ, a salvation which has already been achieved, should not blind us to the fact that his references to the subject generally speak of it as future.[2] Salvation belongs to the last day. It is "ready to be revealed in the last time" (1.5). This passage is most illuminating. True to character, Peter once again interprets salvation in terms of the Old Testament revelation, only here it is not a matter of comparison but of contrast with the earthly Canaan. The land of Canaan is often in the Old Testament spoken of as the "inheritance" of the people of God (e.g. Ps. 79.1). "But unlike Canaan", so runs Selwyn's splendid comment, "the promised possession of the Christians is not subject to the ravages of war or calamity (cf. 1 Chr. 20.1, Isa. 24.3, 4, Dan. 9.26), nor to the idolatry and the sensual vices that accompanied it (cf. Jer. 2.7, 23, 3.2, Ezek. 20.43, Hag. 2.13, 14), nor to the wasting effects of time or unkind seasons (cf. Job 15.30, Wisd. 2.8)."[3] For the Christian inheritance of the heavenly Canaan will not be spoiled, cannot be defiled, and never grows old; a wonderful picture of future salvation.

But between the past and future in salvation history, the Christian has to live in the present. He is intended to have a constant experience of the keeping power of God (1.5). This is his birthright since he was initiated into the realm of salvation by his baptism (3.21). Just as certainly as Noah found the way to safety through the waters of the flood, so the Christian finds salvation through the waters of baptism. Not, of course, that baptism in itself has any quasi-magical powers, as

[1] See Wünsche, *Bibliotheca Rabbinica*, ii, p. 135.
[2] So 1.5, perhaps 1.9, 10 and certainly 2.2 (if "unto salvation" should be read there).
[3] *Op. cit.*, p. 124.

Peter is quick to point out. The baptism of which he speaks is "not the putting away of the filth of the flesh, but the answer of a good conscience towards God". That is to say, when the condition of trusting obedience to God's way of salvation is present as it was in Noah, when there is the soldier's pledge of sincere loyalty to God[1] – granted *that*, then baptism saves. This is not only because it is the initiatory rite of Christianity, but because it sums up all that Christ has achieved for man in his death, resurrection and ascension; all this God "makes over" to us, as it were, in baptism. It will be remembered that the link between baptism and salvation was a characteristic of Peter's preaching as recorded in Acts.

If baptism is the way into God's salvation which is at once realized and anticipatory, how, we might ask, is it maintained in this present life? 1 Pet. 1.5 gives the answer. It is God who protects us here and now, just as the past and future aspects of salvation are his work alone. It is God who not only brings us into but keeps us in his salvation. This may well be the thought uppermost in the writer's mind in 1.9, 10. The verse could, of course, mean, as Selwyn is inclined to take it, that we shall receive our salvation, like a prize, at the appearing of Jesus Christ. He is surely right in asserting that the salvation of 1.10 "of which the prophets have enquired and searched diligently", covers the whole range of the Messianic deliverance, past, present and future. But it seems to me that attention both to the present tense of *komiz-omenoi* and to the context, suggests that Peter has our present salvation primarily in mind. His words, if taken in this way, are certainly para-doxical, but emphasize the eschatological tension, characteristic of the earliest Christians, between what we already have and what we still await. Faith is, indeed, the mode of realized eschatology. As we suffer testing to our faith, as we look for Christ's return, as we rejoice with him and trust in him, we receive here and now, albeit only in a measure, the fullness of God's salvation. And the more we grow in faith, the more we appropriate of this "salvation of our souls".[2] That, of course, is the meaning of 2.2 if, as seems highly probable,[3] it should read "desire the sincere spiritual(?) milk that ye may grow thereby *unto salvation*". The need for progress along the Christian way is every-where safeguarded in the New Testament. The lives of those experiencing salvation are dominated by gratitude for Christ's

[1] This I take to be the most probable background of the difficult *eperōtēma*. But see Selwyn's discussion (*op. cit.*, p. 205) and G. C. Richards(*J.T.S.*, Oct. 1930).

[2] Of course, *psychē* in 1 Peter is never a psychological term (as it is in Paul) contrasted both with *pneuma* and *nous*. Sometimes it refers to man seen as a spiritual being (1.22, 2.25), and sometimes it means broadly "a person" (3.20, 4.19).

[3] εἰς σωτηρίαν is not omitted by a single early MS.

redemption and by the expectation of Christ's return. Salvation necessarily affects behaviour, and demands progress.

There is, perhaps, a touch of the reverse side of realized eschatology in 4.18, "If the righteous scarcely be saved, where shall the ungodly and the sinner appear?" One of the ineluctable strands in the biblical teaching about the last day is judgement. And judgement, like salvation, is not only future but present. God's judgement on his "household" is demonstrated by the trials they bear here on earth. So Hort comments on 2.2, "Salvation in the fullest sense is but the completion of God's work upon men, the successful end of their probation and education." The righteous, says Peter, quoting the LXX of Prov. 11.31, are indeed being saved, but only through tribulation and difficulty. It is no simple, easy matter for God to refine his gold in the furnace of affliction. Peter is asserting in this passage that both wrath and mercy, salvation and judgement, are future realities which belong to the last day, and are yet anticipated in time (cf. Rom. 1.17, 18). Stibbs seems right in taking the meaning of 4.17, 18 to be that "those who share in God's judgement on sin here will find salvation hereafter, whereas those who live here in ungodliness and sin must face terrifying final judgement hereafter".[1]

It will be apparent that the theology of salvation that meets us in 1 Peter is profound, rooted in the Old Testament Scriptures and the work of Christ, and consonant with the speeches attributed to Peter in Acts, though in several ways more developed. A notable characteristic of the teaching of the Epistle on salvation is that it preserves the tension of primitive eschatology.

What, then, is the case with 2 Peter? This is not the place to argue the provenance of the book. Professor C. C. Bigg, writing in the *I.C.C.* in 1915, was the last author of a major commentary in English to maintain its authenticity. There has, in all conscience, been little enough work done on it since that date, nevertheless it has come to be regarded as certainly spurious, and belonging to the mid-second century A.D.[2] The reasons which give rise to this widespread assumption appear to me not to bear the weight of the hypothesis they support, as I have indicated elsewhere,[3] and I am inclined to the opinion that to regard it as pseudepigraphic raises greater problems than it solves.

However that may be, the salvation terminology of 2 Peter is

[1] *The First Epistle General of Peter* (1959), p. 163.

[2] Thus a scholar usually as careful as C. E. B. Cranfield can regard the subject of authorship as closed, and dismiss it in a couple of pages (S.C.M. Torch Comm., 1960, pp. 148, 149).

[3] See my *2 Peter Reconsidered* (1961). Since then, D. Guthrie, *New Testament Introduction*, ii (1962) and E. F. Harrison, *Introduction to the New Testament* (1964) also incline with me to the Petrine authorship of 2 Peter.

certainly different from that of the First Epistle. "Salvation" comes but once, the verb "save" not at all, while the attribution of the title "Saviour" to Jesus, which we have seen to be rare in the New Testament, comes no less than five times. Three times we meet the phrase "our Lord and Saviour Jesus Christ" (1.11, 2.20, 3.18), once "our God and Saviour Jesus Christ" (1.1), and once simply "our Lord and Saviour" (3.2). This usage is regarded by Käsemann,[1] for example, as indicative of the late date of the Epistle. He draws attention to the stereotyped nature of the phrase, its application to Jesus rather as though he were a cult deity, and parallel forms of adulation applied to Jesus by second-century Christian writers. Cullmann gives qualified agreement, and instances Ignatius, the Martyrdom of Polycarp, and the Gospel of Peter as using this *Sōtēr* language of Jesus.[2] However, arguments of this kind are indecisive. As Cullmann recognizes, the attribution of this title to Jesus is certainly pre-Pauline (Phil. 3.20 makes this plain), and on any showing 2 Peter was not written before Philippians! Furthermore, it will be noticed that there are variations in the title; it comes, as we have seen, in three forms in 2 Peter. And this gives pause to the ready assumption that we have to do with a fixed stereotyped phrase. Furthermore, the most common of the three Petrine attributions, "Our Lord and Saviour Jesus Christ", is by no means common in the sub-apostolic age. Indeed, I have not noticed it at all in the literature of the first half of the second century;[3] the nearest is Ignatius's phrase "the Saviour, our Lord Jesus Christ" (*Philad.* 9.2), and the description in the *Martyrdom of Polycarp* of "our Lord Jesus Christ, the Saviour of our souls and the Governor of our bodies" (19.2). Thus arguments for the lateness of the title based on second-century usage are precarious, particularly when both "Lord" and "Saviour" individually are predicated of Jesus well before A.D. 50. And when we examine the contexts in which the word is used in 2 Peter, its use appears not in the least stereotyped, but rather, highly apposite. The whole Epistle is written to people who claim Jesus as Saviour, but do not obey him as Lord. That appears to be why the writer significantly combines the roles of Lord and Saviour. It comes twice in ch. 1, at the beginning and end of a stirring appeal to backsliders. He starts from the *dikaiosunē*, the impartial fairness, of our God and Saviour Jesus Christ, which has given to the readers a faith equal

---

[1] *Essays on New Testament Themes* (1964), pp. 169-95.
[2] *Op. cit.*, p. 243, viz. Ign., *Eph.* 1.1, *Magn.* 1.1, *Smyrn.* 7.1, *Philad.* 9.2; *Mart. Poly.* 19.2, *Gospel of Peter* 4.13.
[3] "Our Lord Jesus Christ" occurs six times in *1 Clem.*, five in *Polyc.* and once in *Ign.*, but never with "Saviour". "Jesus Christ our Saviour" comes in *Polyc.* 1.1, Ign. *Smyrn.* 7.1, *Magn.* 1.1, *Eph.* 1.1.

in privileges to that of the apostles. They are nothing less than partakers of the divine nature (1.4),[1] and as such they must show forth their pedigree in the quality of their lives (1.5-11), so that they need not be ashamed when their Lord and Saviour Jesus Christ consummates his kingly rule. It is through the action of the Lord and Saviour that they enjoy the privileges of being children of God. And yet their entrance upon the *basileia* of the Lord and Saviour is still future. What is this if not the characteristic primitive tension between the "now" and "then" in salvation, the realized and the future in eschatology?

2.20 has something of the same tension. They have escaped the pollutions of the world through coming to know[2] Jesus Christ as Lord and Saviour. If they cease to allow him to be Saviour from sinful habits, they are "denying the Lord who bought them" (2.1) and their last state is worse than their first. 3.2 looks formalized at first sight, but may it not refer to the future element in salvation which the scoffers scout? Jesus is not only Saviour from the past (1.1-4), and in the present (2.20) but for the future as well. To deny the parousia of Jesus, is to deny Jesus as Saviour.

3.18 reminds the readers that the way of growth in grace is by deepened knowledge[3] of Jesus as Lord and Saviour. To submit to his mastery as Lord is to discover his power as Saviour. Indeed, it is a remarkable thing that each of the five references in 2 Peter to "Saviour" is applied specifically to Jesus, thus emphasizing that Christ is the centre of Christianity, which both begins and develops in the knowledge of him – a theme which remains constant in the various streams of early Christianity (Jn. 17.3, Phil. 3.8-10, cf. Acts 8.5, 35, etc). This holds good even of the lone and rather curious reference to salvation in 3.15. It seems to mean that the patience of the Lord (Jesus), displayed in the merciful delay of the parousia, is designed to lead men to salvation. He gives them time to repent and be saved. When the parousia dawns, it will close the day of salvation and mean judgement, the final

[1] On the background of this phrase, see Deissmann, *Light from the Ancient East* (1910), p. 322 and *Bible Studies* (E.T. 1901), pp. 360ff.; Green, *op. cit.*, p. 23.

[2] It is important to note that in this verse and 1.4 men are not said to become partakers of the divine nature *in* escaping the natural world, as Käsemann and Bultmann take it (neglecting the aorist participle *apophugontes*), but *after* escaping the "world" in the sense of "mankind in rebellion against God," which is the characteristic New Testament meaning of the word.

[3] So far from sitting back in comfortable assurance of their knowledge of Christ, for that very reason (αὐτὸ τοῦτο, 1.5) they are to add to their faith virtue (1.5ff.) and become in practice what they already are in Christ. The emphasis on knowledge in this Epistle is no more "incipient gnosticism" than it is in 1 Corinthians. The apostolic writers are combating a γνῶσις that emancipates from morality, with a proper γνῶσις χριστοῦ which is the very basis of Christian ethics, and the very heart of Christian development.

separation of the just from the unjust.[1] And what could be more primitive teaching than that?

Before leaving 2 Peter, a word should be said about 1.1. The natural reading of that verse makes the writer call Jesus God as well as Saviour. The two nouns are held together by a single article.[2] It looks as though "God" is here used as a variant for "Lord" that "name above every name" given Jesus at his ascension (Phil. 2.9-11), for in the other references in 2 Peter it is as Lord and Saviour that Jesus is presented to us. If this is so, it would be a rare designation, though not unparalleled, and it would be fully in line with the whole biblical revelation that God is the one who saves, while doing justice to the conviction of the early Christians that Jesus can be no less than God.

A further small point is that in 2 Peter "Saviour" appears only as a supplement to "Lord"; the "name above every name" naturally tended to swallow up any other title that pointed in the same general direction. And "Saviour" was one such title, for it was, like "Lord", an Old Testament designation of God, and was applied to Jesus because of the conviction brought about by the resurrection that he was indeed Lord.

THE EPISTLE OF JUDE

Together with 2 Peter we must take Jude. Between the two Epistles there is an undoubted literary relationship, either of 2 Peter on Jude, as Mayor, Abbott, M. R. James, Chase and most moderns think; or of Jude on 2 Peter, as Spitta, Zahn, Plummer, and Bigg prefer; or else of both on some common source. Be that as it may, Jude speaks of our common salvation as early as verse 3. What he makes of it appears more clearly in verse 5. Christian salvation is historic, like the Exodus. Like that great event, it is the work of God. The Christian experience of salvation, like the Jewish, is dependent upon perseverance. For whilst all the people were delivered from Egypt, some apostasized, and in rejecting the loving faithfulness of God, had to face its complement, his judgement. "All those men who have seen my glory, and my miracles which I did in Egypt and in the wilderness, and have tempted

---

[1] Indeed, the excellent balance of the eschatological tension in 2 Peter could not be better shewn than by the contradictory contentions of Bultmann and Käsemann. The former complains that there is too great an emphasis on future salvation in 2 Peter, while the latter attacks the author for dwelling on the saved condition of the citizen of heaven! Both scholars have grasped one element in the truth. See Green, *op. cit.*, p. 20.

[2] Bigg comments, "Though σωτήρ is one of his favourite words, he never uses it alone, but always couples it with another name under the same article. There is strong reason for thinking that the two names always belong to the same person; undoubtedly they do in four cases out of the five" (*op. cit.*, p. 251).

me now these ten times, and have not hearkened to my voice; surely they shall not see the land which I sware unto their fathers" (Num. 14.22f.). God[1] saves men from their plight and he will preserve them to the very end, provided they continue to trust and obey their Saviour. No man will be in heaven against his will. That is why the antinomians with whom Jude is dealing must not presume on the grace of God. They appear to have regarded salvation as an assured religious possession of their own, rather than as a constant manifestation of God's grace – and that attitude is the foe of true Christianity, indeed it is a manifestation of the anti-God spirit.[2] The historic element in salvation cannot be used as a sanction over God, any more than the Jewish Torah could (see Rom. 10.1-3). The Christian life begins and ends with faith making response to grace. God will keep men. But men must trust him to do so, and want him to do so. Hence the solemn warning of the possibility of apostasy, which is repeated in many places in the New Testament. A particularly close parallel is provided by 1 Cor. 10.5ff., a passage which alludes to the same Old Testament incident as Jude. It would seem that the Corinthians were making the sacraments into guarantees of salvation, almost independent of the God whose grace they represent. This is magic, not faith; for while faith seeks to cooperate with God, magic seeks to manipulate him. Paul has to warn them that there is no method of securing salvation other than by keeping in living contact with the Saviour. The Old Testament church, too, had a historic deliverance. They too were baptized into solidarity with the deliverer (Moses); they too ate the heavenly food. But they rebelled against God – and so they fell in the wilderness. That is why the man who thinks he is standing secure should take care lest he fall. Why, even Paul himself dare not presume. If he were to live an undisiciplined and undedicated life, in repudiation of the Saviour's proffered grace, he too might have to face rejection at the day of testing (1 Cor. 9.16-27). For salvation is not a historic possession but an eschatological experience. To be saved or to gain salvation is neither a possession which can be obtained nor a proposition which can be proved (or even assented to), but an existential relationship with the Saviour. And one of the marks of the man who has truly entered this relationship is that he has a desire to save others from the awful loss, the separation, the state of rebellion against God which they are in. This is emphasized both by Paul and by Jude (1 Cor. 9.22, 10.33, Jude 23). The "saved" man manifests the love of the "Saviour" God for sinners. That is how

[1] The variant readings, "Jesus", "Lord" and "God" in verse 5 are an interesting reflection of the second-century views both of Christology and soteriology.

[2] See the magisterial indictment of this attitude in a modern setting in D. Bonhoeffer's *The Cost of Discipleship*.

he can be distinguished. Instead of slipping back to the ways of the world, he is always at work for God attempting to bring others to the Saviour. But lest this human sense of saving be misunderstood, Jude ends his letter with one of the noblest paeans of praise to be found anywhere in the New Testament. It is God who is able to keep you from falling. It is God who is able to bring you to final salvation. To God the only Saviour, *our* Saviour, be glory and majesty, dominion and power both now and for ever (24, 25).

THE EPISTLE OF JAMES

We shall not expect to find coordinated doctrine in an Epistle directed to intellectualists[1] whose main need was not to know more, but to put into practice what they knew full well; nevertheless the sidelights which emerge from James's approach to the subject are interesting and arresting. He never speaks of "Saviour" or "Salvation", but on five occasions he uses the verb "save", and in each case with a different connotation.

Perhaps we should begin with 4.12, for it expresses the central affirmation of both the Old Testament and later Judaism. Salvation is of the Lord. It is the prerogative of God to save and to destroy. He is sovereign in his world; therefore we should leave him to judge, and not arrogate that function to ourselves. He is sovereign in his world; therefore we should trust him, and not act independently of his will. James is reiterating here a great truth about God revealed to Moses long ago, "I kill, and I make alive; I wound and I heal; neither is there any that can deliver out of my hand" (Deut. 32.39). Jesus said much the same, "Fear him rather who is able to destroy both soul and body in hell" (Matt. 10.28). Divine Judgement and mercy, salvation and destruction are always held together in Scripture in an inescapable dialectic. Man must choose.

This leads naturally on to James's second contention, namely that faith (coupled with works) saves (2.14). Few passages in the New Testament have been so misunderstood as this one. It is James's apparent denial of the Pauline doctrine of justification by faith that made Luther dub this "a right strawy epistle", and consign it to an appendix to his New Testament. Whether or not James is implicitly attacking Paul[2] in these verses is partly dependent upon the relative dates of their writings, and that of James is quite uncertain. There were certainly

---

[1] On this background to James, see J. Jeremias, in *The Expository Times*, September 1955, and J. B. Lightfoot, *Galatians* (1869), p. 162.
[2] This is most unlikely, as the article of Jeremias cited above makes plain. Paul and James use πίστις, ἔργα and δικαιοῦσθαι in different senses; they refer to different occasions in the life of Abraham, and they write against a different background.

those who twisted Paul's doctrine of free grace into an excuse for antinomianism (Rom. 3.8), and James may have such people in mind when he denies that faith alone can save. But the point to notice is the article ἡ πίστις. Bede has caught the meaning of the Greek when he paraphrases it "*fides illa quam vos habere dicitis*", and so has the N.E.B. translation, "Can that faith save him?" James is not denying that faith in the sense of *fiducia*, or "loving trust", is the proper response on the part of man to the saving activity of God on his behalf; what he is attacking is faith in the sense of *assensus*, cold intellectual assent to credal formulations which makes no difference to the behaviour of one who professes it. He insists that authentic, saving faith must issue in works of love (2.14-18), just as Paul in Gal. 5.6 stresses "faith which worketh by love" as the only thing that will stand the test of God's scrutiny. The total initiative and self-giving of God in salvation demands the total response of man in faith and works. The faith that saves is the faith that shews itself in works of love.[1] The absence of a transformed life, on the other hand, is proof positive of the absence of salvation. And if that were the only contribution made by the Epistle of James to the doctrine of salvation, we would have ample cause to be grateful for so searching a warning.

But in fact James has a good deal more to say upon this subject. In 1.21 he says that the "word", or Christian message, saves. The context would appear to be a baptismal one; the evidence has been set out, with parallels from other parts of the New Testament, in Selwyn's *First Epistle of Peter*, pp. 390, 391, 394. And despite Mayor's warning[2] that nothing is said about baptism here, such a background is made probable by the way James speaks of the gift of God, his Fatherhood, the new birth for a life of holiness, and the need to "lay aside filthiness and naughtiness", a phrase which is strongly reminiscent of 1 Peter 3.21, and that passage, of course, is explicitly baptismal. Baptism, however, is grounded on the word, or the truth of the gospel, as it is variously described in different parts of the New Testament.[3] And thus while Peter stresses baptism as the instrument of salvation, James very properly stresses the "word" which underlies it.[4] Salvation is to be found through the Christian message. But there are conditions. It is not gained by action, but by quiet waiting upon God, the giver of

[1] It is interesting to note the different content given to "works" in Paul and James. James is advocating the loving deeds which prove faith (see 2.8, 1.25) while Paul is attacking acts performed to win merit from God (cf. Rom. 4.2-4).
[2] *The Epistle of St. James* (1913), p. 62.
[3] See 1 Pet. 1.22, 23; Jas. 1.18, 21; Jn. 17.17, Col. 1.5 etc. as cited in Selwyn; it should be noted however that baptism has often to be inferred in these verses!
[4] John 15.3 is usually regarded as an allusion to baptism, and yet what is said is that the disciples are made clean through the *word* spoken by Jesus, cf. 17.17.

all good gifts (1.16-19). The saving message must be received, and furthermore it must be allowed to take root in the heart so that it actually grows there,[1] and produces the changed life of which 1.26, 27 speak; for hearing without doing never saved any man; such frivolity merely increases his condemnation.

There remain two references in ch. 5 which are by no means unrelated to what has gone before. In 5.15 it is said that "the prayer of faith shall save the sick, and the Lord shall raise him up; and if he have committed sins, they shall be forgiven him". As is well known, commentators have been divided over the meaning of this verse. Does it mean that, in answer to prayer and the anointing of a dying man, God will raise him up at the last day with his sins forgiven, as most Roman Catholics take it?[2] Or does it mean, as the Greek more naturally suggests, that in answer to prayer and the anointing of a sick man, God will bring him back to health again?[3] I wonder if these two interpretations are as mutually exclusive as they are usually taken to be. Ought we, perhaps, to set the problem in a wider perspective, and regard the word "save" as deliberately ambivalent? The God revealed to us in the Bible is concerned for the whole man, as is the Jesus who confronts us in the Gospels. It would not therefore be surprising if this verse spoke both of physical recovery and the forgiveness of sins; both matter to God. In this case, James would be reminding his readers that God saves in both physical and spiritual senses in answer to prayer. Indeed, this verse reminds one irresistibly of the teaching and practice of Jesus. In answer to the believing prayer of the man's friends (Mk. 2.3-5), Jesus raised the sick of the palsy (2.11f.), and declared that his sins were forgiven (2.5). These are the two results of believing prayer which James envisages here. And the Marcan parallel makes it very likely that the sins in question are those which caused the illness.[4] Mayor[5] appropriately quotes *Nedarim* 41a, "No sick man recovers from sickness until his sins have been forgiven." Thus while there is no warrant in this passage for supposing that the illnesses and sins of

[1] Particularly if the unique ἔμφυτον should be taken proleptically.

[2] In order to find a scriptural basis for extreme unction.

[3] This would not necessarily mean that all sickness would be healed. We must take seriously James's words in 4.15; the "if the Lord will" must apply no less to healing than to any other activity. Nowhere in Scripture is it suggested that all sickness is outside the permissive will of God; indeed there is some evidence to the contrary (e.g. 1 Tim. 5.23, 2 Tim. 4.20, 2 Cor. 12.7ff.).

[4] That there is some connection between sin as a whole and suffering as a whole is the plain teaching of Scripture. It is no less clear that in *some* cases there is a direct causal link between sin and suffering (e.g. Acts 8.23) though it is repeatedly denied that the presence of suffering implies the commission of great sin (Jn. 9.1-3, Lk. 13.1-5).

[5] *Op. cit.*, p. 162.

men will be removed in answer to prayer, irrespective of whether they repent, there is every reason to take seriously its assertion that God is concerned to save the whole man, seen as a physical no less than a spiritual being, and that his will can be furthered by the believing prayer of those who are right with him. For the prayer of such people avails much in its working (James 5.16).

The last reference to salvation in James is as arresting as all the others. 5.20 says that "he which converteth the sinner from the error of his way shall save a soul from death and shall hide a multitude of sins". That is to say, one man may save another. As it is applied here, it is the reclaiming of the backslider that is in question, but no doubt the same holds good of the man who leads another to Christ for the first time. Such a man saves a soul from death. This work of salvation through evangelism is attributed to the human agent elsewhere, particularly in Paul (Rom. 11.14, 1 Cor. 7.16, 1 Tim. 4.16). The remarkable thing about this verse is that it is a backsliding Christian who is the object of this saving activity, rather than someone who is not yet a Christian. The apostasizing Christian *ipso facto* cuts himself off from the source of life and chooses death.[1] The implications of this teaching must be squarely faced; it raises acutely the question of perseverance, with which we shall attempt to grapple in the final chapter. But unless we are to take the exegetically unsatisfying and theologically improbable interpretation adopted by Moffatt,[2] and suppose that it is his own soul that the Christian worker saves by the reclamation of the backslider, the fact must be faced that James does suggest that a Christian who falls away is in peril of spiritual death. It is, as we are discovering, a constant element in the New Testament doctrine of salvation, that a man is only safe as he is in union with Christ. There are many verses which make it certain that Christ will never repudiate the man who trusts in him, but there are others which make it plain that becoming a Christian does not rob a man of his self-determination, and if he chooses to sin against the light in departing from the safety of relationship with God, God will respect the integrity of his free will even in the hell of his own choosing. What James is saying is that such a man is not gone beyond hope of recall. He can, by loving friendship and patient counsel, be won back. The Christian brother who undertakes this work can rest assured that it is perfectly possible, as well as vitally important. "We can well imagine," says

[1] Cf. the plea in Deut. 30.19.

[2] In his commentary on the *Catholic Epistles* (1928) he writes on 5.20, "Such forgiving, redeeming love for a brother will atone for a great deal. It is a good work which the loving God will allow to count in favour of the true Christian" (p. 83). For trenchant criticism of this view see Mayor, *op. cit.*, pp. 223f., and Tasker, *The General Epistle of James* (1956), p. 144.

Mayor in the closing words of his great commentary, "that such a promise might have been a great encouragement to those who were dispirited at the state of the backsliders in the church to which they belonged, and doubted whether it was possible to renew them again unto repentance."[1]

But for all his unusual approach to this subject, and despite his complete disregard for the eschatological significance of salvation,[2] James is at least in line with the Old Testament conception of salvation, as something which is supremely the prerogative of God, although he may use human agencies to bring it about. The four agencies he mentions are the Word, faith, prayer, and personal evangelism, and these four remain high among the means God uses to bring men to salvation.

HEBREWS

When we turn to the Epistle to the Hebrews, we find that the noun "salvation" is used seven times and the verb "save" twice. Moreover, just as in the Old Testament salvation was nowhere connected with the cultus, the same holds good in Hebrews, which is, of course, very much concerned with the cult. However, we notice that the redemption terminology which is sometimes used in connection with sacrifice in the Old Testament is three times so used in this Epistle.

First, the two verbs. In 5.7 Jesus offers up "prayers and supplications with strong crying and tears to him that was able to save him from death". At first sight it looks like a natural and neutral use of the word in the old Hebrew sense of "keep alive". On second thoughts its reference to the agony in the garden no less than its context suggest a deeper interpretation. On the one hand it is obviously attached to the Melchisedec allusion in 5.6 (culled from that mine of early *testimonia*, Ps. 110), and, in view of the use to be made of this figure in ch. 7, suggests the ideal priest. On the other hand this verse looks forward to the salvation (5.9) which Christ procured for men. We are moving in the realm of ideas suggested by the evangelists' record of the mockery on the cross: if he was to save others, he could not save himself. Thus we should, perhaps, take *sōzein ek thanatou* not as "deliver from physical death" but rather "bring safe through death", especially as *ek* not *apo thanatou* is the preposition employed. This would put on our Lord's lips a prayer that was assuredly and gloriously answered, in the resurrection.

And now that he is risen from a sacrifice made once-for-all, he has "an unchangeable priesthood" – unchangeable because it belongs to the age to come. He is able therefore, *sōzein*, to keep safe, all those

---

[1] *Op. cit.*, p. 224.
[2] He does not, of course, display a disregard for *eschatology* (5.1-8).

who come to God by him (7.25). His living presence at the Father's side is the guarantee of their acceptance with God. "The thought here," writes Westcott, "is the working out of salvation to the uttermost in those who have received the gospel. Thus the present (*sōzein*) as distinguished from the aorist (*sōsai*) has its full force. The support comes at each moment of trial."[1] Because he lives for ever, he can save for ever.

With these verses in mind, let us see what our writer means by "salvation". His usage is somewhat independent, but nevertheless retains the characteristic New Testament eschatological tension. It is used as a general description of the Christian way (1.14, 6.9), but as both of these verses suggest, the emphasis is primarily future. Salvation belongs to the eternal world which our author contrasts with the empirical. Christians are even now only about to inherit salvation (1.14). And the salvation of which he believes there are signs in his readers (6.9) is also evidently future, like the ultimate judgment on sin with which it is contrasted (6.8). The emphasis is again on the future in 9.28. Just as surely as judgement succeeds death, so will salvation follow Christ's parousia. There are two surprises for us here. One might have thought, in the first place, that the writer would have regarded Christ's bearing the sin of many (9.28 from Isa. 53.12) as the work of salvation; but apparently not. So taken up is he with the ultimate salvation to be revealed at the end of the age, that he restricts the term to that; salvation is for those who look for him to appear "the second time unto salvation".[2]

The second surprising thing is this. Salvation so fills the canvas of his mind that he does not mention its obverse, and say that Christ will return to judgement, though this is, of course, the obvious correlative. But here, like the author of Revelation (1.7, 22.20), his mind is fixed with singleness of gaze upon the Lord who will appear, and the people who will be expecting him (cf. 1 Jn. 3.2, Phil. 3.20). That coming will be *chōris hamartias*, nothing to do with sin, which was dealt with by his first coming; likewise he sees it as having nothing to do with sinners. Indeed in this Epistle Christ is never said to be the Judge of sin. God does that (10.27ff.).

Whilst, however, the main thrust of the teaching of Hebrews on salvation points to the future, it does not do so exclusively. In 5.9 we are told that Jesus became "the procuring cause" (*aitios egeneto*) of the salvation of the age to come for all believers. Clearly this is something

---

[1] *Hebrews*, p. 191.
[2] Perhaps the *Sitz-im-Leben* of the readers is responsible for this. If they drew back from Christianity into Judaism they would forfeit the Messianic salvation despite having tasted its first-fruits (ch. 3, 6.4-12, 10.26-39).

already achieved, and open to men here and now. How it was accomplished is hinted at, rather than stated. It is, the contest tells us, the work of his royal priesthood, the fruit of his suffering, the crown of his obedience, the seal on his completed work.[1] But we can go farther. "Eternal salvation" is a quotation from the Old Testament. Jesus is seen as fulfilling the prophecy of Isa. 45.17, and yet another Old Testament *testimonium* is brought to the service of the New Testament doctrine of salvation. There it is Israel that shall be saved in the Lord with an everlasting salvation. Here it is all those who obey him; for he *is* Israel. And he is at the same time the "God of Israel, the Saviour" (Isa. 45.15). Thus the two Old Testament strains of God's King being his Servant find their focus in Jesus. It is by incorporation into him ("saved in the Lord") that Israel will be saved for ever.

There is another interesting point here. Salvation is said to be "caused" by the priestly work of Christ.[2] This does not contradict our previous conclusion that found no link between the cultus and salvation. It is no Aaronic priest, but Christ as eternal high-priest after the order of Melchisedec, who offers eternal rest to those who will go his way. A similar phrase is used of Christ again in 2.10. Here the thought is slightly different, for the emphasis is not so much upon the lonely eminence of Christ's work on our behalf as upon the solidarity of the many sons with their captain of salvation. The customary New Testament juxtaposition of sufferings and glory is very evident here. If "glory" is the description of the salvation which we shall share with him, then sufferings are the necessary schooling for that perfection which will be able to enjoy it. The form in which this verse is cast is undeniably Hellenistic,[3] but this does not alter the thoroughly biblical doctrine that the salvation of mankind is the supreme purpose of God's will and of Christ's sufferings, and that mankind reaches this by means of union with the Saviour both in sufferings and glory. Just as for him the *teleōsis* was not complete until after death and resurrection, so it will be for those he is not ashamed to call his brothers (2.11).

2.3 takes us farther, and, as van Unnik has suggested,[4] has curious parallels with Acts.[5] The writer is making an appeal to his readers. If

[1] *Teleiōtheis* presumably refers to Christ's resurrection and heavenly session, particularly in view of the use of Ps. 110.4.

[2] This typically Greek way of thinking is found in Philo in two interesting passages. The brazen serpent in the wilderness is said to be *aitios sōtērias (de Agric.* 22.1.315) and so is Noah in relation to his family (*de Nobil.* 3.2.440).

[3] E.g. the ἔπρεπεν αὐτῷ., cf. Philo *Leg. All.* 1.15.

[4] *Novum Testamentum,* 1960, pp. 46–48.

[5] Thus ἥτις ἀρχὴν λαβοῦσα λαλεῖσθαι διὰ τοῦ κυρίου is paralleled by Acts 1.1, and the text contains several elements which are prominent in Acts; σωτηρία, συνεπιμαρτυροῦντος, σημεῖα καὶ τέρατα, πνεύματος ἁγίου μερισμόις, and ἀρχηγὸς τῆς σωτηρίας (cf. Acts. 5.31, 3.15).

those who rejected the Old Testament law received a just retribution, "how shall *we* escape if we neglect so great salvation?" He explains that the author of this salvation is Jesus, and that there is a solid bridge between the saving activity of Jesus and the people who belong to a later generation. The solidity of this bridge consists in those who confirmed the message of salvation with signs and wonders as God worked through them. This salvation, this liberty as sons of God, is man's proper destiny as created by God (2.6-10), but it is a destiny from which mankind as a whole has defected; indeed it has been achieved by only one man, Jesus. He has fulfilled the primal role of man; all things are subject to him in virtue of his death for every man and his coronation with honour and glory after his resurrection. He is the proper man, the *archēgos sōtērias*, and salvation for man comes through incorporation in him. This, of course, is now largely dependent upon man's own choice. God for his part has made salvation possible. To lose so great salvation man has only to neglect it. To gain so great salvation man has only to accept it, for it is the gracious gift of God.

When we remember that this Epistle was written to Christians, and Christians moreover who were in danger of apostasizing, this verse 2.3 has obvious implications on the difficult subject of perseverance. Can those who have tasted the first-fruits of salvation possibly miss the final harvest? Can the Christian fall away? This question has for more than two hundred years been a divisive one among Christians who have tried to be loyal to Scripture. It separated Arminus from the followers of Calvin, it split Wesley from his friend Whitefield. Today it is generally, though wrongly, dismissed as a pseudo-problem. If man be genuinely free in decision after conversion even more than before it, the possibility of falling away cannot be discounted, while if God is both sovereign and loving he cannot allow the person committed to him to be lost. The problem is real enough, and we shall have something to say about it in the final chapter. But a reading of Hebrews certainly suggests that apostasy is a possibility seriously to be reckoned with in the readers, who were apparently toying with return to Judaism (10. 19-39). Initial commitment to Christ, the author of salvation, does not dispense with the necessity for continued reliance on Christ. It does not mean a man can reckon on future salvation whatever happens. For salvation means, in the last analysis, solidarity with Christ in obedience, in suffering and in glory. Union with the person of the Saviour gives the present anticipation of future salvation. God will assuredly never revoke this; he cannot be untrue to his character of faithfulness and love, and he will certainly keep the trusting soul — as befits him who is able to "save to the uttermost". But that does not mean that he will keep the man who does *not* want to be kept, or that he will constrain to salvation the Christian – if such there be – who is determined to "draw back unto perdition". If there were no possibility of this happening, it is passing strange that the Epistle to the Hebrews should ever have been written; for its whole aim was to be a dissuasive against apostasy.

The rest of the letter has not much to add. 11.7 reminds us that Noah was a man of faith and an agent of salvation. He was warned of a peril he could not see; he believed God that it was real, and so he prepared an ark at God's command and of God's design[1] "for the salvation of his house". In so doing he "condemned the world" in the sense of showing up the unbelief of those who would not believe God. In this passage the primary meaning of "salvation" is clearly "deliverance" in the natural sense, but the context in which it is placed and the way in which the author uses this incident makes it certain that he is thinking of salvation at a deeper level. Doubtless the teaching of Jesus (Matt. 24.37-9, Lk. 17.26f.) influenced the early Church to see Noah as a type of salvation (cf. 1 Pet. 3.20, 2 Pet. 2.5, 1 Clem. 7.6, 9.4[2]). Faith, obedience, and incorporation in the ark (the appointed means of salvation) are the points on which the New Testament writers fasten to illuminate the nature of the salvation which a greater than Noah has brought.

In the same ch. 11 we find another word connected with salvation, *apolutrōsis*. It reappears in a simpler form in 9.12, 15. The reference in 11.35 speaks of the deliverance from torture and captivity which the saints of the Maccabaean period might have enjoyed had they not held firm. But 9.12, 15 are more apposite to our theme. They present us with a striking contrast. The cleansing offered by the Old Covenant availed only in cases of ceremonial defilement and sins of ignorance, but had nothing to offer the man who sinned "with a high hand". Christ's redemption, however, which was achieved by means of, and at the cost of, his death belongs to the age to come, and is efficacious at every level. The Old Testament sacrifices merely brought sin to remembrance, but could not take it away (Heb. 10.1-3). Christ's death provides release both from the bondage and from the doom of sin (9.12-15). It is the reality, of which the Old Testament sacrifices were, as Hebrews graphically expresses it, "the shadow".

It is interesting that in both 9.12 and 9.15 the price of redemption is made plain, as indeed it is in 1 Pet. 1.18, 19. This is hardly surprising when we remember the identical emphasis in the Hebrew *go'el* and

---

[1] He thus takes his place among the "saviours" of the Old Testament, men whom God raised up to do his work of rescuing others.

[2] "Noah was found faithful in the service he rendered in proclaiming a new beginning for the world, and through him the Master saved the living creatures which entered in harmonious unity, into the Ark."

padah of which the *lutron* group of words are the Greek equivalent. Both verses lay stress on what it cost Christ to redeem and save mankind: salvation was not cheaply accomplished (cf. Heb. 2.10, 5.8-10). In fact the exalted Christology of Hebrews is matched by so strong an insistence on Jesus's complete humanity as to drive W. L. Knox[1] to suggest that the writer fails in this Epistle to harmonize two fundamentally irreconcilable views of his person. This, surely, is to miss the whole point of the Epistle's soteriology, which asserts that Christ's work of salvation is rooted in his person; it hangs on his being both divine and human. Christ's mediation between God and man stems from the fact that unlike Moses, Aaron, and Joshua on the one hand, or the angels on the other (chs. 1-4), he is in solidarity with *both* sides. Upon the link between his deity in ch. 1 and his humanity in chs. 2 and 5 depends the whole efficacy of his redemptive work. And in union with him (2.10f.) the Christian experiences in this mortal life the first-fruits of that salvation which reaches beyond the grave to immortality.

I JOHN

Never once do the words "save" or "salvation" occur in the Johannine Epistles, but the title "Saviour" is applied to Jesus in a single, important verse, 1 John 4.14. The burden of the writer's experience and his testimony is that "the Father sent the Son to be the Saviour of the world". It is part of the content of the Christian confession (4.15). Just once in the Gospel John represents the Samaritans as making the same confession. They believe on the ground of personal experience "that this is indeed the Messiah, the Saviour of the world" (Jn. 4.42). The term is singularly appropriate on the lips of the cosmopolitan Samaritans. Against the Hebrew element in their heritage the term would mean that God, the author of salvation, had sent his promised deliverance by the hand of Jesus. The words of Isa. 62.11 had come true, "Behold, the Lord hath proclaimed unto the end of the the world, Say ye to the daughter of Zion, Behold thy salvation cometh." On the other hand, the Hellenistic element in their background would enable them to understand this claim that Jesus is Saviour of the world in another way; it would come as a sharp challenge to the imperial myth that proclaimed the Roman emperor to be the *sōtēr tēs oikoumenēs*.[2] As Westcott notes,[3] the word "Saviour" carried such varieties of meaning that no one word could express it, especially in Latin. Thus Cicero,[4] attacking Verres a century before, upbraids him for the use of the title *sōtēr* in these terms,

[1] *Harvard Theological Review* (1948).
[2] See ch. 4 on the Hellenistic background to this term.
[3] *The Epistles of St. John* (1892), p. 154.   [4] Cicero, *In Verrem* 2.2.63.

"Hoc quantum est? Ita magnum est ut Latine uno verbo exprimi non possit."[1] Certainly in this context in 1 John there is a wide range of meaning in the term. The passage from 4.9-14 is bound together by the thrice-repeated "the Father sent the Son". The mission of the Son springs from the love of God, and he comes to bring life to the world, to be the propitiation for our sins,[2] and thus to be the Saviour of the world. "Saviour" must obviously be interpreted in the light of the other two parallel phrases. As Saviour Jesus removes the barrier and the defilement caused by sin; as Saviour he does not merely give safety (in contrast to, or development of Jn. 3.17, the other Johannine passage which describes his mission) but mediates to men the very life of God. Are we to see here the old Hebrew meaning of salvation, as bringing men to a place of enlargement, freedom and fulfilment? The nature of the new life is described subjectively in terms of love, and objectively in terms of the Spirit within us (1 Jn. 4.12, 13). All this is strongly reminiscent of the early Christian preaching, although it probably dates from late in the first century. For it insists that it is as Son of God that Jesus is Saviour; salvation is the very purpose of his coming into the world; it is worldwide in its scope; it is the work of God in him; it is designed to liberate men and enable them to enjoy life at its best; and it was all achieved through the Son's sinbearing on Calvary.

THE APOCALYPSE

The last book of the Bible was written to Christians who were going through persecution because of their faith in Jesus. It was penned by a

[1] The title was, of course, common in Greek for both gods and heroes, cf. Eurip. *Herc. Furens* 48, Aristoph. *Plut.* 878, Polyb. 1.5.9, etc. The Latin *salvator* or *conservator* is a late translation of the Greek word, and still requires explanation at the time of Tacitus (the very end of the first century A.D.) Thus (*Annal.* 15.71) he writes, "*Milichus praemiis ditatus Conservatoris sibi nomen, Graeco eius rei vocabulo, adsumpsit*". Indeed, the whole idea of salvation is foreign to indigenous Roman religion, which it only permeated from Greek sources.

[2] The attempt of C. H. Dodd (*J. T.S.*, 1931, pp. 352ff.) to show that the 'ἱλάσκομαι root should be translated as "expiate" rather than "propitiate" in New Testament usage is of very questionable validity despite the wide acceptance it has gained. It is subjected to a damaging analysis in L. Morris, *The Apostolic Preaching of the Cross*, ch. 4. From an exhaustive study of the root, he concludes, "It would seem impossible for anyone in the first century to have used one of the *hilaskomai* group without conveying to his readers some idea of propitiation." The basic meaning of "propitiate" is to turn away wrath through the offering of a gift. This could easily degenerate into a completely un-Christian conception if the Bible ever suggested that man or Christ offered some gift to God which secured his favour. What this verse (and Rom. 3.25) makes so clear is that God and none other has provided a way, through the cross, whereby his rightful wrath against sin may be averted. As ever, it is God to the rescue. See J. R. W. Stott, *The Epistles of John* (1964), pp. 84ff., "Additional Note: the biblical concept of propitiation".

prophet named John who drew deeply on apocalyptic symbolism in his message of encouragement and hope. He wrote in order to lift up the eyes of his readers from the depressing political and economic scene, where all seemed weighted against the Christian, to the heavenly realm where God, not the emperor, was on the throne. It is, consequently, a book which is permeated with confidence in the sovereignty of God and the ultimate victory of his cause. At the same time it is a book which derides with superb irony and courage the megalomania of Domitian, and pours scorn on his "deity", his "eternal realm", his "lordship" and his "salvation". One has only to read the poems of Martial to see how every conceivable term of flattery was heaped upon the emperor by his grovelling courtiers. The mood of the times has been aptly caught by E. Stauffer in his *Christ and the Caesars* (especially ch. 11). Against such a background it is perhaps not surprising that the noun "salvation" rather than the verb should occur in the Apocalypse, and that it should always be a cry of worship to the heavenly *Imperator* in contrast to the shout of adulation to Domitian in the circus. For the Apocalypse is one of the most fiercely polemical treatises ever written. John cannot bear anyone to claim the place which belongs of right to God and his Son.

Three times the word "salvation" occurs; each time it seems to be a cry of the redeemed in the heavenly realm; it is through and through eschatological. Each time, moreover, it heads a list of praises to God; it is clearly the most expressive and comprehensive word with which John can describe the mighty works of God. Indeed, it has often been suggested that these outbursts of heavenly praise in Revelation are projections of the forms of worship used by the Christians in Asia at that time. This is probable enough and, if so, shows what a prominent place was given to the theme of salvation in the worship of the primitive Church.

But although each of these three shouts of salvation comes in an outburst of praise to God, they have distinctive nuances of meaning, and each appears to isolate, or at least emphasize, one particular aspect of salvation. The same might be said of a fourth instance (5.9, 14.3), where "redemption" language is used.

(i) *Salvation as Forgiveness* (7.10)

Set in the context of the stubborn rebellion of the world, and the righteous judgement of God, John sees a vision of the blessed in heaven. Actually, it is a double vision; first the elect of Israel, the 144,000, are brought before our eyes, and then the great multitude (? of the Gentiles) "which no man could number of all nations and peoples and tongues". They stand before the throne of God – the very thing that struck terror into the hearts of the wicked (6.16). Unlike the wicked, who know only the "wrath of the Lamb" (6.16) they can stand before him, and enjoy his companionship. Unlike the wicked, who are so conscious of their spiritual nakedness that they cry "to the mountains and rocks, Fall on us, and hide us from the face of him that sitteth on the throne" (6.16), they are clothed with white robes. There is no doubt what this simple symbolism means. The angel explains: "These are they who have washed their robes and made them white in the blood of the Lamb" (7.14). That is why it is possible for them to stand before the throne of God (7.15). No wonder they cry, "Salvation to our God which sitteth upon the throne and unto the Lamb." Salvation is the word used to describe the total process by which they are brought into eternal enjoyment of God. And it is all his work; they ascribe salvation to God, the Saviour and ultimate disposer of all history, and to the Lamb, the Saviour who died and rose again. They owe their all to God who intervenes to rescue his people, and to Jesus in whom God intervenes.

It is, I think significant that the word "salvation" is missing from the angelic doxology in 7.12. They worship the same God, they praise him and are tireless day and night in his service. But they cannot praise him for their salvation, for they have never fallen. John joins with Paul (Eph. 3.10) and Peter (1 Pet. 1.12) in asserting that the very angels can be taught something by the Church – the nature of salvation. For the rescued, reinstated sinner knows something of the grace of God to which unfallen beings must always be strangers. He can demonstrate what God can do in saving the frail, fallible man who trusts him implicitly. Salvation, as ever, is of the Lord.

It is interesting that John, with his awesome sense of the majesty and sovereignty of God, should associate Jesus with him in salvation. But this is the characteristic Christian conviction, which we have seen throughout the New Testament. It is through and in Christ that God saves men. All the Old Testament acts of rescue were anticipations of what God would do in the person of Christ, supremely in his cross and subsequent resurrection to the throne of the universe. And John expresses this truth in a remarkable and memorable way. He speaks of the Lamb as sharing the throne of God (7.10) or being in the midst of the throne (7.17). He has introduced this thought in 5.6, where the seer expects to see the Lion of the tribe of Judah step forth to unroll the scroll of human destiny. Instead he sees a Lamb, with the marks of slaughter upon him, in the midst of the throne of God. A Lamb, and yet a Lion; slain, and yet in the midst of the throne. In that remarkable set of contrasts we see to the very heart of God's nature and his salvation. Christ is indeed the Lion, but his strength lay in suffering as the

Lamb, and so "redeeming us to God by his blood" (5.9). It is the man Christ Jesus, once slain and for ever alive again, who is in ultimate control of world events. *That* is the character of "him that sitteth upon the throne". And it is because of what he is, and what as Lamb of God he has done in bearing away the sin of the world (cf. Jn. 1.29), that the great multitude have the right to stand in heaven and before the throne. Their gratitude for his rescue is shewn in the new song of the redeemed which they are always singing. They can never get over the wonder of his love and sacrifice for them. This is evident in the title "the Lamb" given to Jesus twenty-nine times in the Apocalypse. It is a complex and significant title, and goes back to the earliest days of Christianity (cf. Jn. 1.29, 1 Cor. 5.7, 1 Pet. 1.19). The Aramaic word for lamb, *talya*, can also be translated by the Greek *pais*, a "Son" or "Servant", and this will have had an important effect on Christology, leading back to the Servant Songs of Isaiah (cf. Acts. 3.13, 4.27, 30). But of course, the word also takes us back to the Passover Lamb of Ex. 12 and possibly to the victim which bore away sin on the Day of Atonement (Lev. 16.21f.). It was a composite symbol to express the expiatory work of Christ and the fact that he voluntarily took our place, as Servant of the Lord.[1]

But if there were any doubt that the sacrificial and vicarious death of Christ was a major theme in Revelation, the occurrence of the word "blood" should dispel it. It is because of the shed blood of Christ that men can be loosed from their sins – released both from the guilt and the power of them (1.5). It is by washing in the blood of Christ that the robes of the redeemed are made clean (7.14). The blood is the means, the price of redemption (5.9). So far from being set against the love of God, it is the blood of Christ which puts content into the word *agape* (1.5). It is by the blood of Christ that the martyrs overcome; nothing less accounts for their victory (12.11). It is clear that any theology which shrinks from the concept of the blood of Christ does less than justice to the witness of the New Testament. And it is equally clear that the blood of Christ does not mean his life released for further usefulness (that "strange caprice" of Westcott's which has proved so influential and of which Denney once said, "I venture to say that a more groundless fancy never haunted and troubled the interpretation of any part of Scripture"[2]) but his death. Any who doubt this should look at the other references to blood in the Apocalypse where the meaning of death is grimly evident, and the idea of the release of life

[1] For the centrality of the "Lamb" in the Christology of the Apocalypse, and its roots in Isa. 53, see P. A. Harlé, *L'Agneau de l'Apocalypse et le Nouveau Testament* (1956), and Cullmann, *The Christology of the New Testament*, pp. 71f.
[2] *The Death of Christ* (1950), pp. 149f. See above p. 164.

for further usefulness quite preposterous (6.10, 12, 8.7, 8, 11.6, 14.20, 16.3, 4, 6, 17.6, 18.24, 19.2, 13). There can be no doubt that John sees the blood of the Lamb as the means whereby men are saved from the wrath of the Lamb. Indeed, it is perhaps important to note that each reference to salvation in Revelation occurs in a general context of the wrath of God to which it is the counterpart; thus 7.10 is related to 6.15, 16; 12.10 to 11.18; and 19.1 is shortly followed by 19.15. Swete is clearly right in his cautious summary, "Whatever may be the exact meaning of these words [the blood of the Lamb], it is clear from them that the writer attached the greatest importance to the death of Christ; His sacrificed life was the price of man's redemption from sin to the service of God."[1]

(ii) *Salvation as Victory* (12.10)

This chapter gives, in apocalyptic terms, a conspectus of the whole history of salvation. The "woman" of the Old Testament Church, crowned with the twelve stars of the tribes of Israel, is about to reach the very climax of her existence, and bring forth the man-child. This, of course, provokes the intense enmity of the serpent, and he bends all his wits towards the destruction of this child, but all his attacks are foiled. "The child was caught up to God and to his *throne*." The coronation of the man-child meant the expulsion of the serpent; he was cast out of heaven, and limited to the earth for his activity (12.9). Smarting from his defeat he attacks the remainder of the seed of the woman (12.17), and the faithful Christians have to live a wilderness existence (12.6, 14). But this is no bad thing for the Church. She learns dependence upon God alone, and she learns to overcome, even as her Master had. The way of victory, though hard, was not impossible, for Jesus had demonstrated it, Jesus had achieved it. And his followers knew now that the serpent was a defeated foe. They knew they could overcome because of the ascension of the man-child to the throne of God. They could shout of full salvation (12.10) *now*. Had not Christ faced the very worst that the serpent could do, and risen victorious? That victory, then, was the ground of their own; "they overcame him by the blood of the Lamb." And the experience of the forgiveness and the victory spelt by this blood of Christ constrained them to tell others; they could not keep silent. That is how the victory was extended, and the knowledge of salvation spread; "they overcame him by the word of their testimony." And such was the transforming power of this message that it conformed them to the pattern of the life of Christ; like him, "they loved not their lives unto the death".

That is how they overcame; the death of Christ, witness and

[1] *The Apocalypse of St. John* (1906), p. clxiii.

213

consecration is the threefold secret of their shout of "salvation". Although it cost them much toil and pain and agony, it is interesting that they ascribe the victory to God. Salvation is his work. They know full well that their own defeat of evil was derivative not intrinsic. It stemmed from the victory of Christ throughout the period between the incarnation and the ascension (12.4, 5).

In consequence of the victorious ascension of the man-child the cry goes up in heaven,[1] "Now is come salvation, and strength and the kingly rule of our God and the power of his Messiah." Well might the voice acclaim this signal triumph, determinative as it was of all future history. The crowning of the Christ meant the defeat and death-warrant of the serpent. Henceforth each act of witness and sacrifice on earth progressively unveils the extent of Christ's kingly rule and of the serpent's rout.[2]

(iii) Salvation as vindication of God's righteous judgement (19.1)

The last shout of "salvation" in the book comes in 19.1. It is induced by the final triumph of right and the final judgement on evil. The persecuting, totalitarian, seductive world-power to which John gives the significant name *Babylon* has at last been judged and destroyed (ch. 18). The immediate reference of this figure is, no doubt, to Imperial Rome, seen now not only as idolater and persecutor but as seductress (17.1-6). But John is merely reapplying what in its day was true of Babylon,[3] Tyre,[4] Jerusalem[5] and many another city; the essence of the Babylon spirit remains as the embodiment of worldly seduction away from God. It is the ultimate annihilation of this principle which John foresees, and at which he rejoices. The dirge of judgement over Babylon (18.21-23) is now answered by this paean of praise to God. Arethas, the ninth-century commentator, calls it heaven's *Te Deum* at the righteous judgement of God. The seer was certainly not so squeamish as a twentieth-century writer would doubtless be at the overthrow of evil. But perhaps this reflects more on our apathy towards moral values than on his vindictiveness. Should we not rejoice at the destruction of evil? Let us hear Bishop Hans Lilje, who himself suffered under Hitler in concentration camps. "The idea of vengeance must find some expression in the last days, not in the sense of petty revenge, but to protect the holiness of God who, while he forgives the penitent

---

[1] It is not clear whose voice this is, but it can hardly come from the angels or the living creatures, for reference is made to "our brethren". Doubtless the speaker is one of the Elders, representing the Church.

[2] See a parallel vision of Jesus in Lk. 10.18f., where the defeat of Satan is attributed to the coming of Christ and the mission of his followers.

[3] Isa. 13, Jer. 50 and 51.   [4] Isa. 23.17, Ezek. 27.   [5] Matt. 23.35-37.

sinner a hundredfold, still makes it clear, at the end of history, that his honour has not been left at the mercy of ungodly hostile forces, however often in the course of history this may seem to have been the case" (*The Last Book of the Bible*, p. 218). Such was the strand in "salvation" which the "voice of much people in heaven" is here celebrating – the final banishment of evil from God's world.

(iv) *Salvation as possession by God* (5.9, 14.3)

In the Old Testament we saw that salvation was "to God" as well as "from" various enemies. So it is in the Apocalypse. This is strongly brought out in the redemption language which we meet in 5.9 and 14.3, 4, a metaphor so common in primitive Christianity, and so meaningful both to Jew and Gentile. Like Peter (1 Pet. 1.18) John knows that the death of Christ rescued man from alien ownership at the cost of his own life. Although made by God, man has constantly refused to acknowledge this allegiance. "Other lords beside thee have had dominion over us" (Isa. 26.13). Man in revolt inevitably sells himself to the "prince of this world". The cross of Jesus secures our release from this bondage and brings us again within God's possession, so to speak. We are purchased *for God*. We belong to him by right of creation and of redemption. We owe him all. That is why the redeemed are conceived as a kingdom where God has unquestioned sway, and as priests who not only offer to him the praise and spiritual sacrifices that are his due, but also mediate the knowledge of the Saviour God to the heathen nations (5.10). Such is the very purpose of redemption. Men are saved by God, henceforth to be his possession both in service, in worship and in fellowship. It is the latter two themes which predominate in 14.3, 4. The redeemed are with the Lamb (14.1), sealed with the mark of his ownership upon their brows; they follow the Lamb, and are utterly dedicated to him (14.4). They find their joy in the worship of their Saviour (14.2), and they are characterized as "first-fruit" to God and the Lamb. The exact meaning of this is obscure; they may be the first-fruit in contrast to the harvest of the created world (cf. Jas. 1.18); or they may be the first-fruit dedicated to God while the rest of the world is seen as the remainder of the harvest, destined for profane use (i.e. rejection). At all events *aparchē* means not only that they are the first-fruits of the harvest, but that they are employed in the worship of God. Instead of bringing their first-fruits to the Lord (Lev. 2.12), they bring themselves in adoring worship and consecration. Nothing less could satisfy the purpose of redemption.

Much the same thought is brought before us, with a wealth of descriptive imagery, in the final visions of the book. A variant reading is Rev. 21.24 reads, "And the nations *of them which are saved* shall walk in the light of it." This reference to the saved is almost certainly a pious gloss, but it is extraordinarily appropriate at the very climax of the Bible's teaching on the destiny of Christians. Three pictures of final salvation are brought before us in rapid succession; the safety of the city, the marriage of the bride and the satisfaction of the garden. Each stresses the intimate relation between the Lord and his redeemed people. The I–Thou relationship of Christian salvation is maintained to the end. Salvation is neither absorption into the Ultimate, nor the flight from the alone to the Alone. It is both personal (hence the bride) and corporate (hence the city). Although the writer must perforce use human language, if not to describe, at least to lift up the hearts of his readers to what "eye hath not seen, nor ear heard, neither have entered into the heart of man, the things which God hath prepared for them that love him" (1 Cor. 2.9), he is nevertheless most restrained. Almost nothing corresponding to the sensuous enjoyment of earth is mentioned. Heaven will be a place of intimate communion with God (21.3), a place where every thirst is quenched (21.6), where pain and sorrow and death are banished, where there is no more sea – that eloquent symbol of danger and unrest to the land-loving Hebrew (21.1, 4). It will be a place from which all evil is excluded, and nothing spoils the family relationship of the sons of God with their heavenly Father and each other (21.7). What a profound conception of future salvation! Heaven is seen not so much as a place as a relationship, where the saved are indissolubly linked with their Lord like a bride with her husband, in an atmosphere of perfect love.

The metaphor of the city which mingles with that of the bride (21.2, 9, 10)[1] is no less moving. The city has the glory of God (21.11). That is enough. The unveiled presence of God, whom now we know by faith, will be the Christian's destiny and reward. The succeeding description stresses the perfect symmetry of the city and its vast dimensions, in contrast to the pettiness and disharmony that so often disfigure relationships in the Church on earth. It is a city of perfect purity (21.18), of brilliant and harmonious variety (21.19-21). This is not merely the city of the saints; the city *is* the people of God in their mutual relationships of love. In the security of this relationship (21.25) the nations of the saved bask in the glory of God and of the Lamb, and make his worship their delight (21. 22-26). Once again we are reminded that their redemption is the ground of their worship. Those whose names are written in the Lamb's book of life will praise him for it eternally. The link between redemption, possession and worship remains.

[1] For the city of the heavenly Jerusalem is the true bride – unlike the apostate Jerusalem on earth which had proved so disloyal to God throughout its long history.

It is just the same with the third vision of the glorified Church (22.1-5). The perfect Paradise or garden of God is the complete counterpart to the Garden of Eden. The tree of life which there had brought curse to disobedient men when they lusted after it, the curse of exclusion from God's presence, now brings healing to the nations (22.2). Men share God's life as a result of his gift, not of their effort. Again, in Eden God's throne had been slighted; his servants had disobeyed and hidden from him in shame, and a guilty mark appeared on Cain's forehead. In Paradise, however, God's throne is honoured, and his servants serve him (22.3). They have no cause to hide from him; they see his face, and his name is in their foreheads as the seal of the Spirit which marks them as his own. God is reigning once more over *all* his world, and his servants share his work and rejoice in his love for ever and ever (22.5). Paradise Lost has become Paradise Regained. Such is the last picture of salvation in the Bible, the fitting culmination of God's work of rescue.

CHAPTER 11

Salvation: Some Current Problems Considered

There are several questions on the subject of salvation which are constantly cropping up in some guise or another, and it would be cowardly not to attempt some sort of an answer to them in the light of the biblical material discussed in the previous pages, although on some of them Scripture does not admit of a precise and definitive conclusion being reached. It is as well to remember that the Bible is not a book designed to answer all the questions we should love to ask of it, but rather to show us "things that pertain to life and to godliness through the knowledge of him" (2 Pet. 1.3). "The secret things belong unto the Lord our God; but those things which are revealed belong unto us and to our children for ever, that we may do all the words of this law" (Deut. 29.29). With this proviso, then, let us examine first:

A. SALVATION AND HEALING

It became apparent when we were considering the teaching of the Gospels on salvation that the word "save" was often used ambiguously to refer both to physical and spiritual healing. It is clear that Jesus and the apostles healed the sick as well as preached the gospel. The demon-possessed (Lk. 8.36), the paralysed (Mk. 3.4), and the sick in general (Mk. 6.56) are said by the evangelists to have been *saved* through their contact with Jesus, and the play on the word is emphasized by the usual addition that they were saved by their *faith* in Christ. The burning question for us is this: Does the precedent set in the Gospels provide a norm, a paradigm for Christian work, today? Should the Church be as noted for its healing as its preaching?[1]

This question must be examined with some care, if rash conclusions are to be avoided. In the first place, we have noted throughout this study God's concern for the whole man, for his physical no less than his spiritual condition. Health is seen throughout the Bible as one of God's good gifts to men, and disease as one of the manifestations of evil, as part of the structure of the demonic, which Jesus came to overthrow (Lk. 13.10-17). In this particular passage Jesus specifically

[1] On this whole subject, see Dorothee Hoch, *Healing and Salvation* (1958).

attributes the woman's condition to Satan. Again, when the Seventy returned from a successful mission of preaching and healing, Jesus rejoiced in it as a demonstration of Satan's fall from power (Lk. 10.17ff.). He banished the demonic powers of disease in token that the kingdom of God had broken in, that the spoliation of the Satanic realm had begun (Matt. 12.26-29). When Matthew sees in the healings evidence that Jesus fulfilled the role of the Servant ("himself took our infirmities and bare our sicknesses", 8.17), it is probable that the same *Christus Victor* theme is in his mind; not only in the cross, but throughout the ministry Jesus is the Servant who overcomes by suffering, and at whose hand the forces of evil are continually defeated. As Douglas Webster put it; "Health stands in the same relation to the divine kingdom as does disease to the demonic kingdom. The gospel avers that the demonic is being smashed by the divine."[1]

This brings us near to the heart of the significance of Jesus's healing miracles. Of course he was "moved with compassion" for the sick and suffering, but the import of his healing ministry was theological rather than purely philanthropic. These mighty acts were carefully called *sēmeia*, "signs", by the Fourth Evangelist, who connects each of seven healing miracles of Jesus to a discourse which makes plain the spiritual and eternal significance for all men of what Jesus has just done on a temporary and physical plane for one individual. The healings are signs both of the break-in of the kingdom and of the person of the king; they belong to the warp and woof of *revelation*. In the synoptic gospels we have the same point brought out in a different way. Jesus, in reply to the doubts of John, draws attention to his performance of those very miracles which the Old Testament had prophesied would characterize the days of salvation, the very deeds predicted of the Servant of the Lord (Lk. 7.19-23, cf. Isa. 35.5, 6, 32.2-4, 42.7, 61.1). For the perceptive, the healing miracles were mute attestations of his person, and as such cannot necessarily be expected to continue in later generations.

Furthermore, it is perhaps significant that although there are no recorded instances of Jesus refusing to heal, there is a good deal of evidence that he deprecated the quest for mighty works and signs (Mk. 8.11, Matt. 12.38, Jn. 4.48, 6.26, etc.), and that he was limited in their performance by unbelief (Matt. 13.58). Both points emphasize the integration of the healings with his person, and their purpose as signs. What is more, there is a progressive decline in the number of healings as the Ministry progresses. This may, however, merely indicate that the Gospel material is primarily arranged topically rather than chronologically. Nevertheless, it can hardly be denied that Jesus

[1] *What is Spiritual Healing?* (1955), p. 13.

subordinated his healing to his teaching ministry; thus not only did he repeatedly enjoin secrecy upon those healed (e.g. Mk. 5.43, 7.36) in marked contrast to the openness of his teaching (Jn. 18.20, 21), but he withdrew from Capernaum where he had healed many, in order that he might be free to *preach* in other towns of the vicinity (Mk. 1.38, Lk. 4.43).

When we come to consider the healing activity of the apostles, there remains equal need for caution. On the one hand, the apostles are specifically commanded to heal (albeit only once during the ministry, in the mission charge, Matt. 10.8), and in the Acts we read a good deal of the healing activities of both Peter (3.6, 9.34, 40, etc.) and Paul (19.11, 12, 20.9, 10). It is very likely, furthermore, that miraculous healing should be reckoned among the "signs and wonders" which attested the true apostle (Rom. 15.18, 19, 2 Cor. 12.12, Mk. 16.17, 18, Acts 2.43, 5.12). On the other hand, the uniqueness of the apostles is repeatedly emphasized in the New Testament. They were called to continue the work of Jesus in a quite special way. Even during the time of his Ministry, their message was his message (to preach that the kingdom was at hand, Matt. 4.17, cf. 10.7), their function was his function (to be the Servant of the Lord and heal the sick, cleanse the lepers and raise the dead, Matt. 10.8, cf. 11.5). They were his delegates plenipotentiary (Matt. 10.40). After the resurrection they were equipped with his Spirit, to extend his work (Jn. 20.21-23). They are even called by the same names as Jesus, being designated as both "foundation" and "pillars" of the Church (Eph. 2.20, Gal. 2.9). It is not far from the truth, therefore, when Cullmann says, "The apostolate does not belong to the period of the Church, but to that of the incarnation of Christ."[1] It is certainly most precarious to argue from the gifts enjoyed by the apostles to what should be characteristic of the modern Christian minister.

Indeed, it is noticeable that the apostles did not, so far as we can see, continue the healing ministry of Jesus. They healed on occasions, certainly. But the references to such healings are few; their preoccupation lay with preaching the *kerygma*, the proclamation of the salvation which God had wrought for men in the death and resurrection of Jesus, that demanded the response of repentance, faith and baptism into the community of the Spirit. We certainly do not get the impression that healing figured high among their priorities. In the Pastoral Epistles the tasks of the Christian ministry are detailed with considerable care, but nowhere do we find the suggestion that the Christian leader should be a healer as well, though we find scores of references to his teaching function. Just once, in Jas. 5.14, healing appears to be associated with

[1] *Christianity Divided* (1962), p. 10. See also my *Called to Serve* (1964), pp. 58-62.

Christian leaders. However, on closer inspection it will be found that the passage does not promise either to Christian presbyters or to the Church as a whole miraculous powers of any sort. The whole chapter is concerned with prayer and its power; the prayer of men who are right with God is powerful in its working (5.16). When a Christian believer falls sick, he is bidden to invite the elders of the congregation to come and pray with him. It is the Lord who heals; it is the Lord who forgives (5.15). It is the Lord who determines the issues of life and death, of recovery and decline. James is just as emphatic upon this point (cf. 4.15) as he is on the efficacy of prayer. The significance of the anointing with oil does not here concern us, but it may well be a medicinal measure, as when the Good Samaritan poured oil and wine into the wounds of the man he rescued, particularly as the word used for "anoint" is *aleiphō* and not *chriō*. Professor A. Rendle Short[1] made the acute observation that in Scripture the latter word is used for ceremonial anointing (e.g. Heb. 1.9, 2 Cor. 1.21) while in none of its New Testament occurrences, and in only two out of its seventeen occurrences in the LXX does *aleiphō* have a ceremonial significance. It seems highly probable, therefore, that James is advocating the use of medical means and prayer in the case of the Christian sick.

With reference to the contingent nature of the promise of divine healing in answer to believing prayer, it is interesting to recall that even the apostles themselves were by no means always able to heal. God was not at their disposal to be manipulated as they willed. He remained sovereign. Paul himself, to look no farther, had to leave Trophimus at Miletus sick (2 Tim. 4.20) and could not interpose in the illness of Epaphroditus (Phil. 2.25-7). Moreover, he advises Timothy to deal with a troublesome gastric condition not by the exercise of a little more faith, but by the use of the appropriate medical means, in this case "a little wine" (1 Tim. 5.23). Paul himself suffered from an eye complaint, if we may judge by his reference to his remarkably large handwriting (Gal. 6.11), by the willingness of the Galatians to have given him their own eyes (Gal. 4.15)[2] and perhaps by his inability, even after peering intently, to recognize the High Priest (Acts 23.1, 5). Probably this was his "thorn in the flesh", "the messenger of Satan to buffet him", which God in his wisdom did not see fit to remove; instead he gave Paul his strength in which to bear it (2 Cor. 12.7-9). Here, then, was a man who knew bodily infirmity and yet he could preach the gospel of salvation day in and day out. Clearly Paul did not regard the removal of bodily ailments as an inevitable concomitant of salvation.

[1] *The Bible and Modern Medicine* (1953), p. 125.
[2] Naturally Paul is speaking in hyperbole at this point. But is the example he uses not significant?

It is worth pausing for a moment to consider what would follow if emancipation from bodily ailments were indeed the birthright of every believer. For one thing it would encourage conversions to Christianity for the basest motives of self-interest. This Christian faith would be the best form of insurance against the ills of life! For another, it would make nonsense of such distinctively Christian virtues as endurance and longsuffering. It would suggest that much as God hates sin, he hates disease even more, since he manifestly does not remove sin from the believer in this life, whilst, on this view we are considering, he would remove suffering. Again, such bodily wholeness would suggest that full salvation was available to us now, whereas it is the constant emphasis of the New Testament that salvation is only partly enjoyed on earth; the best belongs to the life to come. Paul, who looks to heaven to provide the remedy for endemic sin, looks in the same direction for the answer to human bodily frailty. Such is the whole point of Rom. 8.17-39. Finally, of course, this view is faced with the insurmountable surd of death. Why, if disease and illness can never be part of even the permissive will of God for *any* of his children (and the Book of Job shows conclusively that it can) should death be decreed for them *all*? No, those who claim for the Christian full freedom from disease on this earth are making the same mistake as those who claim the possibility of sinless perfection. Both are arrogating to this life what God has only promised for the life to come. They neglect the tension between realized and future eschatology, between the "already" and the "not yet" of Christian salvation.

This is not to deny, of course, that God is the author of all healing. Of course he is (Rom. 11.36), whether with or without the use of means. The New Testament teaches that God has given to some members of the Christian Body the gift of healing (1 Cor. 12.9, 28), but it is not the universal equipment of his people, in the same way that it is incumbent upon all to spread the Gospel (Rom. 10.9, 10). "Have all the gifts of healing?" asks Paul. No, they have not. Healing is one of the gifts of the Spirit to some members of the Body for the benefit of the whole. It is not an indispensable element in salvation.

Nor must we deny that God can heal miraculously still. Of course he can. With God nothing is impossible. However, the God of grace is the God of nature, and he does not interfere at random in the working of his world. To expect him to do so is to reveal a deficient concept of God, to think of him as transcendent, over against his universe, while forgetting that his is no less immanent within it, and that natural processes are *his* processes. We have no right to expect miraculous intervention by God in situations where a "natural" or "medical" means of recovery has, in his good providence, been brought to light – any more than the Christian farmer, who neglects to use the means entrusted to him of plough and corn, has any right to expect a miraculous crop. To neglect God-appointed means, or to expect an alternative to them, betrays not great faith in God but great presumption.

Two or three other points are sometimes raised in support of the view that we must expect miracles of the same *genre* as those of the New Testament today.

Mark 16.18 says, "They shall lay hands on the sick, and they shall recover." But in the first place, this verse is part of the "Longer Ending" of Mark which is universally recognized to come from a later hand than that of the evangelist, and formed no original part of his Gospel. Even if it did, it would not help very much, for it is addressed to the *apostles* and not to the church at large, and the uniqueness of the promise is emphasized in the context; "in my name they shall cast out devils, speak with new tongues, take up serpents, and if they drink any deadly thing, it shall not hurt them." Does *that* apply to the modern faith-healer?

Then there is the command given to the Seventy to heal as well as to preach (Lk. 10.9). But the evangelist (who at this point uses material culled from the charge to the Twelve) makes it clear that this is a particular and extraordinary mission, designed to prepare men for Jesus's own subsequent visit to their villages; the Seventy act for that period as his delegates, his *shelichim*. The temporary nature of this entrusted authority is stressed by Luke's account not only of their commissioning by Jesus, but of their reporting back to him at the conclusion of their task. It would be precarious in the extreme to draw general principles from so particular an incident.

A third tendency sometimes discernible is to lay unwarranted stress on Matt. 8.17, a verse to which we have already referred.[1] It is urged that this verse teaches us that Jesus bore our sicknesses as fully and as finally as he bore our sins. What the evangelist is doing is to show that in his healing work Jesus was giving evidence that he was the Servant of the Lord. While there is a great deal of biblical evidence to show that Jesus has decisively removed from man the incubus of his sin by his death and resurrection, there is no supporting evidence whatever for this strange suggestion that he endured physical sicknesses on our behalf.

If we are to be true to the New Testament, we must conclude that the healing of the body has never been a primary ingredient in the Christian gospel,[2] far less an inalienable part of salvation. Adolf Schlatter is surely right in saying, "In the miraculous narratives of the New Testament,

[1] P. 123.
[2] Although the compassion of Jesus towards the sick and needy, and his concern for the whole man, has always formed a conspicuous part of Christian practice – hence Christian initiative in the creation of hospitals, blind schools, orphanages, and the relief of famine.

miracles are not represented as everyday events that may occur in the experience of all believers, but are valued as a peculiar provision for those who bear a special commission. The Gospels, the Book of Acts, and the utterances of St. Paul regarding his 'signs' (2 Cor. 12.12) all show distinctly that miracles were intimately related to the apostolic function."[1] Edmunds and Scorer follow B. B. Warfield in their further contention that "Scripture uniformly links miracle (in the Bible sense) with the periods of *special revelation*, and this explains both their association with the work of the specially commissioned prophets of the Old Testament, the ministry of our Lord, and the witness of the apostles. It also explains their disappearance."[2]

This I believe to be a fair summary of the New Testament attitude to healing miracles. It is significant that the miracles of Jesus in this field were almost always of organic diseases; they were complete; they did not suffer relapses; they took immediate effect; and they were meaningful, in demonstrating some particular element in the gospel. Can all these claims be sustained for modern "miracles"? Can modern faith-healers, who have not succeeded in producing one properly attested and documented example of an organic healing without means, which will satisfy either the B.M.A.[3] or the Christian Medical Fellowship,[4] follow up their claims to be in succession to the healing miracles of the Lord and his apostles by raising the dead? To ask such a question is almost absurd. Yet those who look to Matt. 10.8 for the commission to heal can surely not escape the exigencies of the command to raise the dead contained in the very same verse.

Where medical knowledge is so advanced as it is in the West, where two thousand years of Christian evidences (not to mention the sacred Scriptures) abound to authenticate Jesus's claims to Messiahship, the conditions would appear to be lacking in which we might have a right to expect miracle in the New Testament sense, though we cannot exclude the possibility. However, in missionary areas, where there is only a tiny church in a vast pagan stronghold, where there is a shortage of medical means, where there may be no translations of the Scriptures available or where the people are as yet illiterate, where, furthermore, there are definite spiritual lessons to be reinforced by it – there, on the fringes of the gospel outreach, we have a situation in which we may expect to see God at work in miraculous ways today.[5] That he does so is attested by all the missionary societies working in primitive areas. But to

[1] Hastings *Dictionary of the Apostolic Church*, i. p. 577.
[2] *Faith Healing* (1956), p. 25.
[3] *Divine Healing and Cooperation between Doctors and Clergy* (1955).
[4] *Faith Healing*, Ed. Scorer and Edmunds.
[5] I owe this point to Dr. D. H. Trapnell, M.R.C.P., Consultant at the Westminster Hospital.

suggest that healing and salvation are always and properly inseparable goes against all the evidence of Scripture, history and experience.

B. SALVATION AND UNIVERSALISM

Here is another issue as topical as the last, in days when an Archbishop of Canterbury has said that he expects to meet atheists in heaven, and when one of the ablest of modern radicals, Bishop J. A. T. Robinson, has argued powerfully for the ultimate salvation of all men in his book, *In the End, God* . . .

We shall not here attempt to assess the arguments from general principles which are normally adduced in this discussion; whether universalism is derogatory to free will, whether it is a necessary part of the happiness of heaven, whether it follows inevitably from God's nature as love, and whether it takes sin with sufficient seriousness or has any real place for the biblical doctrine of the wrath of God. Robinson avoids most of the pitfalls of other Christian universalists; he salvages the integrity of human liberty by supposing that in the end it will bow to love of its own free will, and thus find self-fulfilment; he takes seriously the biblical teaching about hell, but resolves it by supposing that this is truth only for the subject facing decision, but not objective truth about man's destiny; God's love will conquer in the end, and God will be all in all. Nevertheless, to achieve this result, Robinson has to make some remarkable assumptions. He has to assume these two different types of truth; he has to assume that all men are already in Christ; he has to perpetuate the *kairos–chronos* distinction which has been so rudely handled by James Barr.[1] Furthermore, he has to pretend that when Jesus, in the parable of the sheep and goats, speaks of the goats being cast into everlasting fire, or everlasting punishment (Matt. 25.41, 46) he is not insisting on "two endless spiritual states" but rather "the eternal seriousness of the choice before man which we must not objectivize, at the risk of turning the profoundest truth into the final lie".[2] For lack of biblical evidence, Bishop Robinson has recourse to analogy and parable. He may, of course, be right, despite the frailty and speciousness of many of the arguments he employs. But the truth or falsity of universalism, argued on general considerations, is beyond the scope of our subject. The question to which we must address ourselves is, Can it be found in the New Testament teaching on salvation?

It is very difficult to argue convincingly that Jesus taught the ultimate salvation of all men. In the face of all the explicit and terrifying material which teaches the precise opposite, one is reduced to desperate clutching at such straws from the parables as that the shepherd seeks the lost sheep *until* he finds it (Lk. 15.4), or that the unforgiving servant is

[1] *Biblical Words for Time* (1962), pp. 20–46.   [2] *In the End, God* . . . (1950), pp. 121f.

delivered to the jailers *until* he should pay all his debt (Matt. 18.34). It is difficult to see how universalist conclusions can be securely based upon such details from the parables in the face of so much plain teaching to the contrary, which might not unjustly be summed up in the words of the Marcan Epilogue, "He that believeth and is baptized shall be saved; but he that believeth not shall be damned" (Mk. 16.16). The whole Bible teaches that salvation is not something that God owes to any man; it proceeds solely from his grace. It is entirely of his grace that all men are not damned (Matt. 24.22). Mk. 8.35 puts the issue with devastating clarity. A man can either be saved or lost; he can give himself over to Christ or withhold himself from him. Such is the existential decision with which Christ confronts men. This is clearly brought out by his answer to the question, recorded in Lk. 13.23, "Lord, are there few that be saved?" "Strive," he says, "to enter in at the strait gate . . ." He warns them against the awful possibility of exclusion from the heavenly home, with the ringing words, "I know not whence ye are; depart from me" (Lk. 13.27). The *either/or* remains. So it is in Jn. 10.9. It is by Christ that men may enter in and be saved; outside there are thieves and robbers. True, Christ came to save the world (Jn. 3.17, 12.47) or the lost (Lk. 19.10), but that by no means necessarily includes everyone. Jesus speaks sadly of those who will not come to him that they might have life, or salvation (Jn. 5.40). Again, "He that believeth on the Son hath everlasting life; and he that believeth not the Son shall not see life; but the wrath of God abideth on him" (Jn. 3.36). Perhaps the most striking juxtaposition in that famous third chapter of John is verse 17 alongside verse 18, "God sent not his Son into the world to condemn the world, but that the world through him might be saved. He that believeth on him is not condemned; but he that believeth not is condemned already . . ."

No, it is extraordinarily hard to find universalism in the teaching of Jesus, in view of his constant warnings about what J. A. Baird calls the "destruction-negative". Baird makes a careful study[1] of Jesus's teaching about those who meet the eschatological crisis unsuccessfully; he examines the references to hades and gehenna, to fire and punishment, to death, to exclusion and destruction in the teaching of Jesus, and concludes, justly, "It is therefore necessary to reaffirm what many who hold this position [i.e. universalism] admit: there is no valid evidence in the Synoptics for the doctrine of universal salvation."[2] Indeed, both in parable (e.g. Matt. 13.47-50, 25.30, etc.) and direct statement

[1] J. A. Baird *The Justice of God in the Teaching of Jesus* (1963), pp. 215-32.
[2] *Ibid.* (p. 232). There is even less evidence in St. John, where the contrast of life and death, darkness and light, truth and error, resurrection and condemnation is so marked a feature of the Gospel.

(Mk. 9.43-48, Lk. 12.4, 5, Matt. 23.33, etc.) the teaching of Jesus provides more warnings about the reality and awesomeness of final ruin than any other part of the whole Bible.

It is hardly surprising, therefore, to find the same insistence on the need for commitment to Christ as the vital requirement for salvation in the early preaching. On the day of Pentecost, Peter besought his hearers to save themselves *from* the crooked generation of those who had rejected Jesus the Messiah (Acts 2.40). It was the apostolic conviction that in Jesus alone was salvation to be found; "neither is there salvation in any other; for there is none other name under heaven given among men whereby we must be saved" (Acts 4.12). The uniqueness and indispensability of commitment to Christ the Saviour could hardly be more emphatically stressed.

But it is to certain passages in St. Paul that universalists look for support. There are, in the Pauline writings, several passages which are patient of a universalist interpretation, though it is doubtful whether there is one which demands it. These fall into two categories, those which involve salvation terminology (1 Tim. 4.10, 2.4, Rom. 11.26) and those which do not (1 Cor. 15.22, 28, Eph. 1.10, 22f., Phil. 2.10f., Col. 1.20, Rom. 5.18, 8.21). Let us examine the latter first. They fall naturally into two rough groupings.

In the first place, there are those which speak about the reconciliation of the world (2 Cor. 5.19, Col. 1.20). There are two difficulties here. For one thing the Greek *katallassō* does not mean "reconcile" *tout simple*. As we have seen (pp. 168f.) it would perhaps better be translated "remove the barriers to fellowship". It is significant that in the very next verse, 2 Cor. 5.20, Paul beseeches his readers to get "reconciled" with God – proof positive that their reconciliation, in our sense of that word, was not yet complete, although God had been in Christ, *katallassōn* the world to himself. Furthermore, while we are quite justified in seeing a universal scope in the word "world", we are warned against taking it as the whole world with no exceptions, by the usage of Rom. 11.15, where the "reconciling of the world" is explicitly contrasted with the "casting away of" the Jews. Similarly, in 1 Jn. 2.2 the readers are warned against any limitation on the efficacy of Christ's death. He died "not for our sins only, but also for the sins of the whole world"; yet the author of this Epistle is under no illusions that all men are thereby saved. He speaks of false teachers who have gone out from the Christian community "that they might be made manifest that they were not all of us" (2.19). They belong to the ranks of Antichrist (2.18).

Secondly, some passages speak of the universal Lordship of Jesus in a way that could suggest universal salvation. 1 Cor. 15.28 speaks of the day when God will be all in all; but this is expressly said to be after the destruction of every evil force, including the abolition of death itself. It *could* support universalism, but it could equally well fit in with a doctrine of conditional immortality – God being *in* all who remained, i.e. the redeemed, and being everything *to* them. It is interesting that a well-attested variant reading in the same chapter suggests conditional immortality – "we shall all sleep, but we shall not all be changed" (15.51); all will die, but not all will be raised to newness of life. Another of these passages where much is made of the word "all" is Eph. 1.10. It could be argued that this implies universal salvation, and indeed it is one of the proof texts for universalism in Scripture. But it is very difficult to believe that Paul is thinking about universal salvation in this passage, where he is not pointing ahead to some future destiny, but explaining the present significance of Christ's lordship *now*. Lightfoot, commenting on the rare *anakephalaiousthai* variously translated "gather together", "unite" and "sum up" writes,[1] "The expression implies the entire harmony of the universe, which shall no longer contain alien and discordant elements, but of which all the parts shall find their centre and bond of union in Christ. Sin and death, sorrow and failure and suffering shall cease." This is as applicable to the orthodox conception of heaven as to the universalist. God's secret purpose revealed in the Christian dispensation was that the universe should be brought into unity in Christ. "This could," writes Whiteley, "be understood as an indication of eventual universal salvation, but that would be to take the words as an answer to a question which has not been asked."[2] Paul is not thinking of individual inclusion and exclusion. He is wrestling with the old problem of the one and the many, so troublesome to the Greek philosophers, and of the place of the Gentiles, so troublesome to the Jewish thinkers. And he sees Christ as the principle of unity and coherence in the universe, and the Church of Christ as the embodiment of that principle. "The Messiah summed up the Ancient People," wrote Armitage Robinson; "St Paul proclaims that he sums up the Universe."[3]

It is equally precarious to build too much on Phil. 2.10, "At the name of Jesus every knee shall bow, and every tongue confess that Jesus is Lord." These words, drawn from Isa. 45.23, where they are applied to God, clearly teach that in the end there is no Saviour but he (Isa. 45.21, 22); but they are applied by the prophet only to "those that are escaped of the nations" (45.20), that is to say "those who escape judgement".[4] They clearly imply that everything and every being in

---

[1] *Notes on the Epistles of St. Paul* (1895), p. 322.
[2] *The Theology of St. Paul* (1964), p. 95.
[3] *St. Paul's Epistle to the Ephesians* (1903), p. 32.
[4] D. R. Jones in the new *Peake Commentary on the Bible* (1962), p. 522.

existence will own his sovereignty, but neither in Paul's context nor in that of his Isaianic source, is there any suggestion that everybody will be saved. It may well be the same with 1 Cor. 15.22, "As in Adam all die, so in Christ shall all be made alive." Now this could, of course, imply that all men will rise in Christ. But it could just as well mean that all those who are in Adam (i.e. all men) will die, while all those who are in Christ (i.e. the redeemed) will rise.[1] The matter cannot be decided one way or another by this verse, but by what Paul teaches elsewhere (e.g. 1 Cor. 11.32). The same applies to Rom. 5.18, "By the righteousness of one the free gift came upon all men unto justification of life." The apostle is speaking of the cosmic effects of the representative heads of the race, Adam and Christ. He does not say that all men are justified; that would be to deny the whole force of his argument in Romans. He does stress the eternal significance of the representative acts in a verbless, paratactic sentence, "As, by the offence of one, judgement for all men; so by the righteous act of one, righteousness for all men." This righteousness is available for all, but effective only for all who accept it. Such is the only meaning of these words which does not make Paul contradict himself. Surely we have the right to expect internal consistency in a single document of a single author?

When we turn to the three passages where Paul actually speaks of "salvation" in universalistic tones, there appears to be a little more substance in the universalist's case. In 1 Tim. 2.4 it is clearly stated that God wants all men to be saved (so also 2 Pet. 3.9). 1 Tim. 4.10 speaks of God as the Saviour of all men, specially of those that believe. And Rom. 11.26 states categorically Paul's conviction that all Israel shall be saved.

Even these three verses, however, are not free from ambiguities. Certainly God desires all men to be saved. Does that mean, therefore, that all will in the end be saved? It may be so. But on the other hand the writer may be attacking the exclusiveness of a proto-gnostic heresy which restricted salvation to a particular class. In the context it is stressed that no class, neither persecutors, like Paul (1 Tim. 1.15f.), nor women, nor even state officials (1 Tim. 2.1, 2, 15), is excluded from the salvation of God. To prove this universal availability of his salvation, Christ gave himself to be a substitutionary-ransom-price (*antilutron*) on behalf of all (2.6). Nothing could express more clearly the love of God for all men. But does that mean that all men will be saved? The author does not think so. Hymenaeus and Alexander have been delivered unto Satan (1.20). Some have departed from the faith, giving heed to doctrines of devils (4.1), some have already turned aside after

[1] See Whiteley, *op. cit.*, p. 271. He cites parallels adduced by R. H. Charles for this "limiting" construction.

Satan (5.15). The writer knows that it is only by continuance in the Christian life that Timothy will save himself and his hearers (4.16), only by constant vigilance that perdition can be avoided (6.9), only by perseverance in good works and the fight of faith that eternal life can be grasped (6.19). This does not look like the writing of a universalist. It is against this background, therefore, that we have to assess 4.10 which speaks of God as the Saviour of all men, but especially of believers. On any showing this verse distinguishes between all men and believers, by asserting that there is a special sense in which God is the Saviour of the latter. To be sure Paul does not deny that all men may perchance be saved, but his main purpose in the context is to "make it clear beyond all doubting that those who ... lead a Christian life, placing their hope in the living God, will not be disappointed."[1] It may well be the case that *Sōtēr* in this verse has two meanings, particularly if the question of the "faithful saying" ends with "all men", and "especially those who believe" is an addition of the author's. He may mean that God is the Preserver of all mankind, but to those who trust him for eternal life he is also the Saviour, or author of eschatological salvation.[2]

Finally, while Rom. 11.26 ("all Israel shall be saved") *may* equally be interpreted on universalistic lines, once again this is neither necessary nor even probable. Leenhardt writes,[3] "Both formulae, i.e. the *plērōma tōn ethnōn* and *pas Israēl*, the full number of the Gentiles and all Israel, are to be understood as suggesting collectives or groups without prejudging the condition of any particular individual. Paul does not say that all the heathen will be converted, just as he does not say that all the Israelites will be saved." He adds, moreover, an illuminating note, "the affirmation that 'the whole of Israel would share in the world to come' (*Sanh.* 10.1) did not prevent the Jews from thinking that certain categories of sinners, of which a list was drawn up, would be excluded (Strack-Billerbeck IV, pp. 1052-1056)."

In short, whatever arguments there may be from general considerations of the nature of God and man, the solidarity of the race and so forth in favour of universalism, there is little enough solid ground in the biblical language about salvation to enable us to pronounce with any certainty in its favour, and a great deal which warns us in the most stringent terms of the danger of "everlasting destruction from the presence of the Lord" (2 Thess. 1.9) for those who wilfully reject the gospel of salvation.

[1] J. N. D. Kelly, *The Pastoral Epistles* (1963), pp. 102f.
[2] So C. K. Barrett, *The Pastoral Epistles* (1963), p. 70.
[3] *The Epistle to the Romans* (1961), p. 293.

Is it true to say, "Once a Christian, always a Christian"? Is apostasy and final ruin impossible for the true Christian? This was the view of Calvin, and it has had paramount influence in Reformed theology throughout the past three hundred years. Calvin knew very well that Jesus had said, "He that endures to the end shall be saved." He recognized that salvation is completed only in the life to come and that regeneration is merely the entry into salvation.[1] In this he differs from later pietists who tend to regard salvation as identical with either baptism or conversion, according to their churchmanship; in either case it is seen as an inalienable possession of the *élite*. But Calvin never made the mistake of holding an entirely realized eschatology of salvation. He knew it belonged to the age to come, and was only tasted in anticipation while here on earth. The way of perseverance he allowed to be very hard, so hard that but for the grace of God no Christian could possible endure. But endure they would, because God remains God. What he has begun he is bound to complete.[2] "Our salvation," he writes,[3] "is certain because it is in the hand of God." He sees the seed of the new birth with which God regenerates his elect, as imperishable.[4] Though a man may fall into grievous sin, though he may appear to fall away entirely, he cannot be utterly lost, or the death of Christ and the promise and the purpose of God would be frustrated.

This emphasis is very important for the peace of mind of the believer, and undoubtedly it represents one strain of biblical teaching. Does not Christ say, "Him that cometh to me I will in no wise cast out . . . I will raise him up at the last day" (Jn. 6.37, 40), and "I give unto them eternal life, and they shall never perish, neither shall any man pluck them out of my hand. My Father which gave them me is greater than all; and no man is able to pluck them out of my Father's hand" (Jn. 10.27f.)? There are many such promises in Scripture, such as Jn. 3.16, 5.24, 6.51, and the whole of Rom. 8, where the present anticipation of the final verdict of justification, the possession of the Spirit, the status of sonship, the promises and the love of God are all called upon to demonstrate the absolute security of the Christian. "I am persuaded that [nothing] . . . shall be able to separate us from the love of God which is in Christ Jesus our Lord" (8.38f.). We are "kept by the power of God, through faith, unto [final] salvation" (1 Pet. 1.5).

All this is gloriously true. On the other hand, it is idle to pretend there is not a contrary body of evidence, and this cannot be evaded by supposing that it always refers to those who appear to be Christians but in reality are counterfeits. Paul knows that the Galatians had "removed

[1] *Comm.* on Ps. 119.123, 2 Tim. 2.10.   [2] *Comm.* on Ps. 138.8, Jn. 15.6.
[3] *Comm.* on Jn. 10.29.   [4] *Comm.* on 1 Jn. 3.9.

from him that called you, unto another gospel", and anathematizes such with a solemn curse (Gal. 1.4, 8). It will not do to say that these men were not authentic Christians. Paul says they were. They had received the Spirit; they had begun in the Spirit. And yet the apostle fears it may all prove to be in vain (3.1-4). Indeed, he tells them that as they have got themselves circumcized (and thereby show their reliance for salvation on something additional to Christ) Christ will profit them nothing (5.2). Such men, indeed, have fallen from the realm of grace, they have excluded themselves from the company brought into being by the unmerited favour of God to sinners (5.4).

Much the same possibility is often brought before us in the Corinthian correspondence. 2 Cor. 11 speaks at length of false teachers who, Paul fears, have led astray his converts from a sincere and pure devotion to Christ (11.3). If they do turn aside to another gospel, they will perish (11.4, 15; 13.5). Paul knows that it is possible for his Christian readers to receive the grace of God in vain (6.1ff.). In the First Letter to the Corinthians, Paul contemplates for himself the same possibility of ultimate rejection (9.27) as he warns them of in 2 Cor. 13.5, if he should presume on God and not abide in Christ his Saviour. He draws on the supreme example of salvation in Old Testament days, the Exodus (1 Cor. 10.1ff.). All the people of God experienced the same deliverance, all of them received the Old Testament types of the Christian sacraments: "they were all baptized unto Moses . . . and did all eat the same spiritual meat and did all drink the same spiritual drink". To stress the point, he explains this spiritual drinking as participation in Christ (1 Cor. 10.4). And yet with many of them God was not pleased; they apostasized, followed other gods, and perished in the wilderness. "These things," he says, "were our examples" (10.6). "They are written for our admonition . . . Wherefore let him that thinketh he standeth take heed lest he fall" (10.11, 12). He immediately redresses the balance of this solemn warning, by assuring them that God will make a way of escape from every temptation, provided they will take it (10.13). It is interesting that Jude should employ this same paradigm of salvation when issuing his stern warning against apostasy. He reminds them that "the Lord, having saved the people out of Egypt, afterward destroyed them that believed not", in a context which is particularly instructive (Jude 5).

Apostasy is brought before us in the Pastoral Epistles, too. Some have already turned aside after Satan (1 Tim. 5.15), men like Hymenaeus and Alexander who have made shipwreck of their faith (1 Tim. 1.19, 20), men like Demas who forsook Paul and the gospel because of love of the world (2 Tim. 4.10). Apostasy is brought before us in the Apocalypse as well. The Church at Ephesus is warned that its candlestick will be removed if it does not repent (Rev. 2.5). The Church at Sardis is warned that unless there is a change of attitude Christ will come upon it like a thief (3.3), the thief who ransacks the house and causes ruin and dismay (Matt. 24.43). Moreover, the overcomer is promised that his name shall never be blotted out of the book of life; the implications for the apostate are obvious (3.5).

All this, of course, is in line with the plain teaching of Jesus. His injunction to endure to the end and so secure salvation (Matt. 24.13) is set in a context where the love of many grows cold. And the plain meaning of Jn. 15.6 is hard to avoid, "If a man abide not in me, he is cast forth as a branch and is withered; and men gather them, and cast them into the fire, and they are burned." Commentators as different in background as Godet and Barrett recognize that this is the meaning of the verse.

Perhaps it is in the Epistle to the Hebrews that this problem is faced at its most acute. For here was a situation, it would seem, where a whole church (or house-church?) was being tempted to return to Judaism, and the author writes his letter as a strong dissuasive. Not only does he show the supremacy and sufficiency of Christ, but he demonstrates the folly of apostasy from the living God, of forsaking the substance for the shadow, of drawing back unto perdition. It is by no means only a couple of obscure passages in chs. 6 and 10 that confront us here, but much else beside. 2.3 warns against the possibility of slighting the "so great salvation" brought us in Christ, with the question, "How shall we escape if we neglect" it? Now the recipients of this letter were "holy brethren, partakers of the heavenly calling" (3.1); nevertheless he warns them that a like fate could befall them as overcame the Israelites who perished in the wilderness, if they harden their hearts. and tolerate "an evil heart of unbelief in departing from the living God". It is only if they hold fast their confidence steadfast until the end that they will enter into his rest (3.6, 14). He continues his warnings throughout the next chapter (4.1, 2, 11, 14), and 6.1-9 is specific about the danger. The recipients are baptized, they are instructed Christians, they have been "enlightened, and have tasted of the heavenly gift, and were made partakers of the Holy Spirit, and have tasted the good word of God and the powers of the age to come" – and if that does not describe a true Christian, it is difficult to find words to do so! He solemnly envisages the possibility of such people falling away, and says they cannot renew themselves unto repentance so long as[1] they crucify Christ to themselves again. He then likens such people to briars, whose end is to be burned. Such is the severity and

[1] This I take to be the least difficult interpretation of the participle *anastaurountas* (6.6).

233

explicitness of the warning, even though he trusts that none of the recipients of the letter are in this state (6.9). The theme is continued in ch. 10. He says that if we wilfully reject the truth after we have received it, and reject Christ as Saviour, God has no reserve plan, as it were; "there remaineth no more sacrifice for sins, but a certain fearful looking for of judgement, and fiery indignation which shall devour the adversaries. He that despised Moses' law died without mercy . . . Of how much sorer punishment, suppose ye, shall he be thought worthy, who hath trodden under foot the Son of God, and hath counted the blood of the covenant wherewith he was sanctified an unholy thing, and hath done despite to the Spirit of grace? For we know that he hath said, Vengeance belongeth unto me, I will recompense, saith the Lord: and again, The Lord shall judge his people. It is a fearful thing to fall into the hands of the living God . . . Cast not away, therefore, your confidence . . . The just shall live by faith; but if any man draw back, my soul shall have no pleasure in him. But we are not of them which draw back unto perdition; but of them that believe, to the saving of the soul" (10.26–39). And he proceeds in ch. 11 to give examples of heroes of faith in order to encourage them to persevere to the end. But he returns to his task of warning in ch. 12. He reminds them how Essau sold his birthright, and "afterward when he would have inherited the blessing, he was rejected; for he found no place of repentance, though he sought it carefully with tears" (12.16, 17). He ends with a final plea, "See that ye refuse not him that speaketh. For if they escaped not who refused him that spoke on earth [i.e. Moses], much more shall not we escape, if we turn away from him that speaketh from heaven [i.e. Christ, God's last word to man]" (12.25).

Such, then, is the New Testament evidence. On the one hand, many promises to assure the believer of his eternal security. On the other, many warnings against presumption and apostasy. What is the Christian's position? It is important for him to know, and modern indifference to this question of eternal security is really either affectation or frivolity. We must know where we stand if we are to build upon a sound foundation of relationship with Christ a useful building of service to God.

The answer is that we can *know* we are forgiven, saved, in Christ, justified. "These things I have written to you that believe. . . . that you may *know* that you have eternal life," wrote John (1 Jn. 5.13). Assurance of salvation is the birthright of every Christian. It would only be presumptuous if it rested in any way on human achievement. But it cannot be presumption to take God's word of acquittal, of adoption, of salvation as the truth, to believe it and to live by it. "God is not a man that he should lie" (Num. 23.19). But this adoption, this acquittal, this salvation of which we can be assured here and now is only proleptic of the age to come; it is only the first instalment of heaven. Furthermore, salvation, election, justification is only *in Christ*. As soon as I regard salvation as a possession, as something that now belongs to me, I have gone far from the biblical picture of inaugurated eschatology, and have fossilized God's future into a past experience. It is perfectly true, moreover, that Christ will never cast out the Christian, that he will be "with us always, even to the end of the age". No foe can pluck us out of his hand. No sin can drive him from our hearts.[1] The believer's security in Christ is absolute, for in Christ alone is salvation. "He is able to save to the uttermost all that come to God by him", wrote the author to the Hebrews, who has nevertheless expressed such strong views about the possibility of apostasy. Does the solution to this apparent antinomy not lie here? Although no power of circumstance, no force of evil, can separate the Christian from Christ, there is one thing that can; his own free will. If the Christian (whose free will is not inhibited by Christ after conversion any more than it was before) deliberately and finally determines to reject Christ, to cut himself off from all that is Christian, if he says, in the words of Milton's Satan, "Darkness, be thou my light" – surely that is a possibility? There *is* a "sin unto the death" (1 Jn. 5.16), there *is* a sin "which hath never forgiveness" (Mk. 3.29), not because God will not forgive, but because man refuses to be forgiven. It takes two to make (or maintain) a relationship of love. Those who deliberately apostasize and give themselves over to evil may indeed constitute a null class, though neither Scripture nor experience would appear to suggest it. But one thing is certain. It does not alter the security possible for the Christian. It need not worry any doubting soul. For if any man is afraid that he has committed the unpardonable sin, he *hasn't* committed it! His very concern shows that he has not repudiated Christ. So while the possibility of apostasy is put before us as a terrible warning in the Bible, it need not imperil the believer's assurance of salvation, provided that assurance is built upon the Saviour and not upon some past experience, be it conversion or baptism. Salvation is in Christ. All who are in Christ will be saved; even the man who has built upon the foundation of Christ an unworthy and selfish life will at the last be saved – albeit like a man escaping in his pyjamas from a fire which has consumed all his wealth and home and possessions (1 Cor. 3.10-15). Only the man who has deliberately and finally repudiated Christ will fail to enjoy that salvation from which he has wilfully excluded himself.

A somewhat naïve example may illustrate this point. Let us suppose

[1] Paul did not teach either that grievous sin or that the discipline of excommunication (1 Cor. 5.5) would rob the believer of final salvation.

that I am drowning out at sea. There is nothing I can do to save myself. I am not a good enough swimmer to reach the distant shore, nor am I in a condition where I could profit by even the most expert instruction in swimming technique. I need neither good advice nor self-effort; I need to be saved. Now suppose that a lifeboat put out to sea, and reached me just before I sank; I would hold up my hands to accept the rescue they had come to bring. I would be dragged into the lifeboat, and I could properly say, "I have been saved". That would be true, though it might not be the whole truth. I have indeed been saved from perishing by drowning as the result of my own folly, but I have not yet reached the shore. It would be equally true to say that "I am being saved", each moment that I stay in the lifeboat, kept up by the boat from the downward pull of the waves. But I should only ultimately be saved when the boat reached land. Until that moment, it is theoretically possible that I might leap out into the waters again, and resist all attempts at rescue in my determination to drown. The possibility of such a ridiculous action would assuredly not disturb the grateful tranquillity of any rescued man. He would not be foolish enough to "apostasize", and abandon the means of his salvation. He could say with confidence, as the man in Christ can say, "I have been saved from the consequences of my folly, through the intervention of a saviour; I am being saved from sinking back into the waters because I remain in the place of safety; and I shall be saved entirely when I reach the shore." As St. Paul put it at the close of his life, "I was delivered . . . and the Lord shall deliver me . . . and will preserve me unto his heavenly kingdom; to whom be glory for ever and ever" (2 Tim. 4.17, 18).

D. SALVATION AND MODERN MAN

Finally, we must ask, Is this biblical message of salvation relevant to twentieth-century man? Does it still make sense?

Of course, it does not make sense if words like "save" are used without interpretation. Modern man thinks he knows what is meant by "salvation," and does not want it. The unexplained use of religious language is a major factor in the dismissal by most modern men of Christianity as irrelevant.

Nor does it make sense if appeal is made to needs which are not felt. We do not commonly think today in terms of demons, although there are theologians of the stature of Tillich, C. S. Lewis and Otto Piper who by no means discount the realm of the demonic. Nevertheless, it is hardly the most natural point of approach to Western man, although in missionary areas like the Miao in South-East Asia nothing could be more relevant. Similarly, we are not haunted by the spectre of subordination to Law, which to the first-century Jew was a hard taskmaster indeed. Sin, again, is a word which is normally understood these days to mean immorality or murder, and this makes its use in the New Testament sense more difficult. Nevertheless, it is not true to say that men today have no sense of sin. They have, though it is disguised. They take it not to the clergyman but to the doctor or psychiatrist, and the hospitals of Great Britain alone are more than half-full of patients with no organic ailment at all, who are suffering from various nervous troubles, psychoses, guilt complexes and so forth. Very often the guilt felt bears no relation to the wrong done; but that does not exorcize it! The proclamation of a God who accepts the guilty, who makes himself responsible for their wrongdoing, is the greatest liberating force on earth, and the greatest reintegrator of personality. That is not to say that the cure for all mental and psychological disorders is to be found in commitment to the Saviour; but that is undoubtedly what *some* of the patients need who throng the consulting rooms of the psychiatrists. I recall one such man, who had been attending a mental hospital for shock treatment, being completely healed when he came to see from the New Testament what God the Saviour had done for him, and that he was accepted by God, just as he was. I recall the case of a university student who was not in touch with any psychiatrists, but whose sense of guilt was such that he contemplated suicide. It was wonderful to see in this young man the liberating effects of forgiveness, once he came to see that God in Christ had done all that was necessary for his acceptance.

But the law and sin do not merely bring the introspective and the hag-ridden to God for salvation. There is still nothing so effective for breaking down the self-sufficiency of the common man who has "never done anyone any harm" than to take him thoughtfully through the Law of God, as exemplified either in the Ten Commandments or the Sermon on the Mount. It is still, as Paul discovered, "by the commandment" that sin becomes "exceeding sinful". When man sees himself in his essential selfishness, his indifference both to God and to his fellows, his lovelessness and his arrogance, he begins to recognize the attractiveness of a God who freely pardons the self-despairing. There is no need to seek to inculcate *feelings* of guilt; it is the *fact* of being in the wrong with God who is holy love which needs to be established. And then Christian salvation will seem relevant enough. I have often seen a man who, at the beginning of an evening's conversation along these lines was full of self-confidence, come before its end to an honest recognition of how far short he falls of God's standards for human life and turn with almost incredulous joy to decide for the Saviour who long ago decided for him.

Nor is it only in the sense of forgiveness that salvation speaks to men today. It is no less relevant to the pressures of life and circumstance which beset him. No man lives up to his own standards, let alone God's. If he is honest he will admit this; if he lives attentively in the company of Christians he will see men and women who are progressively enabled to overcome their habitual failings, and are increasingly Christlike in their behaviour. This cannot fail to attract him, as it attracted me, and made me want to know what was the secret of a life so unlike my own. The power of Christ, that is to say, to keep a man from falling, and to transform him – this is something that is immensely relevant to many a man of high ideals who is miserably conscious of his inability to keep them.

I have deliberately written at some length about the relevance of Christ as Saviour both from the guilt and power of sin, because this idea is often scouted today, and dismissed on the grounds that men have no consciousness of sin. It is also, incidentally, the main emphasis in the New Testament teaching on salvation. But of course, there are many other areas of life where man's needs have never changed, and where the biblical message is sorely needed. In a world strained with mistrust, bitterness and alienation, surely the interpretation of salvation as reconciliation cannot be out of place. As Hunter says, this term "has two distinct advantages; first, it states the whole problem in the language of personal relations . . .; and second, it answers to a universal need, for reconciliation to reality – however it be conceived – is something elemental for which all men crave . . . The language of the home will move the men of our day when the language of the slave-market or even the law-court leaves them cold."[1]

Many today are in despair about the world situation. Nuclear weapons and political brinkmanship have made it a very unstable place to live in. Surely this situation calls for a stirring proclamation that the Lord God omnipotent is still reigning in the kingdoms of men, that the Lamb is in the midst of the Throne of the Universe, that the world is under the control of self-giving Love. That is the message of salvation in the Apocalypse, which matched the perplexity and the perils of the times. Yet where, today, does one hear this element in Christian salvation stressed? Communism has an eschatology, and is not ashamed to proclaim it; so has Christianity – a salvation which embraces past, present and future, which is concerned for the whole man, for the society as well as the individual, for the body as well as the soul, for life to come as well as this life. And yet this future side of salvation is muted in most modern Christian preaching. There are times in all men's lives when they are acutely aware of death and concerned about its sequel. The biblical teaching on salvation is

[1] *Interpreting Paul's Gospel* (1954), p. 87.

intensely relevant here; it is the ideal corrective to the materialism and this-worldliness of modern life, which may satisfy while it lasts but offers no hope beyond. And yet we shrink from stressing this element in salvation lest we be thought to present Christianity as "pie in the sky when you die". Have we nothing to learn from the basic realism and the balanced eschatology of Heb. 9.27, 28, "And as it is appointed unto all men once to die but after this the judgement, so Christ was once offered to bear the sins of many; and unto them that look for him shall he appear the second time without sin unto salvation."

Frustration and aimlessness are common experiences today; many people have nothing to live for, no aim or purpose in their existence. Surely such people can be brought to appreciate the value God sets on human beings, when they see that he came to deliver them from this aimlessness, and to deal with the sources of this frustration by putting his Spirit into their lives and personalities and making them his ambassadors, agents entrusted with the furtherance of his cause in a rebellious world?

The sheer grace of salvation as its appears in the Bible, where God intervenes for the unworthy, the unlovely and the ungodly is something that strikes a note of amazement in the many loveless, lonely people of our modern world. The corporate aspects of salvation, too, are intensely relevant to a world which is passionately concerned with *belonging*. As we saw in the Old Testament doctrine of salvation, to be saved means not only to be delivered from fears, enemies and sins, but to be delivered over into the possession of God, to inherit the destiny of living with him and for him. In the Christian Church, the Body of Christ, that corporate nature of salvation can be realized. Every church worthy of the name has among its adherents many who were lonely, deprived of love, and isolated. They find in the fellowship of the church that unity enjoyed by those who know that they belong to God and therefore to each other. This corporate element in Christian salvation is especially compelling to the lonely and shy. I think of a brilliant medical student who had never known what it was to be loved, by parents or by anyone else. She lived for her books, had no friends at all and had three times tried to commit suicide. The love of God was inconceivable to her; she had sat under eloquent mission addresses unmoved. It was when she saw Christianity in terms of the society of the redeemed that it gradually became meaningful for her, and when she eventually committed herself to the Saviour and his Church her very unbalanced personality gradually became integrated and fully *human*.

Guilt, moral defeat, loneliness, anxiety, the quest for meaning in life, death and beyond – these are still foes which plague the human spirit.[1] There is still a hunger for salvation, just as there was in the pagan world at the time of Christ. There are few ways in which the Church could better serve this generation than by a recovery, a translation into modern idiom, and a bold proclamation of the wonderfully comprehensive message of salvation contained in the Scriptures.

[1] F. W. Dillistone in *The Christian Faith* (1964), has an acute analysis of the human situation. He sees men in quest of security, freedom, order and meaning; and he proceeds to show that the triune God is the only adequate Saviour from such a predicament.

Select Subject Index

absorption, 84, 187, 216

Adam, 59, 103, 157f., 165, 172, 174, 186, 189, 229

after-life, 13, 40-44, 61, 78, 86, 131f., 146, 151, 160, 181-9, 216, 222

age to come, 42-45, 58f., 66, 71, 95, 114, 131ff., 143, 146, 151, 153, 157f., 176, 183, 203f., 231, 233, 235

ambiguity, 88, 113f., 120, 128, 143, 201, 218, 229f.

'Am-ha'arets, 109f., 111

Anathema, 145

angels, 61, 211

anointing, 201, 221

Antichrist, 128, 198, 227

Antinomianism, 195, 198

Antiochus Epiphanes, 41, 55f., 66, 69, 75

apocalyptic, 37, 41-45, 55, 58f., 63, 102, 105, 108, 139, 180, 210

apologetic, 128f.

apolūtrōsis, 167f., 207, see redemption

apostasy, 143, 197ff., 202, 206f., 231-6

apostles, 220

asphaleia, 130

baptism, 91-95, 98f., 120, 142, 146-51, 170f., 172, 175, 192f., 198, 200, 231-5

Barabbas, 69f.

Bar Cochba, 56, 71

blood, 54, 106f., 150, 164, 167, 191, 211ff., 234

Canaan, 190-2

Christlikeness, 176f., 180f., 185f., 213, 238

Christology, 115-18, 124-7, 162, 181, 195-8, 208, 211f., 219

Church, 148f., 172f., 177f., 198, 207, 210-13, 216-24, 228, 232f., 239f.

circumcision, 127, 171, 232

civil wars, 72f.

community, 47, 100, 105, 143, 171ff., 184, 187

consecration, 20, 22f., 213ff.

conversion, 113, 185, 222, 231, 235

covenant, 21, 25, 27f., 35, 38, 46f., 49, 64, 99, 107, 170, 234

creeds, 11, 18, 141f.

cross, 98, 106ff., 118, 121-4, 126, 132ff., 140, 144ff., 150, 164-9, 174-6, 207-9, 211ff., 215

cultus, 35, 47, 52f., 77-82, 124, 203, 205

curse, 145f., 164f., 192, 217, 232

Day of Atonement, 53, 212

Day of Yahweh, last day(s), 22, 36-39, 44, 51, 64, 94f., 99, 121, 131, 139, 151, 153, 174, 180, 184, 188, 192, 194, 235

death, 106f., 109f., 117, 121, 131f., 155-8, 167, 174f., 181-92, 202, 206, 212f., 222, 224, 228, 239

Decalogue, 23, 156, 237

deilia, 160

demons, the demonic, 61, 79, 84, 112, 115f., 159, 174, 218ff., 223, 229, 236

development, 182-4, 193f., 196, 206

election, 47, 49, 57f., 178, 184f., 231

endurance, see perseverance

Epicureans, 160f.

eschatology, 34-54, 58f., 66f., 90-95, 98-105, 122, 130-2, 139, 142, 146, 152-6, 171, 179-98, 203f., 210, 222, 226, 230f., 235, 238f.

Essenes, 65-68, 71

eternal life, see life

eucharist, 7, 107, 171f., 198

evangelism, 119, 128ff.

Exile, 23, 34, 38ff., 47f.

Exodus, 16-19, 24, 34, 38, 143, 167, 190f., 232

exorcism, 112, 115f., 123, see demons

expiation, 52, 53, 107, 123, 212, see cross, propitiation, blood

faith, 24f., 52, 107, 111, 114f., 119f., 124, 126f., 150, 163, 165f., 169-71, 182, 193, 195, 198-200, 207, 218, 234

first-fruits, 19, 153, 176, 189, 204, 206, 208, 215, 235

flesh, 159f.

forgiveness, 46-48, 51-54, 91, 107-11, 114, 118, 126, 142, 146, 148, 150, 210-14, 235, 237

Galilee, 59, 91
Gentiles, 23, 30, 38, 47, 49, 55f., 58, 61f.,
  90f., 104, 110, 118, 126ff., 134, 147ff.,
  151, 164, 167, 178, 190f., 210, 228
glory, 103f., 107f., 155, 177, 180, 185f.,
  205, 215-17
gnōsis, 82-86, 103f., 196, 229
'God and Saviour', 74f., 78, 124, 145, 161f.,
  176, 195
Godfearers, 127, 147
go'el, 29-32, 154, 167f., 207
Gospel criticism, 96-98, 113
grace, 32f., 48, 64, 111, 117, 143, 147, 154,
  161-4, 198, 211, 226, 231f., 239

haggadah, 16, 35
halakah, 158
ḥasidim, 44, 66
Hasmoneans, 66
ḥayah, 13-15
healing, 111-18, 120, 123, 128f., 144, 149,
  201f., 217-25
heaven, 102, 104, 117, 121, 128, 183-7, 191,
  198, 210, 222, 225f., 234, 236
Hebrews, 203-8
Heilsgeschichte, 12, 35f.
Hellenistic thought, 59f., 63, 72-88, 116,
  144, 182, 186f., 205, 208
ḥesed, 14, 16
Holy Spirit, 36, 46-52, 93-95, 101, 111,
  123, 133, 139f., 142, 146f., 150f., 153,
  158, 160, 166, 170f., 175ff., 183, 187f.,
  209, 217, 220, 222, 232ff., 239
hope of salvation, 34-54, 179-89, see
  salvation (future)

immortality, 84f., 86, 160, 182f., 186f., 208,
  228; conditional, 228
Imperial Cult, 72-77, 145, 208
Incarnation, 104f., 121, 129, 154, 214, 220
individual, 24, 43, 47, 50, 63, 93-95, 109,
  111, 134, 143, 147, 150, 176
Israel, 55, 57, 60, 64, 69, 118, 128, 134f.,
  142f., 172f., 178, 184, 190, 205, 210,
  229f., 233

jailer, Philippian, 149f.
James, 199-203
Jesus (the name), 124, 127, 129, 139, 144f.,
  147, 176
John the Baptist, 89-95, 98-100, 111, 142,
  219
John the Evangelist, 131-5, 208f.
Jude, 197ff.
judgement, 14, 16, 37, 44, 63f., 92-95, 108,
  133, 142, 194, 196f., 199, 204, 214f.,
  228, 234
justice, 27, 42

justification, 28, 67-69, 111f., 148, 152f.,
  163-7, 199f., 229, 231

katallassō, see reconciliation
katargein, 183f.
kerygma, 113-15, 119f., 126, 129, 139, 143,
  147, 161, 179, 220
kingdom of God, 95, 100-2, 111, 131, 147,
  151, 215, 219
kōpher, 32f., 167f.

Lamb, 16, 94, 191f., 211-16, 238
Law, 61, 64, 91, 109, 148, 155-7, 167, 198,
  234, 236f.
Lazarus, 132f.
legalism, 23, 52, 64f., 69, 109, 147f., 152,
  162, 164, 198, 200
life, eternal life, 13ff., 41-44, 100, 106, 120,
  121-3, 177, 183f., 188f., 209, 226, 230,
  233
liturgy, 8, 17f., 34f., 141
Lord, 124, 125, 127, 140ff., 173, 195, 197,
  227f.
love, 126, 170, 184, 198-200, 209, 212, 216,
  225, 229, 231, 233, 235, 238
Luke, 125-31, 137ff.

Maccabaeans, 26, 44, 56ff., 67, 69, 207
magic, 79f., 171, 198
Maranatha, 141
Mark, 119-22
Matthew, 122-5
Mazzoth, 19
Melchisedec, 203, 205
Messiah, 38f., 44, 50, 56-71, 87, 90-95, 99,
  104, 114, 116-22, 125, 133f., 139-45,
  147f., 150f., 158, 172, 190-3, 204, 208,
  214, 224, 227f.
Messianic banquet, 111, 117, 184
Messianic woes, 45, 121f., 178
Moses, 24, 36f., 61, 66, 91, 124, 134, 148,
  190, 208, 234
mystery cults, 77-79, 85, 160, 171

nephesh, 40
new creation, 38f., 41, 44f., 171, 187
Noah, 47, 150, 192f., 205, 207

obedience, 23, 48, 115, 170, 205, 207
old aeon, 155-161, 174f., 178, 183
Old Testament, reinterpreted, 90, 107, 127,
  139f., 144, 146, 148, 203, 205, 228, 232

padah, 20, 31f., 52f., 90, 154, 167f., 208
parousia, Second Coming, 108, 123, 130,
  132, 154, 160, 176, 178-81, 185f., 188,
  193f., 196, 204, 233, 239
Passover, 16-19, 34, 190ff., 212
pax Romana, 73f.
Paul, 147-89

242

Pentateuch, 134, 156
Pentecost, 19, 101, 126, 139ff., 153, 171, 227
perseverance, endurance, 117, 121-3, 197, 202, 206f., 226, 230-6
Persia, 41f., 59, 62, 103
Peter, 137-47, 190-7
Pharisees, 41, 60-65, 71, 109-11, 115
philosophy, 59, 76, 84-86, 144, 186f., 228
praeparatio evangelica, 12, 71, 81, 150
prayer, 52, 141, 177, 201, 221
preaching, 119, 126-9, 136-51, 170, 174, 177-9, 200, 213, 220, 227, 236-40
priesthood, 16, 53, 57, 66, 73, 203ff., 215
prophecy, 38-46, 94f., 102, 105, 108, 130, 139, 147, 151, 180
propitiation, 209

Qumran, 42, 57f., 65-68, 91-95

rabbis, 50, 97, 115f., 122, 141, 156, 158, 178
ransom, 29, 30, 106f., 154, 167f., 190, 229
reconciliation, 168f., 227, 238
redemption, 28f., 30-32, 38, 90, 104, 137, 167f., 183, 187, 189-92, 203, 207f., 210-12, 215f., 229, 239
regeneration, 84, 170f., 176, 231
religio, 75-77
repentance, 25, 46, 51f., 84f., 92f., 95, 98, 101, 111, 145f., 163, 169, 177, 196, 202, 233f.
response, 23-25, 101, 128, 170, 177, 199f.
resurrection, 107f., 120, 130ff., 135, 140, 144ff., 151, 172-7, 179, 181f., 186-9, 192, 203, 206, 211
righteousness of God, 27f., 35f., 46f., 111, 133, 163-5, 195
Romans, 55f., 60-66, 68-88, 118, 125, 130, 208f.
royal psalms, 21f., 26, 36

sacrament, 53, 78, 151, 157, 172, 198, 232
sacrifice, 52-54, 66, 76, 107, 165, 168, 190, 203, 207, 212
Sadducees, 41, 60-63
salvation
  and healing, 111f., 113-18, 120, 123, 201f., 217-25
  and modern man, 236-40
  and perseverance, 121-3, 230-6
  as power, 142, 174-8, 238
  as protection, 30, 32, 171-4, 193, 216, 231, 235
  assurance of, 231-6
  by knowledge, 82-86
  conditions of, 23-25, 101f., 143, 150, 169ff., 200f.
  corporate, 47, 128, 172, 188, 205f., 216, 230, 239, *see* solidarity

costliness of, 29-33, 126, 150, 167, 191f., 207f., 214f.
  final, 34-47, 108, 117, 143, 151, 153, 176, 192, 199, 205, 222, 225f., 231, 235f.
  from enemies, 20-22, 152-61, 215, 238f.
  from sin, 20, 45-54, 67, 85-88, 108-12, 114ff., 124f., 145f., 154-61, 165-9, 192, 204, 207-12, 227
  future, 21ff., 36-46, 63, 102, 117, 127, 142f., 147, 153f., 179-89, 192, 196, 204, 206, 215ff., 222, 238f.
  God's work, 13-16, 21, 47, 51-54, 87, 95, 126f., 141, 161f., 169, 195-9, 205, 209, 231
  historic, 16-21, 35f., 40, 45f., 120, 126, 130, 140ff., 146, 150, 172, 180, 186, 190ff., 197f., 211ff.
  in Christ, 124, 148, 152, 164-72, 183, 185, 188, 197, 205f., 211, 227f., 235f.
  individual, 46, 216
  man's work, 20ff., 178f., 202f., 207
  means of, 20f., 161-71, 204ff.
  national, 35-40, 44ff., 58, 62, 72-75, 178
  past, 153-71, 190ff., 204f.
  personal, 43, 63, 129, 216
  present, 61, 100, 102, 127, 132, 143, 146, 150, 171-9, 192f.
  purpose of, 16f., 22f., 35, 191, 215-17, 239
  scope of, 47f., 108-11, 118, 126f., 133ff., 147, 151, 229
  See also, cultus, Servant of Yahweh, Son of Man, universalism
Samaritans, 61, 92, 118, 134f., 208
sanctification, 174-7, 185
sanhedrin, 61, 128
Satan, 19, 106, 116, 159, 213-15, 219, 221, 229f., 232, 235
satisfaction, 28f., 45, 117, 209, 216f.
"Saviour of the world", 73, 118, 127, 133-5, 208f.
secular and sacred, 13, 40, 63, 112, 120, 124, 126, 168f.
self-sufficiency, 86ff., 111, 237
Seneca, 85f.
sense of sin, 237ff.
Servant of Yahweh, 23, 39ff., 43, 48-52, 58, 67, 90, 93ff., 101, 105-8, 113, 123, 133, 138-40, 146, 150, 172, 192, 205, 212, 219f., 223
Seventy, the, 219, 223
shalōm, 41
shemah, 18
sheol, 42-45, 60
shipwreck, 128
signs and wonders, 130, 139, 206, 219f., 224
solidarity, 17, 47, 50f., 104, 120, 148, 150, 166, 171f., 174f., 184, 187, 189, 205f., 208

243

Index of Authors and Non-Biblical References

Index of Scripture References

252

253